Sisters against the Empire

Eva's bookplate by Constance from Prison Journal

SISTERS AGAINST THE EMPIRE

Countess Constance Markievicz and Eva Gore-Booth, 1916–17

Patrick Quigley

Patrick Quigley (signature)

The Liffey Press

the liffey press

Published by
The Liffey Press Ltd
Raheny Shopping Centre, Second Floor
Raheny, Dublin 5, Ireland
www.theliffeypress.com

© 2016 Patrick Quigley

A catalogue record of this book is available from the British Library.

ISBN 978-1-908308-87-0

All rights reserved. No part of this publication may be reproduced or transmitted in any form or by any means, including photocopying and recording, without written permission of the publisher. Such written permission must also be obtained before any part of this publication is stored in a retrieval system of any nature. Requests for permission should be directed to The Liffey Press, Raheny Shopping Centre, Second Floor, Raheny, Dublin 5, Ireland.

Printed in Spain by GraphyCems.

Contents

Acknowledgements	vii
Prologue	1
1. 'The Hour So Anxiously Awaited…'	4
2. Eva and Constance – 'The World's Great Song'	12
3. The Rebellion Begins	20
4. 'The Red Angel of the Revolution'	31
5. In Kilmainham	42
6. Two Trials	54
7. 'My Sister's Dead Body …'	67
8. Eva and Esther in Dublin	76
9. Sorting Out	84
10. 'Paying the Price…'	96
11. Roger Casement	107
12. Aylesbury: 'It's Queer and Lonely Here…'	117
13. September 1916	129

14. 'Life's Secret Forces…'	145
15. Settling Accounts	153
16. Christmas 1916 – 'What I Was Born to Do'	164
17. 1917 – 'Dim Sunshine and Pearly Waves…'	174
18. 'In Prison All Her Life…'	185
19. 'Where I Would Like to Be…'	200
20. 'The Brave Soul'	210
21. 'She Is the People's Countess'	220
22. Aftermath	235
Endnotes	241
List of Illustrations	252
Bibliography	256
Index	262
About the Author	269

Acknowledgements

This book began when Sandra Heise, Curator of the National Museum of Ireland, 1916 Collection, showed me the two volumes of Constance Markievicz's Prison Journal. The pages of beautiful drawings and sketches gave an unparalleled insight into Constance's inner world during her long months in Aylesbury Prison in 1916-17. Sandra and her colleague, Brenda Malone, made me welcome as I explored the fascinating memorabilia in their protection. I am grateful also to Dr Audrey Whitty and Finbarr Connolly of the National Museum for their help in securing images.

I am grateful to Conor Lenihan for his enthusiasm and considerable expertise in helping to launch and promote the book. And to Constance Cassidy, Eddie Walsh and family for their marvellous work in restoring Lissadell and maintaining the Lissadell Collection for future generations. During the writing the historian Ray Bateson generously helped with his encyclopaedic knowledge of the 1916 Rising and shared his research on the events at St. Stephen's Green. The book would not have been possible without the Gore-Booth family records in the Lissadell Papers stored in the Public Record Office of Northern Ireland (PRONI) in Belfast; I am grateful to Sir Josslyn Gore-Booth for permission to use the material. During the period of the research many curators of the national cultural institutions responded to my requests when under pressure from many demands; I want especially to thank Mary Broderick of the Prints and Drawings Department and the staff in the National Library; Aoife Torpey from Kilmainham Gaol Museum; Maedhbh Murphy from the Royal College of Surgeons Archive;

Brother Brian Kirby, Provincial Archivist of the Capuchin Archives; Noelle Grothier, Archivist with the Bureau of Military History; Rosemary King and Brother Brogan from the Allen Library; Harriet Wheelock of the Royal College of Physicians Library for Kathleen Lynn's Diary and for showing me the beautiful wooden tray carved by Constance.

Thanks also to Sonja Tiernan, tireless promoter of the life and works of Eva Gore-Booth for information on *Urania*, to Niamh Nestor for assistance with Eva's plays in UCD and to Ana Conlon and Kate Daly of Video Productions, who included me in their documentary film on the life of Constance. I can't forget Kimberley Campanello, author of a work on Constance and Eva, and Doris Daly for encouragement on our meetings in London. Thanks a second time to Ana Conlon for work on the cover and Barry O'Carroll for adding colour to the flag.

Michael Barry and Turtle Bunbury gave advice and encouragement and Michael McCarthy allowed me a tour of St. Mary's. Larry Mullen of Sligo has always supported Markievicz-related work. Many thanks to Jaroslaw Plachecki of the Irish Polish Society for his support and contacts in Poland. Edyta Dolan, currently Chairperson of the IPS, generously provided me with a translation of Casimir Markievicz's Declaration of Polish Citizenship. In Warsaw I have been encouraged by visits to the Constance Markiewicz Gymnazjum in Bemovo and the hospitality of the teachers: Beata Swiatkowska, Krystyna Szymkowska, Aneta Rzeszutek and former principal, Jolanta Rozycka. Thanks also to Tadeusz Malkiewicz of Krakow, grand-nephew of Casimir Dunin-Markievicz, for his knowledge of the family history and for fascinating material on Constance in Ukraine. I much appreciate the courtesy of the staff in the Public Record Office in Kew, the London School of Economics and the Imperial War Museum.

Thanks especially to my wife, Mary, for her patience and support during the book's long gestation.

This book is dedicated to the memory of Frank Mahon of Chicago, aficionado of *The Quiet Man* and author of a play about Constance on which work was cut short by his tragic death in 2015.

Prologue

Leonard Cohen has performed in many different venues but an open air concert at Lissadell House is a unique event. The stage is protected from Atlantic winds by a wall of trees while the stone head of Ben Bulben watches from the north. Cohen appears energized by Lissadell, the setting for the opening lines of W.B. Yeats' elegy, 'In Memory of Eva Gore-Booth and Con Markiewicz', as he recites:

> The light of evening, Lissadell,
> Great windows open to the south,
> Two girls in silk kimonos, both
> Beautiful, one a gazelle.

The poem transports us to the autumn of 1894 when the Gore-Booth sisters entertained Willie Yeats in the room with tall windows facing south. The young poet was delighted to be a guest in the great house and was aware of his inferior social position. Constance, at twenty-six, was the eldest daughter of Sir Henry and Lady Georgina Gore-Booth, while Eva was twenty-four. They had talent in abundance – Constance sketched, painted and played the piano while Eva wrote poetry and plays which they performed at Lissadell.

Yeats was fascinated by the house that contained a music gallery, marble pillars and walls covered with paintings in antique Florentine frames. The visits to Lissadell made a deep impression: 'I had escaped from my class.' Many years later he would revisit the sisters in the opening lines of his memorial poem and embalm them as symbols of an aristocratic way of life. In the following stanzas he would scold them for their devotion to social and political causes – Constance by 'conspiring among the ignorant,' while Eva dreamt of 'some vague Utopia.'

Con and Eva as milkmaids in 1890s

The sisters were not contented with luxury; they left the great house and became poets and revolutionaries. They engaged in the political struggles of the age – there was much more to them than French windows and silk kimonos. Eva is mainly remembered as a poet of the Celtic Renaissance who lived in England and agitated for women's trade union rights and suffrage; Constance is famous as Countess Markievicz, condemned to death for her part in the 1916 Easter Rising. Her sentence was commuted to life imprisonment. After a year of isolation, in which she struggled to retain her sanity and spirit, she returned in triumph as 'Ireland's Joan of Arc'. She was the first woman elected to Westminster and a Minister for Labour in an underground state.

Constance lived at a headlong pace like an actor playing different parts – leading lady in drawing-room comedies; chain-smoking organizer of soup kitchens during the Dublin Lockout; gun-slinging rebel trading shots

Prologue

with snipers; frail woman carrying bags of turf up tenement stairs; solitary artist sketching Celtic gods and heroes in her darkened cell. It is pointless to ask which is the real Constance – they are all aspects of her quest for a life of purpose. She created more than one myth out of the material of her life, but underneath was a woman with a sharp wit and sense of humour and a need to believe in a cause. She wrote to her brother, Josslyn, after the Easter Rising: 'My enemies will make a monster out of me, my friends a heroine, and both are equally wide of the truth.'[1]

Her prison journals from Aylesbury Women's Prison in 1916 and 1917 are a rich trove of drawings, poems and sketches that bring us into her vivid inner world and give an insight into the beliefs which nourished the revolutionary generation. On another level the journals record the journey of a soul from despair towards hope and the exhilaration of freedom.

The story of Constance's prison year would be incomplete without her sister. Eva was a pacifist and vegetarian who lived with her partner, Esther Roper. Eva and Esther were highly motivated and idealistic exemplars of the self-improving and idealistic philosophies that believed society could be improved by communal effort. Their lives were inextricably bound up with events in Ireland and England; Eva was at home in Manchester and London as much as in Sligo and Dublin. During the fifteen months between Easter 1916 and June 1917 both were deeply affected by the events of 1916. Eva damaged her fragile health to help her sister in a time of greatest need; Constance was deeply influenced by Eva's love of humanity and claimed, 'I once held out and stopped a man being shot because of her.'[2]

Sisters against the Empire is a study of the relationship that sustained Constance in the traumatic months between Easter 1916 until her triumphant return to Ireland in June 1917. The story of their creative collaboration takes many strange turns and shows the sisters in dramatic situations that illuminates their minds and souls – it is one of Ireland's greatest stories.

1

'The Hour So Anxiously Awaited...'

'What do you think of my rigout?' she asked.

She wore a dark-green woollen blouse with brass buttons, dark-green tweed knee-britches, black stockings and huge heavy boots. Around her waist was a cartridge belt; from one side hung an automatic pistol, from the other a convertible Mauser rifle; a bandolier and haversack crossed her shoulder. She stood tall and straight, a fine military figure.

'You look a real soldier, Madame,' said Nono, admiringly, and Madame beamed as if she had received a tremendous compliment.'[3]

Madame was Constance Gore-Booth, the Countess Markievicz, and her admirer was Nora 'Nono' Connolly, twenty-three-year-old daughter of the leader of the Irish Citizen Army (ICA), James Connolly. It was April 1916; the two women were sharing tea and bread in the kitchen of Constance's home, Surrey House, in the Dublin suburb of Rathmines. She was Chief Scout of the Fianna, the nationalist scouts organisation, who made tea and sandwiches around them as they debated how to dress for a revolution.

Constance was also a founder of the Irish Citizen Army and is credited with designing the green uniform with the distinctive slouch hat. Nora's outfit was similar to Constance's with the exception of puttees and shoes studded with nails. She wondered if she should wear a tam o'shanter on the barricades.

'This will be my hat,' said Madame, putting on her best hat, a black velour with a heavy plume of coque feathers.

'You look like a field-marshal with that,' laughed Nono.

Constance was an experienced actor and knew that revolution was a performance in which the image was as important as the deed. She had discussed the thorny question of a woman wearing trousers in public with her friend, Dr Kathleen Lynn. In the days before Easter 1916 she avoided con-

'The Hour So Anxiously Awaited...'

troversy by wearing a skirt over the trousers in public.

Surrey House was a centre of revolutionary activity where writers and actors mingled with trade unionists and revolutionaries. Michael Collins was a visitor as were Con Colbert and Sean Heuston, rebel leaders executed in 1916. A window was left open at night so that any passing friend would have somewhere to sleep. The boys and young men of the Fianna were protective of their Chief Scout and made her house their unofficial headquarters.

Nora was about to transport guns into the city when two police detectives arrived at the door. She ran to the kitchen and summoned Constance who came out and reduced the hall light to a glimmer. The policemen entered the porch and stood inside the door; they were there to deliver an order under the Defence of the Realm Act forbidding her to enter 'that part of Ireland called Kerry.'

Constance in ICA uniform

'What will happen,' asked Madame, her fingers caressing the butt of her Mauser pistol, 'if I refuse to obey the order and go to Kerry? Would I be shot?'

'Ah now, Madame; who'd want to shoot you? You wouldn't want to shoot one of us. Now, would you Madame?'

'But I would,' cried Madame gaily, 'I'm quite prepared to shoot and be shot at.'

The banter suggests the detectives were unsure whether to take Constance seriously. It suited them to pretend she was a harmless eccentric. Her official title was the Countess Markievicz, but they knew her well enough to use the more familiar 'Madame'. She was used to visits from the police. She was out when they called to raid the house in January and confiscated a disused printing press and a stack of Munsey's magazines. They were still searching when she returned and presented them with a rusty rifle 'to lend a colourful and dramatic touch to their visit.'[4]

Some days after the raid the police returned and requested she register as an alien since she was married to Casimir Dunin-Markievicz of Polish nationality, a citizen of the Russian Empire. She told them, 'more forcibly than politely, that she was an Irishwoman and before she would register as an alien she would see the police in hell.'[5]

With the revolution a matter of days away she was keen not to antagonize the detectives and reminded them politely that they should stay away if they wanted to avoid being shot.

'None of us are fond of you,' she warned, 'and you make grand big targets.'

Their visit threw Constance into a quandary. Should she defy the police order and appear in Kerry? She was under orders from Connolly not to go as she was sure to be arrested; he wanted her in Dublin. She was one of Connolly's 'ghosts', ready to take his place if he were arrested or killed. Nora suggested she write a speech and send a substitute; they settled on Marie Perolz who dressed in Constance's clothes and went to Kerry. Perolz was one of the fearless young women who surrounded Constance. She joined the ICA and worked in a fruit shop but spent most of her time delivering messages and persuading British Army soldiers to sell guns. The activities of two Countess Markieviczes in different places at the same time would be a cause of confusion in police reports. There was a lot of rebel activity in Kerry that April, the location for a delivery of guns and the arrival of Sir Roger Casement from a German submarine.

As the day for the Rising approached there were divisions within the Irish Volunteers but the smaller ICA was determined to go ahead. Thomas O'Donoghue was a private:

> I remember distinctly, about three weeks before Easter Week 1916, he (Connolly) called a number of us together and gave us commissions…. I received the rank of Lieutenant which was the same rank as he gave Countess Markievicz on this occasion, although she was one of the Council of the Citizen Army.[6]

The commissions were to take effect when the rebellion started. The ICA turned their headquarters, Liberty Hall, into a centre of operations. The young Frank Robbins remembered frequent visits from Constance at teatime with a bag of cakes. One day he heard her remark: 'I have already overdrawn my bank account for my next quarter's allowance to the extent of £45, and if this bally revolution doesn't take place soon I don't know how I'm going to live.'[7]

When Constance married Casimir Dunin-Markievicz in 1900 she was allocated an income from the Lissadell estate which was invested in stocks and shares. The shares were held in transport companies, mainly rural railways, and dividends were paid into her bank account in Coutts of London. She overdrew on her account by feeding families of locked-out workers in 1913. Among other commitments were a hall in Camden Street for Na Fianna, a cottage in the Dublin Mountains where the scouts could practise rifle shooting without disturbing neighbours, and a weekly newspaper, *The Spark*, as well as other revolutionary activities.

The Spark, April 1916

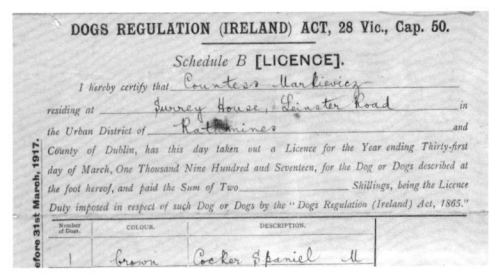

At one stage she provided the seed capital to nourish a commune in Belcamp Park near Raheny. By early 1916 her finances were in a distressed state with many bills unpaid. One bill she made sure to pay on time was a dog licence for her cocker spaniel, Poppet.

Poppet's dog licence

Connolly's deputy in the Transport Union, William O'Brien, told of a visitor to Liberty Hall on Easter Saturday. The lady was surprised at the amount of people coming and going and queried Constance.

'Rehearsing, I suppose?'

'Yes,' replied Madame with a knowing smile.

'Is it for children?' enquired the lady.

'No,' said Madame, 'for grown-ups.'[8]

The rebellion was planned for Easter Sunday; the leaders expected arrest at any time and Constance stayed in the home of Jenny Wyse Power, President of Cumann na mBan, the women's organization attached to the Volunteers. On Sunday morning she saw the notices in the *Sunday Independent* announcing the cancellation of Irish Volunteer parades. She was dismayed and raced on her bicycle to Liberty Hall where she met Sean MacDermott and Tom Clarke in Connolly's bedroom. Clarke told her that the Volunteer's Chief of Staff, Eoin MacNeill, had deprived them of the rebellion, but the plotters were determined to reorganise and take over the country on Monday. The arrest of Casement in Kerry and the loss of thousands of German rifles threw a shadow over the possibility of success, but the conspirators were determined.

'The busiest day I ever lived through was that day in Liberty Hall,' she wrote.

> Messengers came and went, and the Provisional Government of the Republic sat the whole day in Connolly's little room. I was in there for one moment on business....They were all quite cheerful. The cloud had passed.[9]

During the day the printers prepared copies of the Proclamation of the Irish Republic. According to legend Constance took a copy wet from the press and staged an impromptu reading in front of Liberty Hall. Max Caulfield, an early historian of the Rising, wrote of her holding the thin poster in her hands as she read to the curious crowd, 'with characteristic hauteur, disregarding the detectives who mingled amongst them.'[10] If she did read it she would have recited the stirring phrases in a high-pitched English accent. The official announcement of the Republic would take place on Easter Monday at the General Post Office. 'Many of us could almost wish that we had died in the moment of ecstasy when, with the tricolour over our heads we went and proclaimed the Irish Republic, and with guns in our hands tried to establish it,' she wrote.

The Citizen Army leadership decided to allay police suspicions by staging a route march. Shortly after four o'clock the tiny army led by Commandant Connolly and his Chief of Staff, Michael Mallin, left Beresford Place and marched through the city. Constance walked in her green uniform with embroidered buttons and feathered hat. The route led through the dusty streets past the imposing buildings of Dublin's Georgian inheritance – the Bank of Ireland, once seat of the native Irish Parliament, past the pillars of Trinity College to the elegant buildings around St. Stephen's Green. The route led through cobbled streets to the gates of Dublin Castle, headquarters of the British administration in Ireland. The sentry on duty called up the guard, but the column marched along the street past Christchurch Cathedral and back along the Quays.

A journalist, J.H. Cox, met the marchers and wrote after the Rising:

> To the eye of the populace the leaders of the startling insurrection were not at all known. Countess Markievicz of whom such florid descriptions have appeared in the English papers was never to outward seeming a personality. When she and James Connolly passed me on Easter Sunday evening on their usual weekly march with the Citizen Army I did not suspect the notoriety they were to achieve at noon next day.[11]

Cox understated the degree to which Constance and her scouts were known, but few could guess that this display was anything other than a piece of street theatre from a woman well-used to the stage. The gossips claimed her husband went to fight in the Great War rather than live with her; others said he was a Polish charlatan who abandoned her when she squandered her inheritance. C. Day Lewis caught the mood in his elegy:

> Fanatic, bad actress, figure of fun –
> She was called each. Ever she dreamed,
> Fought, suffered for a losing side, it seemed
> (The side which always at last is seen to have won.)[12]

The marchers returned to Beresford Place where Connolly made his last public speech from the steps of Liberty Hall; he called on the Citizen Army to stand ready to defend the Republic. The army could rarely count on more than 300 men and women at full mobilization. Margaret Skinnider, a young school teacher in Glasgow, had taken a week's holiday when Constance hinted that something big was coming at Easter. Skinnider was thrilled to hear Connolly announce: 'You are now under arms. You will not lay down your arms until you have struck a blow for Ireland.'[13]

Constance sketch of Margaret Skinnider

He told them to hold on to their guns as some of their allies in the Irish Volunteers would not share their goal of a socialist republic. 'If we succeed,' he told a comrade, 'all our sins will be forgiven; if we fail, all our virtues won't save us from the gallows.'[14]

As they prepared for revolution the conspirators contrived to maintain a screen of normality. They put on an improvised concert of songs and sketches in Liberty Hall to obscure the preparations. Constance was a regular organizer with experience from helping Casimir design and make sets for his plays in Dublin. She performed recitations, especially rousing speeches from *The Memory of the Dead*, the historical work Casimir called his 'bloody play'. She wrote songs for the ICA based on traditional Polish songs; a favourite was *Armed for the Battle* or *On the Battlefield*:

> We are ready to die for the Ireland we love
> Be the chances great or small;
> We are willing to die for the flag above
> Be the chances nothing at all.

Instead of going home Constance went with Connolly's secretary, Winifred Carney, to sleep with the family of William O'Brien. During the night the household was awakened by a gunshot. Constance was unloading her Belgian automatic when it went off and sent a bullet through the door. In her excitement she may have neglected the rules of gun handling learned from her father in Lissadell many years before.

Early on Monday morning she went with Carney to Liberty Hall where the Volunteers and Citizen Army members stood on parade with full arms and equipment. There has been much debate on the status of women in the ICA. Constance was adamant that women should be on an equal footing:

> There were a considerable number of ICA women. These were absolutely on the same footing as the men. They took part in all marches, and even in the manoeuvres that lasted all night. Moreover, Connolly made it quite clear to us that unless we took our share in the drudgery of training and preparing, we should not be allowed to take any share at all in the fight.[15]

Constance's Mauser pistol, 'Peter the Painter'

She was prepared for action with her Browning automatic pistol supplemented by a Mauser pistol with a detachable carbine stock, nicknamed 'Pete Painter', appropriately named given her training as an artist in London Paris. The gun was a present from Casimir according to her biograp Anne Marreco.

Connolly, Pearse, McDonough and Plunkett were dressed in full military regalia, but Constance remembered the frail figure of Thomas Clarke.

> The hour so anxiously awaited, so eagerly expected, had come at last. Our hearts' desire was granted to us and we counted ourselves lucky. Happy, proud and gay was Tom Clarke on that day. His life's work had borne fruit at last…we met for a few minutes just before the time fixed to march out. It seems queer, looking back on it, how no one spoke of death or fear or defeat. I remember saying good-bye to Tom Clarke just at the door of Dr Kathleen Lynn's little surgery, which we had all been having a look at before we started. We then went downstairs, and each man joined up with his little band.[16]

The intention was to seize key positions which would be a signal for a national uprising. Despite the mishap in Kerry the rebel leadership hoped the German navy would prevent British reinforcements arriving and might even send troops. 'Padraic Pearse and James Connolly addressed us and told us that from now on the Volunteers and the ICA were not two forces, but the wings of the Irish Republican Army,' she wrote. It was the last time she would see her close friends Clarke, Connolly, MacDonagh and the other rebel leaders alive.

Easter Monday was warm and bright as the groups of armed men and women started for their destinations. Due to the confusion over the countermanded orders the numbers were much lower than expected. Despite the desperate nature of the undertaking Constance had no doubts:

> I stood on the steps and watched the little bodies of men and women march off, Pearse and Connolly to the GPO, Sean Connolly to the City Hall, all marching proudly, confident that they were doing right, sure at last that they had made the subjection of Ireland impossible for generations to come.

2

EVA AND CONSTANCE – 'THE WORLD'S GREAT SONG'

Eva was born at home in Lissadell in 1870, a year after her brother, Josslyn, and two years after Constance. An intense bond developed between the sisters, much closer than their relationship with Josslyn or the later siblings, Mordaunt, another boy, born in 1878, and the baby, Mabel, two years later. The two eldest sisters were united in having strong creative and intense natures. As they grew older Constance was the leader of the little band and Eva her closest companion.

From her early years Eva had a strong sense of the spiritual life. She wrote of her childhood self in the third person in *The Inner Life of a Child*:

> Time flows on through streams of monotonous orderly years, but it seems as if every now and then an Angel troubles the waters. The immortal events of the inner life shine to us out of the simple past.[17]

She was especially close to her maternal grandmother, Lady Frances Charlotte Arabella Hill, who died at Lissadell on 3 August 1879. Eva lay in bed knowing it was still daylight outside.

> Without any warning the child became suddenly conscious that a 'door had opened in the air,' and that her grandmother was standing beside her. Oddly enough, the child who in theory was terrified of ghosts, had no thought of fear, nor did she ever think it strange, she was simply delighted to be with her. Again and again the spirit came.

Many of her childhood experiences brought her to an inner state she described in a poem as 'the borderland of consciousness.' Her nurse was another woman to whom she developed a close attachment:

> If she fixed her mind on the old nurse upstairs in the nursery, and cried out to her with her will and her imagination, she could almost draw her downstairs to see her...

The connection persisted when the nurse left Lissadell:

> ... the child did not even know she was ill, but she was warned by a very vivid dream of her friend's approaching death.

Esther Roper thought Eva had an unhappy childhood, not for lack of affection or material things, but because she was haunted by the conviction she had to atone for actions from an earlier existence. This sense of a reincarnated soul is explored in her poetry and the play, *The Buried Life of Deirdre*. It would develop into an intense social consciousness and propel her into political action. 'She seems to have been haunted by the suffering of the world,' Esther wrote, 'and to have had a curious feeling of responsibility for its inequalities and injustices.'[18]

She was aware of the story that their grandfather, Sir Robert Gore-Booth, had cleared lands of tenants by sending them to Newfoundland on an unseaworthy ship which sank with great loss of life. Despite a lack of documentary evidence the story has persisted, a reminder of the grievances of the peasantry against the landlord class. The sensitive and intelligent sisters were aware of such stories and the unrest of the Land War of the 1870s and 1880s.

Eva and Constance closely resembled each other in looks although Eva was slightly taller. Constance was robust and outgoing while Eva was introspective. The artist Sarah Purser visited in 1880 and painted a joint portrait of the sisters in a woodland setting. Constance stands among the trees with an armful of flowers and

Sarah Purser's painting of Eva and Constance

a look of proud determination on her young face. Eva is crouched on the ground, her attention focussed on a tiny flower as though she could, like William Blake, see eternity in the fragile growth. Purser was a woman who provided for herself in a society with few outlets for women. Constance decided she would become an artist and worked hard to improve her skills at sketching and drawing.

There was always a complementary aspect in the relationship between Eva and Constance. Constance was impetuous and fearless; Eva was shy and reserved. Stories clustered around the 'Miss Gores' – people said they gave away their clothes to poor children they met on the road with Constance donating her shoes and Eva her coat. Their artistic temperaments marked them off from their siblings. In contrast Josslyn was earnest and worked hard to make Lissadell a model estate. Mabel followed her idealistic sisters when they formed a branch of the women's suffrage movement in Sligo, before settling down to respectable married life in Margate, Kent. Mordaunt set himself apart from his siblings by becoming a resolutely ordinary person. He went to England and worked in an engineering firm in Sheffield.

The sisters shared an ante-room at Lissadell called the 'Glory-hole' where Eva wrote poems and plays and Constance worked on her sketches. It was probably on one of those West of Ireland days when the rain falls endlessly that Constance scratched her name into the glass of a windowpane. Eva suffered bouts of illness in her teenage and young adult years. Constance wrote in her diary of January 1892: 'Eva's toothache very bad. I slept on the old sofa in her room.'[19]

Constance was presented to Queen Victoria when she was nineteen years old in March 1887. She was now officially eligible for marriage if a suitable match could be found. Eva was ill with scarlet fever in August 1888 and was presented to the Queen in 1889. Mother and daughters spent the social season in London each year and then in Dublin. Constance was the belle of the parties and matchmaking sessions, although she rarely met a suitor that pleased her. There seems to have been less concern about finding a match for Eva; she avoided the parties and preferred to attend concerts and the theatre.

The young Willie Yeats visited Lissadell in the winter of 1894 and in early 1895. He had been in contact with Constance in London in June 1893 where she reminded him of his unrequited love for the beautiful Maud Gonne. She was shorter and smaller than Maud, but Yeats was struck 'by a very exact resemblance in voice.'[20] In the summer of 1894 he arranged a session with a London fortune teller for Constance and a friend. When he visited Lissadell he was delighted with the sitting-room as big as a church and Eva's poetry.

> I have been staying at Lissadell for a couple of days and have enjoyed myself greatly,' he wrote to his sister Susan. 'I was busy telling stories – old Irish stories, first to one, then the other.... Miss Eva Gore-Booth shows some promise as a writer of verse.[21]

Eva's 'delicate gazelle-like beauty reflected a mind ... subtle and distinguished. Eva was for a couple of happy weeks my close friend, and I told her all my unhappiness in love.' He felt for the first time that he had 'broken out of my class ... into that of county,' but the omens were not positive. 'I threw the Tarot, and when the Fool came up, which meant that nothing at all would happen, I turned my mind away.'[22]

Throughout the 1890s Eva sent poems to Yeats who encouraged publication. He responded to her first collection, *Poems*, published in 1898:

> I think it is full of poetic feeling and has great promise... 'Weariness' is really most imaginative and is ... about the quietness of eternity and of dreams...[23]

Her health deteriorated in the mid-1890s; the family feared consumption and sent her to recuperate in Italy. She stayed in Bordighera in 1896, the seaside location near the French border, where she met the companion with whom she would spend the rest of her life, Esther Roper.

> Was it not strange that by the tideless sea
> The jar and hurry of our lives should cease,
> That under olive boughs we found our Peace
> And all the world's great song in Italy?

Esther was born in Manchester in 1868 to an English preacher with the Church Mission Society and an Irish mother. She was one of the first women to attend Owens College where she secured a BA in 1891 with first class honours in Latin, English Literature and Political Economy. She took a paid job as Secretary to the Manchester National Society for Women's Suffrage and dedicated herself to the cause and to improving working conditions for women factory workers.

She became ill due to overwork in 1896 and was in Italy to recover when she met Eva beneath an olive tree. The Gore-Booths owned estates at Salford, near Manchester and Eva was consumed by curiosity about the living conditions of working women. 'We spent the days walking and talking on the hillside by the sea,' Esther wrote. 'Each was attracted to the work and thoughts of the other, and we became friends and companions for life – she made up her mind to join me in the work in Manchester.'[24]

Sketch of Esther Roper by Eva

There are conflicting views as to whether the relationship was platonic or physical, but there can be no doubt that they loved each other deeply. Eva left Lissadell in 1897 and lived with Esther in Manchester, but remained in contact with the family and the pair often visited Ireland. Meanwhile Constance decided to study art in Paris in the footsteps of Sarah Purser in the Academie Julien. In 1899 she met Count Casimir Dunin-Markievicz and they were married in London on 29 September 1900. Eva and Mabel were the bridesmaids.

Eva kept up connections with Ireland and the poets of the Celtic Renaissance. AE (George Russell) included her among his 'canary birds' in the anthology *New Songs* in 1904. Constance wrote to Eva from Paris, keeping her informed of the courtship with Casimir in which she made the running. 'Although often separated for months, and even for years, the deep devotion of the sisters remained unchanged,' remarked Stasko Markiewicz, Casimir's son by his first marriage. 'Each was always ready to come to the assistance of the other, whether the crisis was an illness, a political campaign, or other emergency.'[25]

Eva became a mentor to Cristabel Pankhurst, daughter of the campaigner Emmeline Pankhurst, but ended the relationship as she opposed the violence of the suffragettes. She was an effective agitator and Constance came to her aid in Manchester in 1908 when they fought a bye-election campaign against a government bill that discriminated against the employment of barmaids. Their campaign contributed to the defeat of the Liberal candidate, Winston Churchill.

Eva maintained links with artistic life in Ireland, but Yeats was replaced as mentor by the more paternal figure of George Russell who wrote of her:

> Though her life was spent mainly outside Ireland since her girlhood, her affection for the country never seemed to weaken, and when she writes about Ireland her verse becomes less abstract and more intimate...[26]

Eva looked on her sister's militant nationalism with equanimity, but was happy to live as an English nonviolent agitator for change. 'Both were rebels against all that they regarded as mean and unworthy,' wrote R.M. Fox. 'Their passionate selfless sincerity drove them in different directions.'[27]

The north of England climate was hard on Eva's health and in 1913 she and Esther moved to London and rented the top two floors of an elegant house at 15 Fitzroy Square. They were near the heart of London's cultural life in Fitzrovia and mixed with suffrage activists, artists, philosophers and writers. In the same year Roger Fry established the Omega Workshop downstairs for aspiring artists.

Eva continued to produce poetry, lectures and pamphlets as well as studies in the history of religion and mysticism. Like Constance she had an income from her Lissadell inheritance which gave her a large degree of personal freedom, although she sometimes had to call on brother Josslyn for a loan. She campaigned against an attempt to ban flower sellers from Oxford Circus and once gave 300 oranges to an East London club for girls at Christmas.

15 Fitzroy Square

The author, suffragette and nationalist Hannah Sheehy-Skeffington first met Eva at Surrey House in 1912:

> Eva was almost absurdly like Constance – taller, willowy where Constance was little. She was more short-sighted which gave her a detached, removed air. Their voices even were alike – & yet differ-

ent – Con's high-pitched and ringing like a bell, Eva's lower & slower tempo with a certain breathlessness.[28]

In another passage she remarked:

Constance was a little smaller & more boyish looking and robuster in physique.

Hannah's feminism brought her close to Eva, but she shared Constance's desire for Irish independence. Hannah and Eva believed in the necessity for women's suffrage, but Constance felt election to Westminster was a diversion from national independence. Surrey House was a place where books and ideas were appreciated and Hannah shared literary evenings with the sisters:

Eva and Esther in Paris

> When one could induce her (Eva) – it was not easy – or trap her into reading or quoting poetry its lovely sensual quality came out.

During Eva's visits to Ireland Hannah was struck by the strong connection between the sisters:

> I know no example of two closer affinities than that of these two: even the Bronte sisters were not as closely linked. Alike in fundamentals they had many striking differences of temperament, yet these seemed but to heighten and intensify the love and complete understanding between Constance & Eva Gore-Booth.

The outbreak of war in 1914 appalled Eva; she was opposed to violence, especially the slaughter of the Great War: 'I am one of those quite hopeless people who do not believe in fighting in any circumstance.'[29] She read an anti-war paper, *Religious Aspects of Non-Resistance*, at a London conference in July, 1915. She asserted that the war was 'causing the most gigantic accumulation of pain and death that the world has ever seen.'[30]

She visited Dublin with Esther in 1915 where they watched a parade of Citizen Army, Volunteers, Fianna and Cumann na mBan at the funeral of the old Fenian, Jeremiah O'Donovan Rossa. 'There were few uniforms, though Padraig Pearse, their leader, was in full uniform,' Esther wrote.

> When it was over, thinking with admiration of all the gifted people in their ranks, I said with relief to Eva, 'Well, thank goodness, they simply can't be planning a rising now, not with such a tiny force.' I had become sadly used to the tramp of endless troops through London on their way to the Front.[31]

3

THE REBELLION BEGINS

While Constance maintained women and men had equal status in the ICA and received military training, Connolly did not envisage that women would take part in the fighting. On Easter Monday he issued revolvers to the females, but Margaret Skinnider was disgusted to be told to shoot only in self-defence. Constance held the rank of Staff Lieutenant and Connolly appointed her liaison officer between the rebel headquarters in the General Post Office and the outposts. It was her hope to fight alongside the men, but she obeyed orders. At this stage she appears to have been dressed in civilian clothes. There are misleading reports of her marching in full uniform into St. Stephen's Green at the head of the Fianna and Cumann na mBan.

'I went off then with the Doctor in her car,' she wrote.

> We carried a large store of First Aid necessities and drove off through quiet dusty streets and across the river, reaching the City Hall just at the very moment that Commandant Sean Connolly and his little troop of men and women swung round the corner and he raised his gun and shot the policeman who barred the way.[32]

Captain Kathleen Lynn was Chief Medical Officer in the ICA. She was a Protestant from Mayo, a distant cousin of Constance, who recruited her into the revolutionary movement. She described her role:

> My assignment was the City Hall. Mme. Markievicz and I were driven in my car from Liberty Hall by Crimmins who was a most reckless driver.[33]

The Rebellion Begins

Kathleen Lynn with Constance

The rebellion was timed to start at noon when the city clocks chimed twelve and church bells rang out the Angelus. Sean Connolly is credited with firing the first shot which killed Constable O'Brien who barred access to Dublin Castle. Connolly was shot dead by a British Army sniper a short time later. 'A wild excitement ensued,' Constance remembered, 'people running from every side to see what was up. The Doctor got out, and I remember Mrs. Barrett and others helping to carry in the Doctor's bundles.'

Dr Lynn remained with the garrison in City Hall while Constance set off in the car with the remaining medical supplies to St. Stephen's Green. She met a group of women from Cumann na mBan in Lord Edward Street and told them to report to the City Hall. She was in the passenger seat beside the driver when they passed Volunteers taking over Jacob's Biscuit factory. Among them was the actress, Maire Nic Shiubhlaigh, who remembered the open two-seater swaying from side to side. Constance stood up, waved her hat and cheered them on: 'Go at it, boys,' she cried. 'The Citizen Army are taking the Green. Dublin Castle is falling.'

The occupation of the park at the centre of St. Stephen's Green has been criticised as an impractical attempt at trench warfare in an urban space, but most combatants of the time were thinking in terms of the Western Front. The Green was a transport hub where a number of major roads entered the city. The twenty-two acres of the park made it the ideal location for organizing men and equipment. Volunteer units from the country would gather here before dispersal to city depots. Despite the reduced numbers on Easter Monday the rebels proceeded to commandeer vehicles and erect barricades to block British Army reinforcements. They began evicting holiday makers from the park and to dig trenches on the lawns.

Commandant Michael Mallin, who had some knowledge of tactics from his service with the British Army, was faced with a dilemma. The original plan to occupy a number of landmark buildings around the Green such as the Shelbourne Hotel could not be carried out. Constance found Mallin struggling with inadequate numbers.

> He said that owing to MacNeill's calling off the Volunteers a lot of the men who should have been under him had to be distributed round other posts, and that I must stay and be ready to take up the work of a sniper.

She would have preferred to be in the centre of the fight in the GPO, but readily obeyed Mallin's order.

> He took me round the Green and showed me how the barricading of the gates and digging trenches had begun, and he left me in charge of this work while he went to superintend the erection of barricades in the streets and arrange other work.

There is considerable confusion around the order of events in the afternoon with participants and witnesses remembering incidents in different sequences, sometimes at different places; all agree that Constance took a prominent role in events. 'This work was very exciting when the fighting began,' she wrote. 'I continued round and round the Green, reporting back if anything was wanted, or tackling any sniper who was particularly objectionable.'

One of her less exciting tasks was to guard the gates to the Green and help remove civilians, some of whom treated the rebellion as street entertainment and refused to leave. There were exchanges of gunfire between the insurgents and British Army officers in the vicinity of the Shelbourne. Fire was returned and a number of guests were wounded before hotel staff moved them to the rear of the building. Further along the north side of the Green a British Army recruiting officer, Captain De Burgh Daly, was observing rebel positions when he found himself in the front line:

The Rebellion Begins

> Countess Markievicz drove up to Stephen's Green in a motor and got out opposite the University Club. She was dressed in a man's uniform, green with a brown belt and feathers in her hat. She apparently was in command or second in command of the S[inn] F[einers] in the Green. About 1 o'clock she leaned against the Eglington Monument and took a deliberate pot shot at me in one of the open windows of the University Club. I was sitting in the window – the distance was about 50-60 yards. She could not tell I was a doctor, but I suspect considered I was a combatant officer as I had ribbons on...[34]

British Army doctors were sometimes fired on as their only distinguishing mark was a small badge on the arm. Constance may have taken De Burgh Daly for one of the 'objectionable snipers' shooting into the Green. The shot would feature prominently at her court-martial. Walter McKay was a seventeen-year old page-boy in the University Club, deputizing for the hall porter who was on his lunch-break.

'I was standing at the Club door,' he testified.

University Club

> From there I could see Stephen's Green and I saw a few rebels dressed in green uniform they were pulling the civilians out of the Green and as they were doing this the accused drove up in a motor car, blew her whistle and leaned out of the car. She gave orders to a Sinn Feiner after he had shut the gates of Stephen's Park. She then drove up towards the Shelbourne Hotel – I saw her again about 1.15 p.m. she was then behind one of the monuments in the Green, she had a pistol in her hand which she pointed towards the club and fired. I raced upstairs and saw where the bullet struck. After firing she walked up towards the Shelbourne Hotel dressed in knickers and puttees.[35]

Constance disputed McKay's evidence, arguing that he could not have seen the alleged target from the doorway. She suggested she was shooting at a sniper in the vicinity of the Shelbourne Hotel, further along the street. Stasko Markievicz claimed he spoke with Dr De Burgh Daly in the 1930s. In this version the officer was at the window of the nearby United Services

Club speaking to a Mr. Best who exclaimed: 'Look out! There's a woman on the Green pointing a gun at us.'[36] The window was slightly open and the shot passed between them.

Another variant has two British officers walking along the Green when one exclaims: 'Why, there's Madame Markievicz holding a rifle! By Jove, she's pointing it over here!' It reads like a comic book episode complete with comic dialogue. They scurry for safety as bullets whiz over their heads. Louis MacNeice attended school at Sherborne where one of the older boys used to boast she fired at him. An army officer wrote to Sir Josslyn Gore-Booth:

> This officer was Dr Daly ... who knew the Countess and she knew him and saw her fire at him – she missed. A policeman was shot and the crowd yelled – 'that is the Countess again' but there is no-one who saw her fire.[37]

The Irish Times and *Irish Independent* ceased publication between Thursday 27 April and Monday 1 May. In the absence of newspapers rumours and outright lies satisfied the hunger for information. 'Rumour has never been so busy and rumour has never been so lying as during the past ten days,' said the *Kildare Observer*. One of the stories about Constance involved the shooting of a Dublin Metropolitan Policeman, Constable Michael Lahiff. He was shot soon after the rebels arrived at the Green and died of his wounds in hospital. The circumstances of the shooting are disputed and are still unclear a century later. The shooting of Constable O'Brien at Dublin Castle was also attributed to Constance and she was reported to have shot two sentries before being shot dead herself.

While many stories have fallen away, the shooting of Constable Lahiff is often quoted to illustrate Constance's bloodthirsty nature. It was not mentioned at her court-martial the following week, nor in the first biography of her by Sean O'Faolain, who was not inclined to let her away with anything. A document appeared from British military intelligence in June 1917 purporting to be an extract from a diary by Miss Fitzgerald, a nurse based at the Jubilee Nursing Home, 101 St. Stephen's Green. She claimed the occupants were sitting down to lunch on the south side of the Green when they heard shooting. Miss Fitzgerald rushed to the window where she saw:

> ... a lady in a green uniform the same as the men were wearing ... the feathers were the only feminine features in her appearance, holding

a revolver in one hand and a cigarette in the other.... We recognized her as the Countess Markievicz ... such a specimen of womanhood. We had only been looking out a few minutes when we saw a policeman walking down the footpath ... he had only gone a short way when we heard a shot and then saw him fall ...[38]

Ms. Fitzgerald did not mention more than one shot while Constable Lahiff was hit three times. She claimed to see Constance running into the Green and shouting: 'I got him.' In his book *The Rising Dead RIC & DMP*, historian Ray Bateson compared the many accounts of the shooting and detailed the inconsistencies. One version, popularised by Max Caulfield and widely copied, located the shooting at the main entrance to the Green at the top of Grafton Street. Constance confronts the constable who refuses to surrender the keys to the park.

> 'Mick, give me the keys to Stephen's Green or I will shoot you,' Constance demands.
>
> 'Countess, act your age like a good lady,' he replies.
>
> She is as good as her word and calmly shoots him.[39]

This story has entered the mythology of the Rising, but it is unsatisfactory for a number of reasons. Who witnessed and recorded the stilted dialogue? Why would she demand the keys when the rebels were already inside? Why demand keys when a single shot could blow the lock apart? In another version the constable was attempting to force his way into the Green. Despite a number of warnings he persisted and the exasperated rebels shot at him. There are almost as many versions of the shooting as bullets flying around the Green.

Constance was still officially liaison officer with the GPO but Mallin decided he needed her to stay. 'About two hours later he [Mallin] definitely promoted me to be his second in command,' she wrote. There were a number of captains in the ICA already; Captain Christopher (Christy) Poole was Mallin's second with responsibility for the Green. Why did Mallin choose to place Constance over him? He may have looked at the small number of rebels and realized success was unlikely. It is possible he chose Constance as a buffer in the event of failure. Her elevation over Poole saved the latter's life as his role was overlooked by the British after the rebellion.

Constance in action

Constance was now in charge of around a hundred Citizen Army men and women, some stray Irish Volunteers as well as women from Cumann na mBan. The women were delegated to look after catering and first-aid, but some ICA women like the nineteen-year-old Lily Kempson took a more militant role – she used her revolver to commandeer vehicles for the barricades and food for the stores. Mallin and Constance sent groups into houses around the Green to set up sniping positions. People saw Constance directing men and were astonished to see a woman in command of a military operation. Many assumed she was in sole command of the forces on the Green.

The Rebellion Begins

'Countess Markievicz supplied the first touch of drama,' wrote Elizabeth Bowen in the 1940s.

> In the uniform of a Colonel of Volunteers she emerged from the Green and marched up and down, gun on shoulder, in full and rewarding view of the Shelbourne windows. This practise – fascinating to many, for lady colonels were rarer then than now – she was to continue for several days of what by degrees became the siege of the Shelbourne.... It is the stern opinion of the hotel staff that the Countess took unfair advantage of her sex.[40]

Some witnesses refer to Constance as 'strutting' and 'parading herself' when it would have appeared natural for a man to walk about to supervise the trench digging. Constance cut a flamboyant figure in her tight green uniform and trousers and feathered hat and many legends about her have gone into the folklore of the Rising. Christy Poole claimed a rebel urged the burning of the Shelbourne, but Constance argued against it as she had stayed there during her debutante days.

Some of the stories of her prowess with a gun come from early Easter week. Over the years she achieved a reputation as a crack shot which matched her teenage exploits as a fearless horsewoman. She must have risked being shot on the north side of the Green as the ostrich feathers would have made her a distinctive target. Ulick O'Connor relates a story where the rebels commandeered a car for a barricade. Constance recognized the occupants from her hunting days in Sligo and apologized for the inconvenience, explaining that the car was needed for the revolution while inviting them to tea in the Green.[41] She was said to have offered tea and cakes to hostages. The story of refreshments may have been inspired by Hannah Sheehy-Skeffington who brought a picnic basket in the afternoon. As Hannah was bringing nourishment to the rebels, her pacifist husband, Frank, was distributing leaflets urging citizens to prevent looting.

Kathleen Behan, mother of Brendan and Dominic, had her own Constance story:

> She started to dig a hole in the Green to defend it against the Brits. Now, although there was all this fighting going on, many people were trying to ignore it and go on working as usual. Near her dugout were some men working on scaffolding, and they started to jeer at this mad woman in uniform digging a hole in the middle of a park.

In the end she couldn't stand it any longer, and loosed off at them with her pistol.... They didn't stay at work after that.[42]

Many of the young Irish Citizen Army members had no combat experience and were nervous on the day. The author, James Stephens, witnessed the shooting by ICA men of James Cavanagh who tried to remove his cart from the barricade. According to Sean O'Faolain, the stubborn Cavanagh was a prominent Sinn Feiner and 'Madame, furious, threatened to court-martial the man who had shot him; but nothing was done in the end.' A latecomer, Liam O'Briain, asked to be allowed across the railings to join the fight. The exchange with Constance neatly reveals the attitude of the participants.

'You know the result if we fail – rope or bullet.'

'I don't give a damn,' he replied.

The image of Constance in uniform became an enduring memory of the week. A Canadian journalist, F.A. McKenzie, commented:

> Those who saw her declare that she made a striking and handsome figure. From the rebel point of view it is a pity she and her people had not spent their time studying military tactics.... Some of the trenches were better fitted for comic opera than for fighting...[43]

McKenzie wrote one of the first accounts of the Rising, *The Irish Rebellion: What Happened and Why*, published in mid-1916. He told another Constance story that found its way into the folklore. Among the prisoners in the Green was a British soldier who took the opportunity to court a Cumann na mBan girl:

> The Countess, walking around soon afterwards to see that all was all right, was horrified to find the young soldier with his arm around a girl's waist. She stormed at the girl ... and ordered the girls to their duties.

About 3.00 pm Constance was in a group headed by Sergeant Frank Robbins which visited the Royal College of Surgeons. The classical building with its stone pillars and statues above the pediment dominated the west side of the Green. Their mission was to search for rifles and ammunition belonging to the Officer Training Corps. According to Robbins the caretaker, James Duncan, opened fire with a shotgun, but was overpowered.

The Rebellion Begins

The rebels piled inside and questioned Duncan who denied all knowledge of arms.

> The patience of our group was soon exhausted. Had not Madame Markievicz intervened he would certainly have had a very rough time.[44]

James Duncan wrote a report with a different slant for the college authorities. He came to the door to answer a Fellow of the College:

> Before your Petitioner could close the door the Countess Markievicz with two other Rebels presented themselves at the Hall door, one of the Rebels firing at close range a rifle at your Petitioner. They broke the glass of the inner door. They then forced their way in, the Countess Markievicz covering your Petitioner with a revolver, saying at the same time 'Where is the roof?' and also 'if you hesitate I will shoot you dead.' Your Petitioner being under constraint and in danger of immediate death showed the way to the roof ...[45]

Duncan refers to himself as 'your Petitioner' as he was accused of stealing in the aftermath of the rebellion and was sacked from the College. The rebels locked him with his wife and child in a bedroom on the top floor while they searched in vain for arms. Constance returned to the Green and the rebels appeared on the roof. From the rooftop Robbins saw a girl with a bicycle waving from across the road. It was Margaret Skinnider who brought from the GPO the green white and orange flag of the Irish Republic that would fly from the roof for the rest of the week.

During the evening Constance and Mallin went for a survey around the Green and surrounding streets. Sometime later Margaret Skinnider was returning on her bicycle from the GPO when she saw British soldiers advancing from Harcourt Street. Two rebels came from the park and stood in the middle of the street; she recognized Constance and Captain William Partridge, a Labour Party Councillor on Dublin Corporation.

> The countess stood motionless, waiting for them to come near.... At length she raised her gun to her shoulder – it was an 'automatic' over a foot long which she had converted into a short rifle ... and took aim. Neither she nor Partridge noticed me as I came up behind them. I was quite close as they fired. The shots rang out at the same moment and I saw the officers leading the columns drop to the

street. As the countess was taking aim again, the soldiers, without firing a shot, turned and ran in great confusion for their barracks. The whole company fled as fast as they could from *two* people, one of them a woman![46]

Fox described a similar engagement, but had Constance accompanied by Captain McCormack. The Royal Irish Rifles were approaching the Green from Camden Street via Cuffe Street.

> McCormack, who reacted at once like an old campaigner, dropped down on one knee in the middle of the road – Cuffe Street – and took careful aim at the attackers, wounding one of them. Madame joined him and succeeded in hitting a second and so stemming the rush.[47]

Despite differences in details there can be little doubt that Constance was an eager participant in the skirmishes. As they walked back to the Green Constance told Margaret about the attack on Dublin Castle. Margaret considered it appropriate that Constance was present as she often attended aristocratic balls at the Castle but had forgone her privileges when she threw in her lot with the rebels. Her testament, *Doing My Bit for Ireland*, published in the USA in 1917, helped to promote the image of Constance as a fearless revolutionary. Margaret included a colourful account of her heroine taking possession of the College of Surgeons:

> She walked up the steps, rang the bell, and, when no-one answered, fired into the lock and entered.

As Constance would predict, her friends were eager to make her a heroine just as her opponents would seize every opportunity to depict her as a monster.

It was a quiet spring evening on the Green. All over the city holiday makers returned to the city after a day at the races or the seaside. There were no uniformed police on the streets and looters prowled 'like night-cats,' according to Sean O'Faolain. From the roof of the College of Surgeons the Tricolour fluttered over the barricaded streets and freshly-leaved trees in the Green.

4

'The Red Angel of the Revolution'

The long bright evening moved gradually into a cold spring night. Margaret Skinnider joined the couriers and first-aid women on the floor of the summerhouse and immediately fell asleep.

> Madam was not so fortunate. She was too tired and excited to sleep. Instead, she walked about looking for some sheltered place, and to get out of the wind, tried lying down in one of the trenches. But the ground was much too chilly, so she walked about until she noticed the motor-car of her friend, Dr Kathleen Lynn, seized that morning for the barricade.[48]

The street must have been quiet with no military activity for Constance to walk outside the railings. She climbed into the car and made her bed on the seat beneath a rug.

> When morning came she could not forgive herself for having slept there all night while the rest of us remained outdoors.

It rained heavily giving the rebels in the park a taste of conditions in the muddy trenches in France; the rain provided cover for the Dublin Fusiliers who occupied the Shelbourne during the night. Other units of the British Army moved into position on the streets around the Green. Constance was awakened early on Tuesday by the sound of machine gun bullets crossing the roof of the car. The rebels replied with rifle fire, but their shallow trenches gave little protection and the fresh greenery left them exposed. A young Citizen Army man was shot and his body riddled with bullets as the line of fire moved back and forth along the grass. A bullet passed through Mallin's hat as he helped a wounded comrade to safety.

Another bullet was supposed to have struck Constance on the heel of her boot. According to legend she provided cover by making a lone attack on a machine gun post. As the bullets struck all around she advanced using trees for cover, firing her machine pistol at the hotel window. She kept firing until she hit the machine gunner and the shooting stopped, allowing the Citizen Army to evacuate the trenches. It is unlikely that anyone could withstand a withering swathe of machine gun bullets, but she most likely fired from cover at the machine gun crew.

Constance aiming her pistol

The dearth of information on the time and place of British Army casualties makes it impossible to verify accounts of rebel 'hits.' Four of the ICA men were killed by machine gun bullets.

Mallin held an emergency conference of officers at which it was agreed to evacuate the trenches. He ordered withdrawal to positions deeper into the park but the gunners soon found the range and the first aid station came under fire. Lt. Thomas O'Donoghue was digging a trench in the centre of the park when he heard a woman calling:

'O'Donoghue, where is O'Donoghue?'

I recognised the voice as that of Countess Markievicz.

I shouted back: 'Madame, here I am in the centre of the little hill.'

She came over to me as if no machine gun were about and told me that we were to retire immediately to Cuffe St. corner. I told her that my orders, received a few hours earlier directly from Mallin, were that I was to hold on and not retire under any circumstances. So Madame said:

'The Red Angel of the Revolution'

'Well, your orders now are to retire; Mallin sent that message over to you.'

'Well, Madame,' said I, 'we are not going to run away. We will have to organise in order to retreat. It would be too dangerous to retire immediately in disorder.'

We reached Cuffe St. corner and Madame told us we were to go to the College of Surgeons. We felt safe at the far side of the Green and so Madame and I were able to indulge in a little conversation. Madame said she never thought that I would turn out in the fight, as she heard that I did not believe in physical force. I then returned the compliment by telling Madame that I didn't think she would turn out and instantly she asked: 'Why?'

I replied that she was too much of a fire-eater and that I always believed that people who spoke strongly were not sincere in their protestations of willingness to fight, but I saw now that she meant everything she said.[49]

During the day the rest of the garrison moved from the park into the College of Surgeons and completed the evacuation by about 3.00 o'clock. Some of the women dragged wounded comrades through the bushes to safety. They brought their equipment into the lecture halls and corridors of the stone building and blocked up windows with furniture and text books. The front door was barricaded, leaving the sheltered York Street door for entry and exit. The rebels wandered through lecture rooms full of laboratory equipment; one room had jars containing body parts and foetuses. The smell of formaldehyde drifted through the building. Mallin instructed them not to cause any damage, but one young man attacked a full-length portrait of Queen Victoria in the Boardroom. For the rebels she was the Famine Queen who presided over the starvation of a million peasants in the 1840s.

Damaged portrait of Queen Victoria

The unnamed youth took a knife and cut strips from the canvas, intending to use the material for puttees. Mallin reprimanded him with a cuff on the ear. O'Faolain is partly responsible for the story that Constance was the culprit. The Examination Hall next door was a huge room with solid windowless walls and skylights making it ideal for a dormitory. A section of the room was adapted as a first aid station while another room was used as a morgue. The kitchen was commandeered to feed the garrison.

> They tore up the carpets into strips and the men slept in them rolled like mummies. Broken chairs and the coal in the boiler-house made excellent fires for cooking. They laid out their dead on old benches from the House of Lords and a rough crucifix, fashioned out of metal breast-plates, hung heavily over the bodies.[50]

The next five days saw the same pattern of trading fire with the British in the Shelbourne Hotel and the United Services Club. British Army snipers operated from other positions around the Green while skirmishing went on in surrounding streets. The British Army commander, General Lowe, decided the man assault would be on the rebel position in the GPO.

'On Tuesday we began to be short of food,' Constance wrote.

> There were no bread carts on the streets. We retired into the College of Surgeons that evening and were joined by some of our men who had been in other places and by quite a large squad of Volunteers, and with this increase in our numbers the problem of food became very serious. Nellie Gifford was put in charge of one large classroom with a big grate, but alas, there was nothing to cook. When we were all starving she produced a quantity of oatmeal from somewhere and made pot after pot of delicious porridge, which kept us going.

They secured supplies of biscuits and sweets from Jacob's factory and Connolly sent three girls from the GPO with bread, cheese and Oxo cubes. The scouts could still move with ease through the streets due to the large number of onlookers. Lt. O'Donoghue and Constance made a grisly discovery:

> When night fell, I was … examining the basement with the Countess; where we were groping in the dark for electric switches, I suddenly heard her exclaim: 'O'Donoghue, there is a body here – I can feel the curly hair. It is like the body of a child'. I shuddered and found

myself unable even to look for the electric light switch, but Madame found it quickly enough and we replaced the cloth over the body of the child. I did not really look at it – I could not.[51]

Constance was concerned that Eva in London would worry and sent a message through Hannah when she visited the College on Tuesday. As the garrison fretted about food Mallin sent units to break through houses towards the Shelbourne to start a fire and smoke out the British. According to R.M. Fox, Constance guided the party. They left the College at 8.00 o'clock on Tuesday night crossing a plank over a thirty foot drop into the alleyway. She got down on hands and knees and crawled across to the Turkish Baths next door.

She had been preparing for urban warfare for years; Stasko remembered coming home to Surry House to find her and Connolly absorbed in a manual on street fighting. The group used sledge hammers to break through the walls into adjoining houses. Other groups had different objectives – one targeted a pastry shop and brought supplies back to the College. Constance was called back to a meeting with Mallin. The moment to start the fires arrived when she crawled through the wall with fresh orders. They were to cancel the plan; Mallin felt they had been compromised and the British were preparing an ambush. The garrison would hold out for as long as possible, but would not go on the offensive.

On Tuesday evening Frank Sheehy-Skeffington was still trying to stop looting when he was arrested by British troops. He was taken to Portobello Barracks in Rathmines where he admitted sympathy for the rebels, but stressed he was a pacifist. On Wednesday morning Captain Bowen-Colthurst had him shot in the yard alongside two journalists. He sent a party of soldiers to ransack the Sheehy-Skeffington home where Hannah was alone with their son. The official murder of the anti-war campaigner would have a deep and lasting effect on his fellow pacifist, Eva Gore-Booth.

Constance slept little on Tuesday night and wandered throughout the halls of the College. According to O'Faolain she made friendships among the garrison that would endure to her death, 'cherished by her as the most precious fruits of her life's work.'[52] As the volunteers slept she talked in low tones with William Partridge. He was worried about his wife who was close to giving birth. Constance promised that if she survived she would look after the child and sent a message to Eva to act as godmother.

William Patrick Partridge, a founder of the Irish Citizen Army and Labour Party Councillor on Dublin Corporation, was forty-three, five foot five with scars on his hands and face from Bright's Disease. Like many of his comrades he had no difficulty reconciling Catholicism with Socialism and led the nightly Rosary. Constance was impressed with his concern for the young rebels, his gentle and caring nature which combined physical and spiritual care. He was, she wrote, a 'brilliant orator and Labour leader, comrade and friend of Connolly's...'

William Partridge

The rebels were well-used to entertaining themselves and Constance took part in concerts with songs and recitations – an anti-recruiting piece such as 'Mike O'Leary' or with a topical anti-war song, *Brit-Huns*. In the College they kept up morale by singing traditional songs to a background of machine guns and answering rifles. Among the favourites were Peadar Kearney's *A Soldier's Song*, the traditional marching sing-along *Step Together* and ballads like *The Bold Fenian Men*. Just across the Green the guests in the Shelbourne Hotel, trapped by the fighting, also amused themselves with nightly entertainments. The tunes were probably similar, but the words would have been quite different.

The rebels appear to have forgotten about James Duncan and his family in the top floor bedroom without food. On Wednesday Duncan was able to shout through the window with a woman in York Street who tied bread and butter to a rope which he drew up.

> Your Petitioner, his wife and child, were that evening by order of the Countess Markievicz, marched under armed escort down to the basement kitchen of the College. They remained close prisoners there until the Sunday following the Rebellion on scanty rations. Your Petitioner was told by one of the Rebels during his imprisonment that the Countess Markievicz and Staff were occupying his dining room.[53]

Margaret Skinnider was delighted to take part in the fighting. She and Constance were on the roof trading shots with snipers in the early stages.

After Private Doherty was caught by machine gun fire and wounded in sixteen places, Mallin discontinued action from the roof. The position in the College remained the same on Wednesday while a fierce battle was fought on nearby Mount Street. Late in the evening Margaret Skinnider went with a group to burn a house behind British Army positions on Harcourt Street. Among them was Joseph Connolly, brother to the late Sean; in later life he would become Chief of the Dublin Fire Service. A machine gun opened up on the group; Private Freddie Ryan was shot dead and Margaret was wounded in three places. William Partridge carried her to the College on his back. Madeline ffrench-Mullen wanted to bring her to a hospital, but she refused. She cried as the medic cut away pieces of the uniform Constance had made for her. As a doctor probed and dressed the wounds Constance held her tightly by the hand.

Examination Hall, College of Surgeons

Unaware that Fred Ryan was dead Constance and Partridge returned to Harcourt Street to rescue him. Partridge created a diversion and two British soldiers inside a house opened fire. According to legend Constance located them by the rifle flashes and killed both soldiers. We can never be certain of the details as each rebel fatality was a potential martyr for commemoration, but British Army deaths were statistics.

Constance seemed to be everywhere in the College – firing from the snipers nest under the roof, checking positions, exhorting volunteers and trying to maintain morale. There was a great gap in age between herself and the majority of the rebels, many still in their teens. She was a heavy smoker and used a wooden cigarette holder. According to Anne Marreco, she was a strict chaperone and made frequent tours of inspection, checking rooms and cubby-holes to make sure all was correct between the young men and women.

A spirit of camaraderie and mutual respect helped to cement the sense of discipline and common purpose in which Constance was obeyed as an officer, but nicknamed 'Lizzie'. Frank Robbins was brought before her when he refused to accept a medicinal glass of spirits from the Medical Officer. He explained he had a conscientious objection to drinking spirits and was excused.

On Thursday 'Nono' Connolly returned to Dublin from a mission to the North of Ireland and went looking for her mother, Lillie. She found her in Constance's rented cottage in the Dublin Mountains, lying unconscious on the floor. Lillie had read in a newspaper that James was dead. From a nearby slope they could see huge fires in the city centre and hear the thump of artillery shells. The British Army had tightened the cordon around the city and brought up a gunboat and artillery to attack the GPO.

By midweek the College of Surgeons garrison could see the flames from burning buildings in the O'Connell Street area. Constance got on the roof to watch the city burning. 'We've done more than Tone already,' she said. Rumours of a nationwide insurrection spread through the garrison. As she lay wounded Margaret Skinnider heard British guns firing on Liberty Hall from the Liffey and thought the German navy had arrived. Partridge walked about with his head bandaged from a falling trapdoor. The garrison did not accept that defeat was inevitable, but planned to change into civilian clothes and carry on a guerrilla war in the Wicklow Mountains. They held a meeting at which Constance bemoaned the lack of bayonets for fighting at close quarters. This gave rise to the story she was looking for scalpels to use as bayonets. Mallin is supposed to have commented with what Marie Perolz called his heavenly smile, 'How bloodthirsty you are.'

In his poem, 'The Statues', Yeats has Pearse summoning the Celtic warrior Cuchulainn to his side in the GPO. It does not take a great leap of the imagination to have Constance invoking the spirit of Maedbh of the Battles as she hurried through the College of Surgeons.

On Thursday the rebels found rifles and ammunition in the basement which provided a boost to morale. Christopher Poole claimed he was with Constance when they found the weapons. The jousting between rifle and machine guns continued. On Friday morning the ship carrying the new military commander, General Sir John Maxwell, along with fresh

Constance:Maedbh of the Battles

troops entered Dublin Bay. General Maxwell was military dictator in Ireland; his mission was to end the rebellion, execute the leaders and crush the spirit of resistance among the population. He was accompanied by Second Lieutenant, Alfred Bucknill, an Admiralty barrister, whose brief was to ensure the military acted within legal parameters. Bucknill suffered from sciatica and was in a low mood:

> We arrived in the very early hours of the morning and steamed up to the North Wall, silent and dark. The Custom House stood out against a background of fire. There were at least four distinct fires burning, and great flames were leaping up in different places as if the whole city north of the Liffey was doomed.[54]

Bucknill and Maxwell

The College of Surgeons was now cut off from the other garrisons with the rebels feeling the strain of confined conditions. After nearly a week of occupation the rooms were cluttered with kit and refuse. Civilians returned to side streets and shouted at the windows that the GPO garrison had surrendered. Pearse made the official surrender to General Lowe in the afternoon of Saturday, 29 April. The British newspapers had a special interest in Constance and highlighted her involvement in the Rising. One headline read:

> Rioting in Dublin: Russian Countess Said To Have Driven Motor For The Rebels

When General Lowe was accepting the surrender from Pearse he enquired about Constance.

> 'I understand you have the Countess Markievicz down there?'
> 'No, she isn't with me,' Pearse replied.
> 'Oh, I know she's down there,' said Lowe sharply.
> 'Don't accuse me of speaking an untruth,' said Pearse in a sharper tone.

'Oh, I beg your pardon, Mr. Pearse, but I do know she's in the area.'

'Well, she's not with me, Sir.'[55]

The GPO garrison were marched into captivity on the grounds of the Rotunda Hospital on Saturday night, but no official communication reached the College. The insurgents refused to believe that the rebellion was over and expected a British assault at any moment. They had fortified the windows and sawed through the stairs to ambush attackers. Constance spent the early part of the night looking after the wounded and various military duties. Sometime during the night the group in the lecture hall knelt to pray for the dead and the living. Many years later, after the deaths of Eva and Constance, Esther Roper wrote:

> A great peace was over them, waiting for the end. Constance wanted to join in the prayers, but at first they could not understand why a non-Catholic should take part in Catholic prayers.[56]

Constance often read the Bible given to her by Lady Hill, but had drifted from religious practice. Esther recognised a mystical streak in her, but thought her extroverted nature worked against the solitude necessary to develop it. All of her life since childhood had been spent in company – her wide circle of family and friends, art school companions in London and Paris. When she married Casimir and lived in Dublin the pace of social life never ceased. Her interest in Catholicism grew after her involvement with the Dublin working class during the Lockout. Esther thought her conversion to Catholicism in 1916 came about because she hated to belong to a church that represented the rich – 'all the peasants being Roman Catholics.'

The intensity of Easter Week appealed to her strong sense of idealism. She began to view religion not as a superstitious remnant, but a belief system that strengthened the urge to courage and self-sacrifice. When her comrades knelt to pray she felt excluded from the manual labourers and clerks, domestic servants and factory girls who made up the majority of the Citizen Army. It is hard for us to appreciate the rigid class snobbery held by the upper and middle classes towards those they regarded as inferior. To consort with the lower classes was considered a symptom of moral collapse and depravity. She was not free from the prejudices of her class, but she delighted in the egalitarian atmosphere of the College of Surgeons. Esther wrote:

But now face to face with death she was deeply impressed by the reality of spiritual things to these men and women among whom she had lived. As she shared their prayers there came to her a vision of the Unseen, which wrought such a change in her that from that moment to her, too, the things that are seen became temporal and the things that are unseen, eternal.

There was a sombre atmosphere in the shadowy Examination Hall with light falling from the panels on the ceiling. The garrison had set up an altar made up of metal plates taken from coffins in the College. Partridge was like a monk with his bandaged head as he recited the Hail Marys in his silvery voice followed by a murmur of Holy Marys. Body and mind were tired after the day, but the soul can emerge at such moments, Leonard Cohen's 'crack in everything through which the light gets in.'[57] It was a defining moment for Constance which she commemorated in her poem 'The Rosary' or 'College of Surgeons':

> The great hall fades away into the gloom,
> As tremulous night falls slowly from above,
> Merging us each in each in tender love:
> One shadow marching onward towards one doom.
> On our rough altar white flowers shine and bloom
> Intensifying dusky waves that move
> Around the tall black Cross. One hope, one prayer
> Filled all our hearts, one perfect Holy Faith
> Lifted our souls. As we knelt humbly there,
> Your silvery voice, soft as a dying breath,
> Was answered by a hundred strong and clear,
> Craving a grace from her whom all hold dear –
> 'Mary! Be with us at the hour of death.'

Early on the morning of Sunday, 30 April, she wrote her will, hastily scribbled it on a single sheet of paper. It was the simplest of documents. Casimir and Stasko were to get one hundred pounds each, Bessie Smith, her domestic from Surrey House, was awarded twenty-five pounds. Everything else was to go to her daughter Maeve Alys. Mallin and Madeline ffrench-Mullen were the witnesses; she placed it in the lining of Margaret Skinnider's coat for safe keeping.

5

In Kilmainham

Mallin was asleep on Sunday morning when Nurse Elizabeth O'Farrell arrived with the order to surrender. Constance accepted the order but appears to have been surprised by the content. Rosie Hackett saw her crying on the stairs, the only time she ever saw her in such a state. She woke Mallin who held a meeting of officers before assembling the company in the Examination Hall to read the order. Many reacted angrily and wanted to continue the struggle; they had been preparing all week for a decisive battle and were ashamed to give up without a fight. Partridge and Constance walked among the angry volunteers and calmed them. 'I trust Connolly. We must obey,' she said.

At one stage a British soldier walked into the hall, bareheaded and smoking a cigarette. It was Captain Harold de Courcy Wheeler of the King's Royal Rifle Corps and a distant relative of the Gore-Booths. Apparently he entered the building to see what was delaying the surrender. Joe Connolly raised his revolver but Constance stopped him: 'Don't Joe, don't. It would be a great shame now.'[58] Along with Mallin and Partridge she convinced the volunteers to surrender by promising them their sacrifice would bear fruit. Margaret Skinnider was carried to St. Vincent's Hospital across the Green before the formal surrender.

Private Seamus Kavanagh remembered:

> On Sunday morning, we were all assembled, and Pearse's letter was read out to us, that it was to save further bloodshed, that we had vindicated ourselves in our protest. He pointed out that some of the leaders might be executed or sentenced to terms of imprisonment, but that the remainder would be sent home. I remember that there was pandemonium and protests. Some of the men got their rifles

and smashed them – including Joe Connolly. A number of them started crying.

> We were asked to kneel down and say the Rosary, which we did. To my surprise, I saw the Countess Markievicz taking out a Rosary beads and reciting the Rosary with the rest of us. She was not then a Catholic, as far as I can recollect, although she used to come to Mass with us when we camped at Belcamp and in the mountains, but I had never seen her with a Rosary beads.[59]

Mallin and Markievicz went out by the side door where they met Wheeler who accepted the surrender. 'I met the accused at the side door of the College of Surgeons in York Street,' Wheeler would testify at her trial.

> Commandant Michael Mallin of the rebels was with her. The meeting took place under a flag of truce. Subsequently the rebels who were in the College of Surgeons marched out and surrendered. The accused was one of the number. She was armed with a pistol and ammunition in a Sam Browne belt. She handed her arms to me.[60]

In later years he included a note when donating the pistol to the National Museum: 'She kissed the pistol when handing it to me.' Her gesture would become a dramatic image of the rebellion, defiance at the moment of defeat. She also surrendered her prized Mauser automatic which was retained by General Lowe and passed on to Wheeler. After handing over the pistol Constance saluted Wheeler and said, 'I am ready.'

As the rebels assembled the young William Oman found Mallin in a philosophical mood. He thought the men would be interned in the Curragh Camp, but he expected to be shot along with the other commanding officers. 'But,' he added, 'I question if they will shoot Lizzie.'[61] A hostile crowd gathered, including the vociferous Separation Women, and began to shout abuse at the disarmed rebels. Wheeler feared for Constance's safety and offered to drive her into captivity in his motor car. 'She refused, and said she preferred to march with the men as she was second in command. About 120 rebels surrendered at the same time as the accused.'

The Irish Times of 1 May said of the Stephen's Green rebels: 'They had held the College building, over which their flag was unfurled on Monday, with considerable tenacity replying with energy to the attack of the military.' As the rebels assembled outside the College a Sligo artist, Kathleen Fox, made a sketch which she developed into a large oil painting. Mallin and Constance stand nonchalantly at the front of their green-clad band surrounded by two columns of British soldiers. Partridge with his bandaged head makes an appearance behind the leaders, bloodied but unbowed. It was the image of a disciplined force the rebels wished to show the world. Journalists focussed their attention on Constance which helped sustain the impression that she was leader of the garrison:

'The Countess Markievicz, fantastically dressed in male attire,' remarked *The Irish Times*, 'was prominent among the one hundred and ten rebels who handed over their arms to the authorities...'

Constance's pistol

McKenzie briefly remarked: 'The Countess Markievicz, the Red Angel of the Revolution, gave herself up today with the group who have been holding the College of Surgeons.'[62]

As they marched into captivity Mallin and Constance are said to have speculated on what fate lay in store for them – would they be shot or hung?

The immediate danger was an attack from the mob that followed through the streets. Constance stood out because of her height, exaggerated by her thin figure and theatrical hat, although the feathers were moulted and flat at this stage. Cries of 'Shoot the bastards' and cheers for the Staffordshire regiment, 'Good old Staffs' followed them down Grafton Street. The inevitable Separation Women were at the forefront of the crowd and directed their scorn at Constance and her breeches.[63]

The playwright and Dublin Fusilier, St. John Ervine, wrote:

> There was a feeling of remarkable fury against the Countess Marckevitz (sic), remarkable because this lady had spent herself in feeding and succouring poor people during the 1913 strike, and one would have imagined that some feeling of gratitude would have saved her from the insults that were uttered against her.[64]

The impression has been fostered that the majority of Dubliners were hostile to the rebels, an impression British propagandists were eager to broadcast, but the situation on the streets was different. Residents of

In Kilmainham

Detail from The Arrest, a painting by Kathleen Fox

tenements in Gardiner Street applauded the rebel prisoners under guard. McKenzie was an impartial witness:

> As I was passing through a street near the Castle cheer after cheer could be heard ... I looked ahead. A regiment was approaching. 'They are cheering the soldiers,' I said to my companion ... I could see that the soldiers were escorting a large number of prisoners, men and women, several hundred in all. The people were cheering not the soldiers but the rebels.
>
> 'Shure,' we cheer them,' a woman told him. 'Why shouldn't we? Aren't they our own flesh and blood?'[65]

This confirms the experience of Kathleen Lynn who was transferred from Dublin Castle on Monday:

> About 50 men and we 12 women marched off via Thomas St. to Richmond barracks, great ovation as we marched along, only separation women hooted.[66]

The Stephen's Green garrison stopped before a freshly-dug trench at Dublin Castle where Robbins thought they might meet their doom, but they were treated to a cup of tea by a relative of Madeline ffrench-Mullen. Elsie Mahaffy, daughter of Trinity's Provost, wrote in her diary about Constance in the Castle courtyard:

> Here 50 men were lying dead – separated from her only by one wall. She showed the most callous indifference, lighting cigarettes and strutting about, as conceited as on old draggle-tailed peacock; she seemed to anticipate no disagreeable consequences for her shameful and silly conduct.[67]

The rebels were again lined up and marched along Thomas Street past the spot where Robert Emmet was hung and beheaded a century before and on to Richmond Barracks in Inchicore where Constance and Madeline ffrench-Mullen were separated from the others. The exercise yard at Richmond Barracks was thronged with prisoners and soldiers. The authorities were in the process of separating leaders from the rank and file. Julia Grennan of Cumann na mBan was brought to the barracks with women from the GPO. Constance ignored the guards to rush over and shake hands and enquire about her friends.

'Remove that woman,' an officer shouted and soldiers separated them. Alfred Bucknill was in the barracks square:

> I saw the Countess Markievicz arrive at the head of her company. When I saw her she was standing gnawing an orange in the Curragh Square with a number of young women prisoners standing behind her. She was dressed in dark green knickerbockers, puttees and tunic and had a green hat with cock's feathers on it.[68]

Brigid Lyons Thornton was among the Cumann na mBan prisoners in Richmond Barracks:

In Kilmainham

> About 7 p.m. we were all marched down to the barrack square where we found the Countess and a number of others lined up.... We were marched out the gate to Kilmainham and the crowds outside along the route gave us a mixed reception, cheering, jeering, booing and making remarks, mostly uncomplimentary. The Countess was the only one in uniform and she attracted most of the attention. We were all a bedraggled lot after the week and certainly did not look our best.[69]

Kilmainham Gaol, a stone fortress on a ridge overlooking the Camac River, opened in 1796 and housed many political prisoners. It was not used as a convict prison since 1910, but had been taken over by the military as an army detention centre. Only sections of the buildings were in use and were not ready for an influx of prisoners. There was no light or heating as the gas had been cut off during the Rising. The atmosphere on that Sunday evening was like a Gothic extravaganza with guards using candles in jam pots for torches to dispel the gloom.

As the prisoners entered they heard shouts and steps echoing down dark stone corridors. Some of the guards were British Army deserters, themselves confined to the prison. A soldier noticed Constance smoking on a landing. 'Put out that fag,' he shouted. She ignored the order and the soldier knocked the cigarette from her hand. The other prisoners wondered at her self-control; she smiled encouragement as she was put into a cell. The other women and some of the male leaders were packed into common cells; Constance was on the same landing, but in a cell of her own. She recalled the day in an account of her trial:

> I surrendered at 12 on Sunday, marched to Castle & there to Richmond Barracks, given biscuits & a cup of tea. Then on to Kilmainham. Solitary confinement at once – Hard 'Sailor's Biscuits' with greasy water (called 'soup') & bad coffee. Wooden beds with mattress divided in three bits that always slipped off.[70]

After forty-eight years of living as she pleased it was her first experience of domination by others; her long captivity had begun. She appears to have been one of the more fortunate prisoners; many of the cells had no furniture and rebels slept on the floor with boots for a pillow.

The initial reaction in Ireland towards the rebellion was anger and dismay, especially from nationalists appalled at the death and destruction.

Unionists were furious at what they perceived as treachery when Britain was at war. Stories abounded about the delusions of the leaders ('the usual stump orators') and the gullibility of the volunteers ('the Larkinite crowd'), but Constance was singled out for opprobrium. She was 'the one woman among them of high birth and therefore the most depraved' according to Miss Mahaffy. In her eyes Constance's main crime was that she 'took to politics and left our class.' Willie Yeats' sister, Lily, wrote to her father in New York:

> What a pity Madame Markievicz's madness changed its form when she inherited it. In her father it meant looking for the North Pole in an open boat.... Her followers are said to have been either small boys or drunken dock labourers out of work, called the Citizen Army.... I would not have followed her across the road.[71]

A rumour that she shot six of her own men went as far as the United States. The *Evening World's* readers learned that the Countess 'in man's clothing and flashing a brace of revolvers' led an attack on the Shelbourne Hotel. The readers of the *New York Times* of 15 May had the benefit of an eyewitness account from a Dr Cecil D. McAdam who saw her 'dressed as a man ... at the head of a band of rebels. I was informed by an Irish doctor that she had shot six of them for hanging back when the soldiers appeared on the scene.'[72]

Evening World Headline

She was accused of taking a bloodthirsty delight in shooting soldiers. Of all the rebel leaders she attracted the most newspaper coverage and was also unique in being the target of propaganda and abuse. Sir Horace Plunkett wrote in his journal that 'her motives were as pure as her methods foul. I met Powerscourt and he was, he told me, begging the authorities to shoot her.'[73]

Powerscourt was Assistant Provost-Marshall in Dublin Castle. *The Irish Times* provided more sober coverage, being more concerned with the condition of the College of

In Kilmainham

Surgeons, especially the damage to Queen Victoria and the state of the carpets in the Examination Hall:

> The caretaker's rooms were reserved as bedrooms for the female invaders. It was here that Countess Markievicz slept, and she and the others seem to have had a partiality for chocolates and other similar articles, many broken packages of sweetstuffs being left behind.

Constance was kept in isolation in Kilmainham but shared the poor conditions endured by her comrades – blankets covered in vermin, lack of washing facilities and poor quality food. Mabel FitzGerald, mother to the future Taoiseach, Garret FitzGerald, wrote to the Archbishop of Dublin, William Walsh, about the lack of sanitary facilities, complaining that 'prisoners who managed to get near a tap and begin to wash were ordered away by soldiers in charge of them.' The day began at 7.00 with breakfast at 9.30 of biscuits so hard the prisoners used them as spoons. Lunch came at noon and consisted of a stew that was, according to prisoners, neither soup nor stirabout. Constance could hear voices and doors opening and closing, but was unable to make contact with her comrades.

Constance's mug shots

The mug shots of her in captivity show a far from glamorous figure. Her face is covered in deep lines engraved into the skin. The dead eyes have the exhausted expression of a woman who has hardly slept for a fortnight. Even the hat is crumpled and the feather lies flat across the brim. The image is the opposite of the determined woman with a gun from Kehoe's studio.

Kathleen Lynn wrote in her diary for 2 May: 'Madam Markiev. here in solitary. We had loan of her comb & soap.'

Constance attempted to maintain her morale by writing poetry on scraps of toilet paper smuggled out by Father Albert Bibby, a Franciscan friar from the priory on Church Street, who transcribed them into a copybook.

In Kilmainham

I cannot sleep, but yet I dream,
I dream and still am sane,
Dear faces white and pallid gleam
Seen thro' a storm of rain;
Of rain or tears? for it would seem
They stood there to be slain.

The military kept information to a minimum and the most lurid rumours flourished.

> Countess Markievicz was described in another bulletin from England as being a sinister figure who had a room in her house entirely filled with human skulls. She had, in fact, from the time of her art-school days a human skull on the mantelpiece. This formed the basis of the fantastic story.[74]

She was held in B Wing where the rebel leaders were kept before execution. Her cell was close to that occupied by Pearse who was moved into Kilmainham on the night before his death. According to R.M. Fox she was able to converse with him across the landing. Pearse was among the first to be shot by firing squad on her third morning in jail, Wednesday, 3 May. She first met Pearse through his involvement in setting up the Theatre of Ireland in 1906, a breakaway from Yeats' Abbey Theatre. She and Casimir visited his school, St. Enda's, in 1909. Two other executions followed in the cold early morning – Tom Clarke, her mentor among the Republicans, and the poet and lecturer Thomas MacDonagh, another friend who printed Casimir's pictures in his journal, *The Irish Review*.

Her poem, 'In Kilmainham', contains a vivid description of her feelings on those bleak mornings:

> Grey dawn and spring; I cannot sleep,
> Despair is in my brain,
> The grey hours through the prison creep
> As if they felt the pain;
> As if they fain would stop and weep
> And time's grim hand restrain.

She expected to share the fate of Pearse and the others and asked the prison chaplain, Father Ryan, to be with her at her execution. He suggested she might like to exchange the soiled uniform for some fresh clothes. 'I fought in these clothes and I'll die in them,' she replied. She found comfort in a crucifix given to her by Father Albert, which she would later pass on to Roger Casement's cousin, Gertrude Bannister:

> My dear Gertrude, I want you to keep this crucifix as a little love token from me. Father Albert gave it to me the first time I saw him & I think it saved me from going mad those awful hours at daybreak when I lay in my cell at Kilmainham listening to the British murdering our leaders...[75]

Father Albert was in Kilmainham on the morning of Thursday, 4 May, for the execution by firing squad of Edward Daly, Joseph Mary Plunkett, Michael O'Hanrahan and Willie Pearse. Major John MacBride, the estranged husband of Maud Gonne, was executed on Friday morning. Brigid Lyons Thornton, a Cumann na mBan prisoner, heard the early volleys: 'Afterwards I always woke up at that hour. I never forgot those volleys.'[76]

A petition written on Constance's behalf some months later gives a picture of her state of mind:

Father Albert Bibby

> She lay awake all night, night after night, till dawn when, each morning, some of her friends were shot under her window. It is perhaps hard for those who have not been through these things to understand, but the fact that two volleys were often necessary to kill them seems to have added a crowning touch of agony to the situation. However strong a person's spirit may be it is surely impossible such an experience should not tell terribly on their nerves...[77]

Constance was held in a cell that did not overlook the execution yard, but the sound of the shots echoed around the thick stone walls. In her imagination she would visit the condemned men as they prepared for death and witness the executions:

> I stood beside them – heard their prayer,
> Last prayer on earth below,
> That God would for his country care
> I saw the cruel foe
> Level their guns – oh I can't bear
> To look more – no, no, no.

She would relive the executions many times and they would be remembered in verse, song and image in Ireland during the coming decades. To observers, including many who opposed the Rising, the programme of execution was like blood seeping from beneath a locked door. Constance again:

> A peal of shots swift pattering crash,
> Breaking the air like hail,
> Silence – more shots – a sickening flash
> Shewed me the volley failed;
> Shewed men with many a bleeding gash,
> Maimed men with faces pale.

During the days in isolation her only outlet was verse and she composed long poems in which she recorded her dismay, tempered by hatred into a steely defiance:

> The dawn glides slowly through my cell
> I sigh, the dream has gone
> I hear a little chapel bell
> Telling that night is done
> Telling of hopes no tears can quell
> Re-risen with the sun.

The lines are imbued with the cult of martyrdom beginning to form around the dead leaders, drawing on the Christian story of sacrifice, death and resurrection. Hannah Sheehy-Skeffington described Constance's poetry as 'dashed off ... they did not work as literature, but there is a fire and quality in them for all that – and, of course, propaganda'[78] as in 'The Men of Easter Week':

> Oh Paudraig dear, & did you hear
> The word that's going round
> The Saxon's dirty flag at last
> Lies trampled on the ground...

Other poems in the same vein were 'A Volunteer', 'The Seagull', 'Easter Week', and 'Manchester Martyrs'. She wrote to reassure herself that despite the military defeat the cause was not lost.

6

Two Trials

When they surrendered some of the rebels thought they would be treated as prisoners-of-war despite assurances from their guards they would be dispatched with bayonets. Stories circulated around Dublin of bodies buried in cellars and a mass grave in the middle of St. Stephen's Green. The military authorities decided the prisoners would be dealt with under the provisions of the Defence of the Realm Act. If the rebels had been German soldiers they would have been marched off to a prisoner-of-war camp. Even though many of them fought in the uniforms of the Volunteers and the Irish Citizen Army and surrendered according to military protocol they would be tried before military tribunals.

General Maxwell held a meeting of chief officers on Monday to sort out the legalities of courts-martial while the authorities at Arbour Hill Prison prepared a large grave, sixty-foot across. 'What actually happened in the trials that followed the surrender is still emerging,' writes Sean Enright in 2014:

> Between 1 May and 3 July over 3,226 men and women were arrested and filtered through Richmond Barracks in Dublin. Of these, 1,867 were deported and 171 prisoners were tried.[79]

The trials took place at a time of frequent courts-martial of British soldiers. In the spring of 1916 five soldiers were executed by firing squad in Macedonia while in May six were shot on the Western Front. The courts-martial were held in camera and the Government refused to reveal the numbers as 'not in the public interest.' Under the Army Act a prisoner could obtain a copy of the trial record but, in a macabre twist of logic, the condemned prisoner was the only person allowed to make the record public.

Two Trials

The courts-martial began on the afternoon of Tuesday, 2 May, in a large three-storey stone building, the Officers' Block, in Richmond Barracks. Prisoners were brought before a three-member military court with high ranking officers for judges. To speed up the process two courts ran at the same time and prisoners were mostly tried in batches. There were two prosecutors, but only one achieved notoriety – a thirty-five-year-old solicitor and Second Lieutenant in the Territorial Army Officer, William Evelyn Wylie, who would become a High Court Judge. Wylie made a statement to the Military History Bureau in 1953 in which he claimed that 'all these courts-martial were drumhead courts-martial in the early stages', and he appears to be quite satisfied that no records were made or kept of these courts-martial. He stated that the three officers constituting the Court made occasional notes but that no official record was taken or kept.[80] Wylie's memory was inaccurate in many respects but his version of Constance's trial has been widely circulated.

The first to be tried were three of the signatories of the Proclamation – Pearse, Clarke and MacDonagh. The verdicts were not notified immediately, but it was death in each case; the sentences were confirmed by Maxwell and they were shot around 3.45 in Kilmainham the following morning. The rebel leaders seem to have been gratified that the officers behaved courteously and allowed them one last turn on the stage of history. Constance, however, was not impressed; she was not at her best on the day of her court-martial – she was dirty, exhausted, hungry and probably out of cigarettes, but she was determined not to placate the military by playing their game.

Each trial had a preliminary session where the prisoner was presented with the charge and a summary of the evidence. There was more preparation than usual in the case against Constance. On Thursday morning, 4 May, she was taken from her cell and brought in a Red Cross ambulance the short distance to Richmond Barracks. She was accompanied by a wardress, Miss McInerney, and a British Army escort. She wrote an account of the trial for her solicitor later in the year:

> Brought to Richmond Barracks I think on Thursday, but it might have been Friday. Was tried twice. First was called by military, 'Preliminary Examination' & was in reality a dress rehearsal for the soldiers.[81]

She was brought to one of the rooms in the Officer's Block. There must have been a lot of activity on the stairs and waiting rooms as thirty-four other cases were dealt with that day. The rooms were small and cluttered with desks and filing cabinets, around which prisoners, witnesses and escorts had to squeeze in and out. Constance's preliminary session was unusual in that both witnesses were present and rehearsed their evidence before her. Alfred Bucknill was involved in collecting evidence against the accused and was active behind the scenes. She wrote two accounts of the trial in prison – a short typed statement and a longer handwritten document that went into the Preliminary Investigation in detail:

Constance walking to the ambulance

There was a preliminary investigation before the trial, presided over by a dark and ugly little clean-shaven man and the same two witnesses [McKay and Wheeler] were examined there. The boy, Walter McKay, said I had a gun, and I cross-examined him to show it was an automatic pistol. He gave a most circumstantial account of where I was standing when he saw me in Stephen's Green, and in cross-examining him I made it clear that his statement was physically impossible. In his examination he said that he lived at the United Services Club, not at the University Club.

Two witnesses were produced: 1st the page United Services Club, who told a long consecutive story of how he had stood on the top of the steps & what he had seen. He saw me drive up and give orders to man at Fountain, (gate with monument opposite to Club). Go on round with the motor, return and enter in 10 minutes time dressed in uniform, fire at Dr Daly in Club windows. Saw Dr Daly retire in time & saw bullet strike top of window just where his head had been. Saw me walk off with Sinn Feiner. I was told I might ask witness questions. Asked how he knew time.

(It must have been two hours before I fired any shots.)

Witness was vague.

Two Trials

> Asked how I was dressed in motor? Did not know.
>
> Asked how I was dressed when I fired? Didn't know.
>
> Could only see my head and rifle.
>
> Asked what I had fired with? Said 'gun'.... started a long rambling statement about my being in uniform & talking to Sinn Feiners.
>
> Asked a lot of questions as to what he could see & as to how did he know I fired at Dr Daly? No answer.
>
> How could he see the bullet strike if he was on the doorstep, and this room on the second floor over his head? He'd been called into the room & talked to by Dr Daly.
>
> The only other witness was the officer to whom I surrendered who spoke the truth, saying that I had accompanied Ml. Mallin, the Commandant, who said I was second in command.

From both accounts it is clear she was concerned with picking holes in McKay's evidence and not so much with the charges against her. The remarks on how she was dressed suggest she was not in uniform when she entered Stephen's Green, which would make sense in a liaison officer. In February, 1953, Bucknill (by then Sir Alfred with a distinguished legal career behind him) gave a statement to the Irish Ambassador in London:

> I saw her again on another day when she was bought to Richmond Barracks from Kilmainham for a summary of evidence to be taken. She was brought over in a motor ambulance attended by a wardress and a guard of soldiers. I took the summary of evidence in her case, and from the statement of a page boy at a hotel facing Stephen's Green it appeared that he saw her fire her revolver at a window in the hotel from which an officer in uniform was looking out. The bullet struck the window sill.[82]

He has no mention of her interrogation of Walter McKay, but includes a touching episode not in her account:

> When I asked her whether she wished to say anything she said, 'We dreamed of an Irish Republic and thought we had a fighting chance'. Then for a few moments she broke down and sobbed.

There is no reason to doubt Bucknill's account, but it would have been no surprise if the defeat of the Rising, the dawn executions and exhaustion had got the better of Constance.

> I was then put into a motor to wait for an hour and a very long hour at that – brought into room – three generals, whose names I forgot, took an oath before me not to divulge what was going to be said at the Court Martial. The charge was read again.

The trial was presided over by Brigadier-General C.J. Blackader, whom she described as 'a fuzzy little officer with his teeth hanging out to dry.' The other judges were Lt. Col. G. German of the Fifth Leicester Regiment and Lt. Col. W.J. Kent, W.S.O. Wylie described the extraordinary opening of the trial in a memoir dictated to his daughter in 1939:

> We quite expected she would make a scene and throw things at the court. In fact I saw the General getting out his revolver and putting it on the table beside him.[83]

Wylie presented Blackader's gesture with the revolver as a sign the court would not brook any nonsense, but it was an excessive and intimidating gesture, and an indication the accused could not expect a fair trial. The gesture appears even more ludicrous when one considers that the 'trial' took place in a room where she was surrounded by armed soldiers. It begs the question why the military would expect she might make a scene – was it because her questioning had shaken McKay's testimony? It appears the military was trying to intimidate her so that she would allow the case to run smoothly. There were a lot of rebels to be disposed of and Wylie and Blackader appear to have been irritated by her unwillingness to co-operate. The gesture with the revolver on the desk indicated the sham of the proceedings and would become a feature of interrogations in later decades by the Gestapo and Soviet NKVD.

Constance took an instant dislike to Blackader but had a brighter opinion of Wylie than his treatment of her would warrant. 'The prosecutor was a decent man but was not present at the preliminary enquiry,' she wrote. She had no way of knowing the account of her behaviour that would be promulgated long after her death. Wylie wrote in a memoir over twenty years later that she cried and begged for mercy: '

> 'I'm only a woman. You cannot shoot a woman. You must not shoot a woman.' She never stopped moaning the whole time she was in court. We all felt slightly disgusted. She has been preaching rebellion to a lot of silly boys, death and glory, die for your country etc. and yet she was literally crawling.

There is no reference to a plea for mercy in the court record. To some Wylie's account was the result of bad memory or misogynistic impulses. Constance's account of the court-martial begins:

> The charge was read again. There were three points as far as I could gather: assisting in a rebellion; assisting the enemies of the Realm. (I interposed: 'Do you mean the Germans? I didn't help them for I couldn't.') They looked surprised and said I could plead not guilty to that. The third charge was: Talking Sedition. They asked me did I plead Guilty. 'I always talked sedition,' said I. 'You always talked sedition,' said one much surprised. In spite of all I could say, they insisted on writing down that I pleaded guilty to the first *two* charges.

The first formal charge was:

> Did an act to wit did take part in an armed rebellion and in the waging of war against his Majesty the King, such act being of such a nature as to be calculated to be prejudicial to the Defence of the Realm and being done with the intention of and for the purpose of assisting the enemy.

The charge was long-winded enough to give the impression it covered more than one offence.

The alternative charge was more succinct: 'Did attempt to cause disaffection among the civilian population of His Majesty.' The same charge was made against the rebel prisoners with talking sedition an extra option in Constance's case. According to the record she pleaded 'not guilty' to the first and 'guilty' to the second charge.

> It then struck me that I should make a protest as to form of trial. They had a man to examine witnesses, were well-fed and experienced. I was starved, worn-out, and utterly inexperienced. So I asked for a solicitor, stating quite civilly that I had no experience and knew no law, and as I guessed I was being tried for my life I considered I should be allowed one.

She had no way of knowing that Eva had employed a London solicitor, George Gavan Duffy, to defend her. Gavan Duffy crossed immediately to Dublin where he consulted with Tim Healy, the Irish nationalist MP and King's Counsel, but the authorities would not allow them access to Constance in Kilmainham. Esther Roper wrote that 'they came away feeling the military authorities meant to take her life.'[84]

'That was refused,' Constance recalled, 'and they offered me an officer. I put all the venom I knew in the thanks with which I declined.'

She put up more resistance than any of the other defendants which would have prolonged the proceedings and would explain the official impatience.

> They asked me if I would have liked to call witnesses. I was afraid of compromising anyone so I refused. They asked me that at the first trial. Mallin could have proved where I was for the first two hours. Then the <u>boy</u> was again produced. He had his yarn carefully altered to make it possible. Dr Daly's name was left out. (He could not have seen Dr D. in the room as he said, also I shot with an 'automatic,' not with a gun. When the time came to question … I said I'd done nothing I was ashamed of, but that little liar made me sick. No notice was taken of this. I said it various times.
>
> I asked the boy where he was at school. 'Meath Industrial.'
>
> I asked was he sent there for lying or stealing.
>
> He began to cry.

McKay's story became a contentious point which she kept returning to over the following year.

> The little boy, however, changed his evidence and burst into tears when I asked if he had been put into the industrial school for thieving.
>
> I again volunteered to say anything about myself, of course stating I would say nothing about anyone else.
>
> I should have liked to have Captain Daly called as a witness, as the boy witness at the preliminary trial swore that I just missed Captain Daly when firing at the Shelbourne Hotel.

This is the only mention of a different interpretation of the incident; it was possible she was shooting towards an 'objectionable sniper' on the north side of the Green and a stray bullet narrowly missed Daly. However this possibility was never explored. She was greatly annoyed when McKay changed his story to say she fired at the University Club.

> The officer [Wylie] examining the boy must have been rather disgusted.... He was by way of helping the boy out with his story.

She refers to McKay as 'the little boy' when he was old enough to enlist and was older than some of the combatants on St. Stephen's Green. He may have been less mature than his years would indicate. The choice of words in his evidence is very similar to words used in the official accounts and would indicate a degree of coaching. She was indignant that the Crown would use an unreliable witness to condemn her when she openly admitted her involvement in the Rising. When she pulled holes in McKay's evidence there was a danger the whole procedure might unravel.

> I blew the little boy's evidence to pieces, and showed that he could not have seen what he alleged from the position in which he stated he was standing – it would have been a physical impossibility. I then asked the boy some questions about Dr Daly and was stopped being told that Dr Daly's name had not been in the evidence. I said I was going to show the discrepancies between the two statements at the two trials.

McKay disappears from the story, an orphan and youngest of three brothers; in the 1911 Census they were all listed as living in a home for Protestant children on Carysfort Avenue, Blackrock.

> I was told that the first was only a preliminary examination and that I could not refer to it! Of course that was enough for me. They asked had I any statement to make which they did at the first trial. I merely told them I stood where I stood before, where I always stood and am as ready to die for Ireland one way or another. I might have said more, but they made me refresh that to get it correct so I remembered it. Miss McInerney could bear me out in all this – she was the matron in charge of me. I was very tired, stupid and unhappy. The officer [Wheeler] was also called & spoke the truth.

Captain Wheeler made a short formal statement on the facts of the surrender: 'I, of course, admitted what the officer swore,' Constance wrote, 'as I was second in command under Michael Mallin in the Stephen's Green area. I gave the fuzzy little officer beans and defied him to shoot me.' The trial record indicates the accused remained calm, responded to the charges and made a short statement at the end.

> The Accused in her defence states -
>
> I went out to fight for Ireland's freedom and it doesn't matter what happens to me.
>
> I did what I thought was right and I stand by it. Statement ends.
>
> C.G.BLACKADER, Brig. General.

Extract from the record

The defiant words do not sound like those of a broken prisoner pleading for mercy – in fact the opposite. There is not the slightest hint of histrionics in the official record, but it does not document the details of the cross-questioning. There is no mention of McKay bursting into tears or the accused pleading for mercy. Constance wrote her account within a year of the trial and it coincides in many points with the official record. Wylie wrote his version over twenty years later. It is possible she was overwrought but Wylie's account does not fit with her behaviour then or afterwards. The historian, Brian Barton, considers it a fictional distortion arising from a deep revulsion that Constance had betrayed her religion and her class:

> Wylie's wilful and scurrilous distortion of her response at her trail is difficult to interpret. It may reflect a personal sense of irritation at her self-assurance and boldness, which he may have considered an insult to the court. Perhaps it reflected a deep-rooted sexual prejudice and rank misogyny on his part.[85]

The military mindset had no difficulty in dealing with schoolteachers, shopkeepers and dock labourers, but it was another matter when one of the ruling class turned and fought against them. It is possible that Wylie was relaying a garbled version of her outburst in front of Bucknill. He threw doubts about the reliability of his memory when he told his daughter:

> I am only telling you what I can recollect myself and I have looked up no records and verified no dates. I think I said already I burned all my notebooks when things got hot in 1920-21-22 so I am afraid as a historical record this is not of much value.[86]

Charles Lysaght, in his review of Wylie's memoir, remarked, 'unless they keep records active men are rarely good witness to the historical events in which they participate.'[87] Wylie's memory has been found erroneous on a number of points but his depiction of Constance at her trial is often presented as an accurate account. There was no hint of a breakdown from Esther or Eva, nor from her first biographer Sean O'Faolain, who spoke to many people of the era.

The story of Constance begging for mercy began to circulate in Dublin. Wylie is the obvious source of the story – he was staying in Trinity College with the Provost, Dr Mahaffy. Elsie gleefully gossiped about the moral and physical breakdown of the one she reckoned 'the worst of all these rebels.'[88] She compiled an account of the rebellion viewed from the Provost's House with a photograph of Constance in jewels and ballgown.

> She was then a lovely tall creature, full of spirits and much admired and made love to at Dublin Castle, where she was a constant guest. Later I lost sight of her but know she went to Paris to study Art, and there lost her shame and her dignity & married a Pole called Dunin-Markievicz ... she was poor. She always looked haggard & I believe her moral downfall was complete, her Art miserably bad & so she took to politics and left our class for Larkin & Connolly... On Easter Monday she commanded the rebels in St. Stephen's Green – she herself said to the gardener there 'I have shot two men & think nothing of it.' She also ordered six poor men who tried to leave her band to be shot that day. So hers are 8 fold murders, the worst of all the rebels.

> At her trail she utterly broke down, cried and sobbed and tried to incite pity in General Blackader: it was a terrible scene – the gaunt wreck of a once lovely lady standing in that bare room in her miserable man's uniform of green all her 'dash' and 'go' left her and in spite of her effrontery she was condemned on the evidence of a little boy, a 'page' from the Shelbourne Hotel who saw her shoot a policeman at the door. She could not frighten or confuse the child who remained clear ...

Here we have the whole cocktail of half-fact, rumour, speculation and prejudice. It is likely that Wylie embroidered the episode with Bucknill over dinner with the Mahaffys, exaggerating details to the immense satisfaction of his hosts. He does not appear to have taken the oath of secrecy very seriously. Over time he may have come to believe his exaggerations were accurate recollections.

There is another interpretation of the breakdown story: the authorities were concerned that the public would discover that Constance defended herself and turned tables on the court. What could be better than a rumour about the Rebel Countess begging for her life? As we can see from Elsie's account of the fall of a once great lady there were many in Dublin eager to believe the worst. In later years W.E. Wylie would become a High Court Judge in the British administration and the Irish Free State, but in 1916 he was not a spectator – he was an important part of the British war machine engaged in eradicating the rebel leadership.

Eva had no doubt there was a campaign from Unionist elements and the security services to destroy Constance's reputation. The most ludicrous stories about skulls in the bedroom and summary executions have fallen away; others have found traction and are repeated without reference to the truth. Constance's recollections were in line with the official record. She wrote in prison:

> I told the court that I had fought for the independence of Ireland during Easter Week, and that I was as ready now to die as I was then.

It would be no surprise if Constance did have a breakdown due to the intensity of Easter Week, the collapse of the rebellion and the executions, but it does appear unlikely. A photograph of her sitting in the rear of a Red Cross ambulance was taken soon after her court-martial. Her faces is calm and composed as she gazes out at the camera. Beside her sits Miss McInerney, a demure woman in a bonnet with head bowed as though she was the one sentenced. Constance should have the last word on her court-martial:

> Now I should not have minded being shot without a trial, but the awful hypocrisy and meanness of the whole sham trial revolted me. They had a right to kill us, but the sickening 'Fair Trial' by 'English Gentlemen' is an insult I resent.

Constance and wardress in ambulance after the court-martial

She was not to know that Michael Mallin, at his trial on the day after her own, tried to avoid a death sentence by claiming he was only a drill instructor:

> Shortly after my arrival at St. Stephen's Green the firing started and the Countess of Markievicz (sic) ordered me to take command of the men as I had been long associated with them.[89]

Mallin had a pregnant wife and four young children and may have reckoned the British would not execute a woman. He was sentenced to death and executed on Monday, 8 May. William Partridge was one of the last to be tried on 17 May. He gambled on the lack of evidence by claiming to have been a reluctant rebel. 'I took no part in the fighting whatever...' he claimed. He was sentenced to fifteen years with five remitted and sent to Dartmoor, in effect a death sentence because of his poor health.

General Maxwell was eager to make an example of Constance by having her shot. He described her as 'bloodthirsty and dangerous ... a woman who had forfeited the privileges of her sex.' He admitted she had a following, but 'we can't allow our soldiers to be shot down by such like.' He indicated clearly in his wire to London on Thursday morning that he would execute her if she was found guilty. He had an ally in Lord French, Commander in Chief of the British Home Forces, who responded: 'Personally I agree with you – she ought to be shot.'[90]

Asquith summoned Maxwell to a meeting of the Cabinet on Friday, 5 May, at which he stressed the executions were to be wound down and insisted that no woman be executed. On his return to Ireland Maxwell commuted her sentence to penal servitude for life. There has always been speculation that the Gore-Booths used their influence among the English ruling circles of prevent her execution, but no paper record exists. Esther wrote:

> Certainly, the day before the reprieve was announced, one of his [Asquith's] secretaries who knew Eva, was allowed to tell her that she might have certain hope that the extreme penalty would not be exacted.[91]

Eva is said to have personally thanked Asquith for his part in preventing Maxwell from executing her sister. The Gore-Booths were connected with many of the leading English families and may have called on some to intervene. George Russell wrote to Eva on 6 May to say he thought the death penalty would be transmuted to penal servitude. Casimir was in faraway Kiev and is reported to have taken a sanguine view; he is supposed to have joked she would not be shot as half of Debretts would go into mourning.

7

'My Sister's Dead Body …'

Up to now Constance had been known in public as a nationalist, but was rarely reported on in the newspapers for her political activities. The rebellion brought her to the notice of the international press and the newspapers immediately linked Eva with her notorious sister. The *Irish Independent* on 8 May inaccurately described Eva as a suffragette in its coverage of the Rising:

> Her sister took an active part in the militant suffragette campaign in England. The Countess herself was of an artistic and highly strung temperament and was well-known in theatrical and literary circles...

In the week after 24 April the English and foreign newspapers carried numerous stories of the rebellion, many based on the rumours circulating in Dublin. *The Daily Mirror* of 1 May featured an unusual picture of Constance and Eva at Lissadell in stilted poses. The headline ran:

> Countess Who Wrecked Two Young Lives: How She Lured the Rebels to Their Folly.

Some of the coverage focussed on Constance as a wild woman, a colourful exotic from whom anything could be expected. Eva was dismayed to read in *Lloyd's Weekly* on the Sunday of the surrender 'a circumstantial account of the finding of my sister's dead body in Stephen's Green...'[92]

Eva's first reaction was shock; she 'had to run up and down London trying to find out if she was really dead.' She was sent from office to office of Army headquarters at Horse Guards Parade, but could obtain no information. Eventually she discovered that Constance was alive, followed by

> *The Daily Mirror*

days of brain and nerve torture when she thought she would be executed at any time:

> And of the terrible days that followed, when I had almost wished the discredited story had been true, so much worse does it seem to the human mind to be executed coldly and deliberately at a certain hour by the clock than to be killed in the hurry and excitement of battle.

Sometime in the following week she wrote a hurried letter to a 'dear comrade' before leaving for Ireland the following week which gives a sense of the shock caused by the news from Dublin:

'My Sister's Dead Body...'

> I am afraid I can't manage the lecture next Sunday. I am expecting a telephone call every moment about going to Dublin to see my sister as they have given me permission & I have a lot to do in between connected with this horrible affair so that it seems impossible to get time to prepare & I would like to put it off.
>
> My sister had a very narrow shave for her life as the courtmartial wanted to shoot her. She led the attack from the College of Surgeons. It was only the politicians here who saved her life.[93]

The remark is a clear indication that Eva believed Asquith's intervention prevented her sister's execution. She was also deeply affected by the murder of her fellow pacifist and peace campaigner, Francis Sheehy-Skeffington:

> The cruelty in Dublin is terrible to think of. A friend of mine was found by the soldiers putting up a poster asking people not to loot, they put him up against a wall & shot him. He is a Pacifist and a non-resister. I got a very sad letter from George Russell, AE, this morning, despairing of my sister's life written before the sentence was commuted & altogether very sad he says, 'My heart is too heavy to write' so many of his friends are being shot, though of course he did not agree with Sinn Fein, he is a great friend of many of them, my sister for instance...

Stasko wrote of Eva 'interceding for Madame's life and hurrying to her succour when, like Joan in the hands of the English, she was sentenced to death.' She dashed off a short letter to Hannah Sheehy-Skeffington:

> Dear Mrs Sheehy-Skeffington, I don't like to bother you with a letter, but I feel I must write. I am so appalled and miserable about Mr. Sheehy-Skeffington. Your suffering is too dreadful. The story is shocking and horrifying everyone here & is causing great indignation. I hope to come over to see Con if I can get permission & shall hope to see you there if you will let me. It is all quite heart-rending. With all my sympathy. Yours Sincerely, Eva Gore-Booth.[94]

For the two days after her trial Constance expected to be shot at any time. When Marie Perolz got into Constance's cell on the pretext of borrowing a comb she told her that she had been sentenced to death. Perolz thought she appeared to be pleased with the verdict. On one of the nights an English soldier on guard waited until the jail was quiet and entered Constance's cell. 'He offered her a cigarette and sat down himself to smoke with her,' Esther wrote.

> He was most kindly and sympathetic, telling her the news and answering questions. She never forgot this human action, coming as it did at a time when she was worn out after a week's violent activity followed by the strain of solitary confinement. She always wanted to thank him, but did not know how to find him and could not make enquiries lest he should get into trouble.[95]

On Saturday morning she was standing on the table looking out the window when a young officer entered. He read from a document announcing she was guilty of the charges and delivered the verdict and sentence in peculiar ungrammatical English:

> Guilty. Death of being shot. The court recommends the prisoner to mercy solely and only in regard to her sex.

Apparently the officer mumbled in embarrassment and she demanded he repeat the verdict. Her response has gone down in the repertoire of Markievicz quotations:

> I do wish you lot had the decency to shoot me.[96]

On Sunday 7 May she was told she was to be transferred to Mountjoy Jail on the north side of the city. According to Captain A.A. Dickson of the Sherwood Foresters the military offered to transport her in a cab, but she declined to travel with soldiers. He remembered her walking along with Countess Plunkett, mother to the executed leader, Joseph Mary Plunkett.

> Accordingly one morning very early ... these two dignified and determined ladies ... set out walking stoically along the middle of the dingy streets, with half-a-dozen soldiers in file keeping level with them on each pavement ... their stately deliberate pace was slow march for us, but my enquiries as to whether this rate of progress suited them were acknowledged only by a silent bow of the head...[97]

Mountjoy was another stone fortress where the prisoners were obliged to change into prison clothes, but they had the luxury of a bath. Constance was examined and her weight recorded as 136 pounds, just under 10 stone, or 61.68 kilograms. She was again placed in isolation. From her cell she

Eva

heard the newsboys calling out the names of further executions. There was a flurry of executions on Monday, 8 May when Eamonn Ceannt, Michael Mallin, Con Colbert and Sean Heuston were shot in Kilmainham. Colbert and Heuston were close friends and among the founding members of the Fianna. She had no access to newspapers, but would have been gratified by a short news item in *The Irish Times* of Thursday, 11 May, based on a Reuter's telegram:

> A representative of the Russkoya Slova obtained an interview with the husband of Countess Markievicz, the Sinn Fein rebel. It appears that he is an artist and dramatist, and was in Durazzo [now Durres in Albania] at the outbreak of the war.

Eva and Esther crossed the Irish Sea on the night of Thursday, 11 May. Another passenger was Prime Minister Herbert Asquith, coming to assess the situation for himself. For Eva and Esther this journey to Ireland was different from the many others they had made over the years. Eva wrote:

> As the *Leinster* steamed into Dublin Bay on that May morning of 1916 the world seemed transfigured with beauty and delight. There was nothing to remind one of that blind will of domination, violence and greed that has for centuries made of these blue waters a highway of destruction. White seagulls flashed against a blue sky and the mountains had about them the radiance and peace of the early morning hours.[98]

She was reminded of the conflict by the khaki clad soldiers crowding the gangway in Dublin. Her thoughts ranged over the centuries:

> An endless procession of soldiers, with every kind of weapon, always on the same errand, always going, as they are going now, to conquer and hold down Ireland.

She recorded their jocular tone on the Dublin docks.

> 'Stay where you are, for God's sake!' I heard a laughing soldier say in mock-tragic accents to a group of civilians who were in too great a hurry to land. 'If I let you go over there, I shall be court-martialled and shot at dawn.'

The jocular remarks did not appear humorous to one whose associates were facing the firing squads.

> Ten minutes after that the world turned black, as I read the words that shrieked in huge letters from every hoarding in the town: 'Execution of James Connolly.' 'James Connolly shot this morning.' In days past I had known James Connolly, most kindly and humane of men. A man who had that quality, rare indeed among politicians,

that however absorbed he might be in fighting for a cause, he did not forget to answer the appeal of individual suffering.

Maxwell was winding down the executions, but was most anxious that the socialist and one of the main organizers of the rebellion should die. On the morning of 12 May the British executed the seriously wounded James Connolly and the crippled Sean MacDermott. Eva and Esther took a cab to the home of Susan Mitchell, a poet and friend of the Gore-Booth family. She was close to Constance and knew Josslyn through her work with the co-operative movement.

'Realization of the happenings of the past weeks rushed upon us in a flood as we drove through the smoking ruins of O'Connell Street,' Eva wrote.

> The driver seemed rather nervy, surly and suspicious, most unlike the usual talking Dublin driver. He confined himself to a long grumble about being starved with his family during the Rebellion.... Driving past Stephen's Green, he began to tell us some rather fictitious details about dead bodies of men and women being carried away at night and buried secretly.

Susan Mitchell had a permit to visit Constance and they set out for Mountjoy Jail. Eva thought that the Dublin streets were terrible.

> They had a sort of muddled desperate look, rather like but infinitely more tragic than the look one used to see in London on an air-raid night ... even the very houses were crouching down, hiding from something.

They found the same cab driver from the morning, but his attitude changed when he discovered their destination:

> 'It's little I thought this morning when I drove you from the boat, it was to the prison I'd be taking you.' From his manner you would have thought (as doubtless he did) that the dingy prison gate was the entrance to some very select Paradise, sacred to the greater saints and the more exalted Archangels.

Eva was familiar with prisons from visits to suffrage protesters and conscientious objectors. 'Prisons are all the same, built after the same dreary pattern,' she wrote. 'Very imposing and grand on the outside, they gradually get squalider and squalider the farther you get into them.'⁹⁹ A porter admitted them through the postern in the main entrance and they passed through an iron gate and across a yard. Eva was anxious about having to tell Constance about the most recent executions.

As I walked through the long corridor, my mind was obsessed by one horrible thought: 'They have shot all her friends ... did she know? Should I have to tell her?'

Susan Mitchell warned her not to mention Connolly's death.

Suddenly there was her face behind a sort of cage: it was cut into sections by the cross-bars. But one could half-see, half guess how calm and smiling she was. She talked very fast, and was full of all sorts of commissions she wanted carried out, asked a great many questions and seemed only really puzzled by one thing: 'Why on earth did they shoot Skeffy?' she said. 'After all, he wasn't in it. He didn't even believe in fighting,' she insisted. 'What did it mean?'

Susan Mitchell by Constance

'At the time I could not answer her: afterwards I found out,' Eva wrote.

Nobody who has not gone through the ordinary prison visit can realise how unsatisfactory it is, nor what a strain it is, to fling one's intimate conversation across a passage with a wardress in it, to a head appearing at a window opposite. And then to know that these few minutes must last one for months, and that one has probably forgotten something important ...

Constance was worried about Mallin's wife, Agnes, who she believed was in hiding, five months pregnant with a large family and no support.

She urged her visitors to find the family in Inchicore, but had no definite address.

> About her own treatment the prisoner had not much to say. She was a 'convict' and a 'lifer' and that was all about it. And anyway, it was splendidly worthwhile. For one glorious week, Ireland had been free … and then back she went to stories of that wonderful time, of the night-scouting and the trench in Stephen's Green and the machine-gun on the Shelbourne and how they were forced to retreat to the College of Surgeons...

Esther's account concurred with Eva's, but included the impact of Connolly's execution. She emphasised the measures taken by the authorities to keep visitors and prisoner apart:

> The three visitors were shown into a bare white-washed room at the end of which was a small barred window opening. Crossing outside this was a narrow passage on the opposite side of which was another barred opening and it was behind this grille that Con's face at last appeared, looking ghost-like.
>
> Con asked at once whether Connolly had been shot. We had been warned on no account must we answer this question. Though no word was spoken she must have seen the answer in our faces, for with the tears running down her cheeks, she said, 'you needn't tell me. I know. Why didn't they let me die with my friends?' It was a terrible moment. Under all other circumstances in prison she kept gay and brave. This was absolutely the only time I saw her show emotion there.... Soon she drew herself up and said, 'Well, Ireland was free for a week.' [100]

Eva's account of the effect of Connolly's death is more perfunctory. She recalled her sister talking of Mallin and Connolly:

> Now he, too, had been shot. At the end of twenty hurried minutes of rapid talk we said good-bye for the next four months, and the oddly becapped head disappeared from the window, vanishing into what unimaginable scenes of dullness, dinginess and squalor.

8

Eva and Esther in Dublin

From Mountjoy the three women went across the city to Surrey House to check on the house and contents – paintings, books, letters, props and costumes as well as valuable furniture. Many of the best paintings by Constance and Casimir hung on the walls, including *The Artist's Wife*, *The Conscript* and *Bread*. When Casimir went to report on the Balkan wars in 1913 he left his garderobe and many paintings in Dublin. Sidney Gifford wrote that the house was:

> ... the theatrical wardrobe of Dublin. Mighty swords suitable for fifteenth century warriors, wigs, top-boots and Georgian costumes were the normal furniture of the Markievicz home.[101]

Esther described the condition of the house:

> The place was in chaos, furniture broken, papers, ornaments, books, pictures, lying smashed on the floor. I noticed a box of lantern-slides which had been overturned and every single slide crushed to bits by someone's boot; a beautiful leather dressing-case ripped across by a bayonet, and so on. The garden had been dug up in search of arms, but nothing was found.[102]

Hannah Sheehy-Skeffington, who lived around the corner in Grosvenor Place, remembered the looting of Surrey House:

> Many of Madam's possessions found their way as 'souvenirs' into soldiers' and officer's kits and were given to their lady friends. A hand press was found there too and smashed up. A manuscript of an article Madame was writing (or reading for some friend) on Catherine de Medici caused anxious query among the soldiers. 'Who was

this woman? A Sinn Feiner?' They were only party reassured when told that the lady had been dead for several centuries.[103]

Even the kitchen utensils had been tied up in tablecloths and taken away. The Fianna banner, a sunburst on a green background, was treated as a spoil of war. In recent times it has been displayed in the Imperial War Museum in London with the caption: 'The banner was discovered in her home at the time of the Easter Rising in 1916 by 3rd Battalion, the Royal Irish Rifles.' A conscientious officer confiscated letters to Constance from the playwright, George A. Birmingham, in which he urged her to wear some clothing for a bedroom scene in his play, *Eleanor's Enterprise*. The majority of paintings were untouched but *The Conscript*, an anti-war painting by Constance from Ukraine, appears to have been slashed by a bayonet, perhaps in revenge for the damage to the portrait of Queen Victoria.

Surrey House

The authorities expected to find incriminating or salacious evidence in Surrey House. Susan Mitchell wrote to Sir Josslyn about the house search:

> A lot of the gossip purported to come from the story of the officer who searched her house and said he found dreadful papers there. This I know to be a lie. I discovered by chance the other day who that officer was. He was ordered to break open all the drawers and receptacles where the papers might be and he hated his task. He found nothing for the reason that there was nothing to find.[104]

'The crowd came later and finished the business,' Hannah wrote, 'until a friend intervened and had the place padlocked.'

When Esther and Eva emerged on Leinster Road they found a crowd of waiting onlookers. The resemblance between the sisters was so close that many thought that Constance had escaped from prison and returned to check on her belongings. People warned her that the soldiers might make the same assumption and shoot on sight. Eva and Esther were more concerned about protecting Constance's property since there was no prospect of her release. Under the Forfeiture of Property Act, 1870, a convicted person's property could be placed in administration with the convict liable for costs and compensation. Constance held a lease on Surrey House and owned a house, St. Mary's, on Frankfort Avenue, which her mother gave her in 1903. She was receiving an income from the Lissadell estate and owned pictures and furniture, not to mention a large amount of theatre props. As well as the house contents Eva was anxious about some precious plants behind the greenhouse and urged Susan Mitchell to have them protected.

They set out the next morning to look for Agnes Mallin. Eva thought that people suspected them of being Government spies as they 'spent many weary hours walking through endless poverty-stricken streets, questioning naturally suspicious and incredulous people...' Eventually they came to the high stone walls of Richmond Barracks:

> ... one of those great fortress-like barracks that seems to overawe Dublin. Round the gates a miserable crowd collected, of patient white-faced men and women, standing under the great gray wall in a sort of hopeless gray dejection.[105]

People told them they expected further executions in revenge for military deaths. They found the Mallin family; Eva left money with Agnes and arranged with Father O'Ryan of Goldenbridge to send money to provide for the family. On their return to Rathmines they visited Hannah who showed them shattered windows where soldiers broke into the house in a vain search for evidence implicating Francis in the rebellion. Eva referenced William Blake when writing about the pacifist:

> All his life Skeffington had never 'ceased from mental fight' against all forms of tyranny, oppression and cruelty. He was a born rebel, a questioner of ancient traditions, a shaker of ancient tyranny.[106]

The murder of Sheehy-Skeffington shook Eva to the core and made her realize she and Constance shared a common enemy – the militarized state at the heart of the British Empire:

> Truly, it was easy enough to understand 'why they shot Skeffy,' though the only crime they could accuse him of was an effort to persuade a hooligan crowd not to loot the shops. Militarism has a true

instinct and a short way with its enemies. But perhaps the future is with Skeffington.

On the day after her visit to Mountjoy Eva composed a poem giving her reactions to the rebellion and her sister's fate:

> And my own sister, through wild hours of pain,
> Whilst murderous bombs were blotting out the stars,
> Little I thought to see you smile again
> As I did yesterday, through prison bars.

According to prison rules Constance was not due another visit from Eva for three months. Alone in her cell she found it hard to settle into prison life. 'When General Maxwell changed my death sentence to one of imprisonment for life I was sent to Mountjoy goal in Ireland,' she wrote in the *San Francisco Examiner* in 1919.

> For these three months I spent a most horrifying time. I was locked up in my cell, with nothing to do all day but walk up and down the narrow space allowed me. For one hour I was allowed exercise in the yard, but the solitary confinement almost drove me mad.[107]

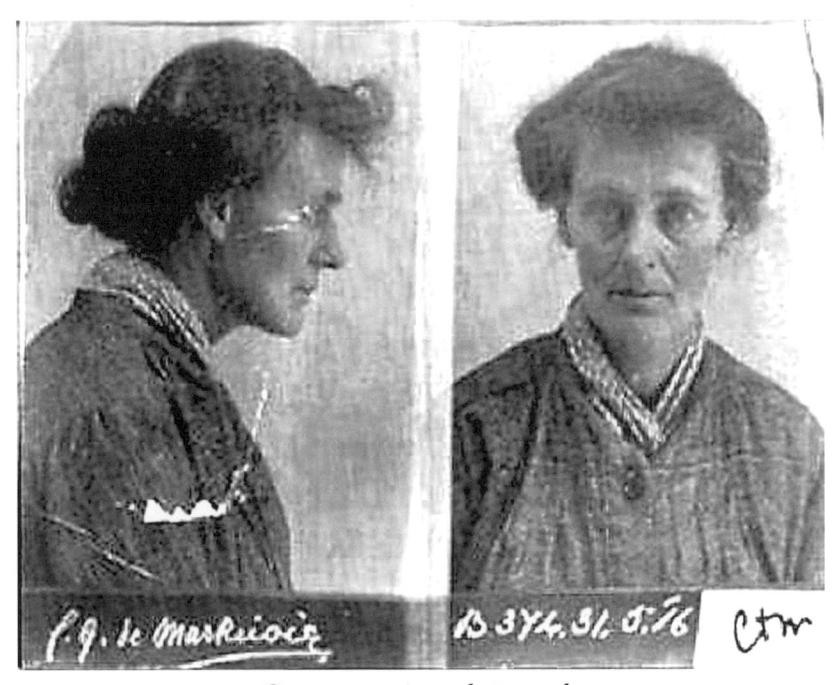

Constance prison photographs

However the Gore-Booth sisters would combine to find ways to fight against the physical and mental prison in which Constance found herself.

Eva and Esther took up residence in the Hotel Pelletier in Harcourt Street and, with the help of Susan Mitchell, began to make the requested contacts and wrote numerous letters to sort out Constance's affairs. The most urgent issues were the women who had worked in Surrey House – Bessie Lynch and Bridie Goff, both now unemployable. Bridie was a member of the ICA and was released after a short spell in Richmond Barracks and Kilmainham. Bessie Lynch did the laundry for the house and was considered the more vulnerable of the two. Eva wrote to Hannah from the hotel:

Eva's note to Hannah Sheehy-Skeffington

Dear Mrs Skeffington,

I have just had the address from Fr O'Ryan of Golden Bridge Chapel, Inchicore, but haven't seen him so couldn't ask if it's the right woman. The address is Mrs Mallin no. 1 Rutland Avenue, off Dolphin's Barn Dublin...[108]

She was unsure if this was the woman due to have a baby in three months. Would Hannah check the details and write to her in London?

There was also the question of what to do with the contents of Surrey House and with the house itself. Should it be sub-let or would it be better to have the lease surrendered? Not to mention the other properties in which Constance had an interest – St. Mary's, a hall in Camden Street which she rented for the Fianna, and a rented cottage at Sandyford. Then there were bills for house insurance, rates due to Dublin Corporation, rents due to landlords, not forgetting income tax on the proceeds from St. Mary's. There were also a large number of outstanding bills to suppliers, some of which had not been paid since 1913. Eva found she had taken on a daunting a task. The outbreak of the rebellion, its suppression and aftermath of repression may have interrupted the course of daily life, but not for very long.

Sir Josslyn Gore-Booth, as the senior male member of the Gore-Booth family, began making enquiries through his Dublin solicitors, Crozier & Sons, about Constance's property. Crozier expected Josslyn to visit Constance in Mountjoy for an interview, but he replied that he would stay in Sligo and deal with her by letter. According to the present Sir Josslyn Gore-Booth, his grandfather was a shy man who preferred to work through others. Constance was hurt by his refusal to see her and raised it in a letter to Stasko a decade later: 'A friend asked him to come to Dublin, but he would not come.'[109]

Josslyn and Molly Gore-Booth with baby

The situation around Surrey House was confused in the first weeks of May. Eva was under the impression that Susan Mitchell and Mrs Russell were looking after things. Crozier wrote to Josslyn that the house was under military control until mid-May when the keys were given to an agent who passed them to Crozier. He wrote to Josslyn on 13 May:

> As we anticipated, all the wardrobes, cabinets, boxes, portmanteaux etc. have been opened and the contents strewn about on the different landings....The oil paintings, of which there are a large number, are not injured, and neither so far as we could see are the various articles of china, of which there is a good number.[110]

They secured the house and were dealing with the landlord. As Josslyn was digesting this information a short letter arrived from Eva on Sunday, 14 May. She told him she had seen Constance in Mountjoy who asked her 'to look after things for her.' She mentioned St. Mary's and Surrey House and told him she was returning to London on Monday night. 'Con looked wonderfully well considering all the awful things she has been through.'[111]

Back in Fitzroy Square Eva wrote a number of letters to the 'dear comrade':

> I don't wonder people should want deliverance from this life. I have just been learning of my sister's tragic experience sitting in her cell at Kilmainham and every morning hearing outside the 'ready, present, fire' & the shots that she knew meant her friends executions. Think of the nights spent waiting for such mornings. Of course she was always waiting for her own turn which she thought certain, but never came. Karma is a strange thing. I am bringing out a little book of her decorations & verses from The Triumph of Maeve and have written a verse dedication to those poor mad Utopians who were after all following something beyond human life with its trivialities.[112]

This is the first mention of *The Death of Fionavar* and indicates the sisters discussed the project in Dublin. Constance worked on the book in Mountjoy, but she may have made previous sketches. R.M. Fox wrote she:

> ... had idly drawn the figures on the border while reading the manuscript of the play. And nothing would please her sister except that they should be published with it.[113]

When Eva and Esther left Dublin they were burning with anger against British injustice. Their idealistic outlook was shocked by the signs of oppression:

> Dublin was a city of mourning and death. Roger Casement had been taken from Arbour Hill Barracks to the Tower. There was a feeling of strain and embarrassment everywhere. People broke down and wept for very little, even in the streets...[114]

Eva wrote again to the 'dear comrade' from Fitzroy Square on 20 May. She was continuing to work on Constance's behalf in London:

> I am so awfully sorry I can't get to the concert today. It sounds quite beautiful. I do wish it was in London but I have still so much to do connected with the Irish business, people to see etc. Ireland was a terrible experience. I will tell you about it when we meet. I saw my sister & she was very brave & cheerful entirely serene about her sufferings. She gave me commissions to find & help other people who I had to hunt for & only found with great difficulty. There was still a reign of terror in Dublin & everybody thought everyone else Government spies. I found out many terrible tragedies. I also saw Mrs Sheehy Skeffington, poor thing & heard a great deal from her.[115]

Eva and Esther in Dublin

The artist Frances Trench ('Cesca') claimed she met Eva on 21 May after a visit to Constance, but she may have confused dates. She noted in her diary the tale of Walter McKay at the court-martial:

> Then this boy broke down, as it was too bad a tale, and they tried again and brought back the same boy with another tale and for that she was sentenced.[116]

Trench was pleased that Constance was still trying to direct events from her cell, sending messages that Kathleen Lynn acted only as a doctor during the rebellion. She instructed Eva to tell Constance that 'we don't believe all the stories people tell.'

'Thank you very much,' Eva replied. 'I shan't see her again for three months you know, but she will be pleased.'

The two friends wrote and lectured on their experiences when they returned to London. Her first biographer, Gifford Lewis, believed that the shock of 1916 sent Eva's health into decline. Eva wrote some of her best poems in response to her experience of Dublin after the Rising:

To Constance – In Prison

Outcast from joy and beauty, child of broken hopes forlorn,
Lost to the magic mountains and parted from all flowers,
Robbed of the harvest moon that shines on far-off fields of corn,
Bereft of raindrops on green leaves, bright wrecks of fallen showers.

Nay, not outcast, whilst through your soul a sudden rapture thrills,
And all your dreams are shaken by the salt Atlantic wind,
The Gods descend at twilight from the magic-hearted hills,
And there are woods and primroses in the country of your mind.

9

Sorting Out

Eva and Esther worked hard to give the impression that Constance was bearing up bravely in prison, but Eva was anxious about her sister's health. Constance was preoccupied with practical matters in a long letter to Eva dated 16 May from: Number B374 Name Constance G. de Markievicz, H.M. Prison, Mountjoy Female, Dublin. As she faced the prospect of a lifetime in prison she was anxious to have her personal affairs sorted out.

> Dearest Old Darling – It was such a heaven-sent joy, seeing you. It was a new life, a resurrection, though I knew all the time you'd try and see me, even though I'd been fighting and you hate it all so and think killing so wrong. It was so dear of Esther to come all that long way too. Susan too, for I expect lots of people will think it very awful of her. Anyhow, you are three dears and you brought sunshine to me, and I long to hug you all![117]
>
> Now to business. Hayes & Hayes, 41-42 Nassau St. are agents for Surrey House. They wrote to me re giving up tenancy, and very decently secured the house, which had been left open. The house is very untidy, as I had no time to put it straight after the police raid. If you could get Bessie Lynch she would be a great help. There is a charwoman called Mrs. Boylan too whom Bessie would know of who is honest.

This must be the raid in early 1916. She was not aware of the looting in the aftermath of the Rising, but had the foresight to leave silver and jewels with an unnamed friend and a trunk with Marie Perolz.

> I am rather unhappy about the pictures. I don't want anything thrown away. Egan, Lr. Ormond Quay, might store those pictures

hanging on the walls, and my illuminated address from the Transport Union. He has some pictures of ours already.

Daniel Egan, picture-framer, was owed money for frames supplied and kept pictures in lieu of payment which he sold to the National Museum of Ireland in the 1930s.

Don't store furniture with Myers: he was a brute to his men in the strike. You'll want to insist on their bringing proper boxes for the books, as they are awfully careless. The china too wants care. Then there are the acting things.

The list was an inventory of mementos from the days with Casimir when they set up the Independent Theatre Company and the Dublin Repertory Theatre. She suggested that Eva buy a tin trunk and store the materials with naphtha balls in anticipation of Casimir's return when everything would be unpacked.

There are wigs in the bottom of the kitchen press and in the cupboard half-way up the stairs.

This must be the collection of used wigs Casimir bought for his production of Shaw's *The Devil's Disciple* which he cleaned and left to dry on the open windowsill. Sometime later Constance was alerted by voices from Leinster Road where passersby were astonished to see human scalps spread across the lawn.

They want to be put by with care. The linen too, such as it is, wants to have the starch washed out before it is put by. If you could only catch Bessie Lynch, she knows the house so well and is such a good worker.

There are a lot of crewel wools in the big press on the stairs: they want to be put with naphtha balls too. If someone could house the wigs and them I'd be thankful.

She went through the contents of the rooms as if packing away her life. There is a poignant aspect to this listing of belongings. She mentioned a desk a small drawer that could be opened without a key, but there was nothing in it.

> Could Susan get my clothes and look after them for me? There is a little brown case with drawing things that Susan might keep for me. I told you that Crozier & Co. are trying to let St. Mary's. I think my name should be suppressed and it should be leased in yours.

Lady Gore-Booth gave St. Mary's to Constance when she came to live in Dublin in 1903. She leased it in 1909 when she rented a house with large grounds, Belcamp Park in Raheny, as a Fianna training camp and short-lived commune.

She continued brightly:

> Of course, my household bills are not paid – John Clarke, S. Richmond Street [£22/10/09 for January-March 1916] is my grocer; Ferguson, Rathmines, my baker; Kehoe, Butcher, Hendrick oilman both Rathmines. I owe two coal bills. One to Clarkin, Tara St, the other to a man I forget in Charlemont St., on the r. side as you face the bridge, but close to the chemist on the corner where the trams pass.

Some of the bills dated back to mid-1913, which would suggest a lot of patience on the part of shopkeepers and suppliers. The other unusual aspect is the degree of recall as if she was keeping a tally in order to pay them when she could afford it. She forget to include a bill for £10 from John Lawlor & Son, 2 Fownes St. from December, 1915 for a 10.22 rifle. She also forgot the long-established Sligo firm, Henry Lyons & Co., which fitted Casimir with a suit, breeches and hat in November, 1913 and were owed £5.6.6. Not to mention a bill of 18 shillings from P. Ceppi & Sons for six frames and mounts delivered to Casimir in 1913.

> I also owe a trifle to Gleeson of O'Connell St. for a skirt and to the Art Decorating Co., Belfast, but there is no hurry in paying any of these. Don't pay anything unless you know the bill is really mine, as people have played queer tricks, getting things on credit in my name before now.

She was unsure when she would be permitted to write again and was trying to do as much as possible. In the middle of the details she paused to pity her sister:

Sorting Out

> You poor old darling. It's such a bore for you. I feel rather as if I were superintending my own funeral from the grave.

She mentioned a valuable music book in the drawing room:

> It might be valuable. If you have time, bring it to a Mr. Braid at P-, and ask his advice about selling it. I promised to let him have a look at it, as he says it is unique. I had not time to leave it with him.

We get some idea of her hectic lifestyle before the Rising from the dispersal of her belongings.

> I left a green canvas suit-case and a small red dressing-case with the caretaker of Liberty Hall. I've had them there some time. I dare say Peter's arrested, but he wasn't mixed up in anything so he may be out. I left my bike knocking round the Hall too.

Peter Nicholl was the caretaker in Liberty Hall. She remembered the dog who ran beside the bicycle through the Dublin streets:

> I miss poor Poppet so much and wonder if he has forgotten me. Poor Mrs. Connolly – I wonder where she is, and if you have got him from her. She was so devoted to her husband. Also she has four children at home and only the two older girls working.

Her immediate concern was for the girl who did her laundry:

> With regards to Bessie Lynch: what I had in mind for her was to start her in a small way in some work after the War. She is a beautiful laundress. Of course she would want another girl with her to do accounts, etc., but you could let her know she is not forgotten, and the ten shillings a week is only to keep her safe and happy until something can be arranged. It's much better for people to earn their own living if they can.

Constance was taking it on herself to organize Bessie's life, but felt she had a responsibility for the younger woman; at the time it was a catastrophe to lose employment and end up on the streets. Constance had reported in Sheehy-Skeffington's *Irish Citizen* of night patrols in central Dublin where she witnessed the sad fate of street prostitutes. Bessie's fate would trouble her executors for some time. There was also her other servant, Bridie Goff, and the Mallin family, to think about.

> Poor Bridie Goff ought to get a month's wages at least. She was arrested with me. Bessie would know where she lives: somewhere in Henrietta Street. If you can't find Bessie, advertise for her in the evening paper. I hope you found Mrs. Mallin. I wish I knew for it worries me so to think of her.

At this stage Constance did not know that Eva arranged to send money to the Mallin family. She was also unaware of the new fund for families of the insurgents under the guidance of Thomas Clarke's wife, Kathleen.

> I nearly forgot the little hall in Camden Street. Mr. Cummins of Richmond Street is the landlord. If things quiet down, I'd like to go paying the rent for them as hitherto. A little boy called Smith, living in Piles building, could find out. The landlord, of course, might know. He was quite nice.

The hall at 34 Camden Street (demolished after a fire in 2014) was the premises where she organized and drilled the Fianna from 1909 when she had to contend with suspicion on all sides – the revolutionaries mistrusted this high-class woman with the English accent; parents and priests suspected she might be attempting to proselytize Catholic boys; and the boys initially disliked taking instruction from a woman. She persevered and with backing of the Irish Republican Brotherhood created an enduring organization.

34 Camden Street

> I feel as if I were giving you such a lot of worries and bothers, and it feels too, that I haven't remembered half. Anyhow, it's very economical living here! And I half feel glad that I am not treated as a political prisoner, as I would then be tempted to eat, smoke and dress at my own expense! In the meantime all my debts will be paid, I live free, and after a time, I suppose I will be allowed to write again and see a visitor. I don't know the rules.

Sorting Out

She once told Gary Holohan, Chief Scout of Na Fianna, that going to prison was not a problem as her allowance would accumulate and she could donate the savings to the cause. Perhaps it was due their privileged upbringing but Casimir and Constance were unable to control spending. She later wrote to Josslyn from prison with the wistful complaint that she wished Casimir had been in charge of household finances and given her pocket money. Casimir was no model of financial responsibility and shared the conviction of many of his class that it was natural to live beyond one's means.

> But do try and get in touch with Mrs. Connolly, Mrs Mallin, and Bessie Lynch for me. I would be sorry too if they thought I had forgotten them, for they were friends.

The tone changed sharply as if she realized the inventory signalled an end to her former life.

> By the way, the garden seat and tools might be of use to Susan. There are a few decent plants, too, which she could take if she likes, and a couple of decent rose-trees. Now, darling, don't worry about me, for I'm not too bad at all, and it's only a mean spirit that grudges paying the price.

She was due a refund of income tax, but could not claim it without Casimir's signature. As her husband was at the far side of war-torn Europe in Ukraine it would have to remain unclaimed for a number of years. We can detect a note of sadness, but she was determined to keep up a brave show before the censor and prison authorities.

> Everybody is quite kind, and though this is not exactly a bed of roses, still many rebels have had much worse to bear. The life is colourless, the beds are hard, the food peculiar, but you might say that of many a free person's life, and when I think of what the Fenians suffered, and of what the Poles suffered in the 'sixties, I realise that I am extremely lucky. So don't worry your sweet old head. I don't know if you are still here, so I am sending this to Susan to forward.
>
> I hope that I shall live to see you again someday and I shall live in hopes.
>
> With very much love to you three darlings. I can see your faces when I shut my eyes.

Josslyn received a letter from Eva on 20 May in which she explained it was necessary to pretend to look after Constance's business in order to be allowed into Mountjoy. Afterwards she visited Crozier and assured him she was not cutting across anything they were doing. 'I didn't want to shove myself in or have all the bother and expense but of course I couldn't refuse Con.'[118]

This gives a different impression from the perception that Eva was displaced by Josslyn. She appears contented to leave the burden of sorting out the financial and property interests to her brother. Another letter followed on 22 May: 'I have just had a long letter of minute directives from Con.' She did what she could without legal powers and found all the people on the list, except for Bridie Goff and 'then there's her dog,' who was being looked after by Mrs Russell.

She wrote to Father O'Ryan in Inchicore from London on 26 May:

> Dear Fr. O'Ryan, Would it be best if you let me know when the money is finished (£3 at 10/- a week) also Mrs. Mallin's new address at Inchicore, then I will go on sending it direct to her. I must thank you ever so much for all your kindness & help. I had a letter from the poor woman herself, it's dreadful to think of her distress. With many thanks and kind regards, Eva Gore-Booth
>
> Mrs M only gives me the Dolphin's Barn address.[119]

We can never know the full story of the whispering campaign about Constance; Eva refers to an objectionable publication in a letter to Hannah from London on 4 June:

> I have got a copy - it's absolutely disgusting. I am writing to my brother to see if he can do anything as I think it would be better to do it in Ireland for various reasons.

We have no further details, but Eva was very upset by the allegations as she makes clear in a further undated letter to Hannah:

> I fear you must be feeling the strain terribly now.... Thanks so very much for telling me about the horrible libel against Con. I think there must be a set of people trying to set these stories afloat as far as one can see. It is indeed mean to pursue a person who because of her present position cannot defend herself.

Sorting Out

In the week before the Rising Thomas Clarke arranged with his wife Kathleen to set up a relief fund for prisoners and their families – the Irish Volunteers Dependents Fund. In early May Cumann na mBan and the Irish Citizen Army created the Irish National Aid Association with similar aims. Both groups amalgamated in August into the Irish National Aid and Volunteers Dependents Fund (INAVDF). As well as helping families the organization would play an important role in rebuilding shattered nationalist organizations and in agitating for improvements in prison conditions. A separate organization, the Irish National Relief Fund, was set up in London with Art O'Brien as Secretary. Eva's name featured on the notepaper as a committee member ahead of clergymen and Irish professionals in England.

Constance wrote to Josslyn from Mountjoy on 22 June about her business affairs:

> I am sorry that you should have all this bother: and I can't conceive why Eva, who is my trustee and therefore the most natural person to look after things should be passed over – I suppose it's because she is a woman! She and I too are always in such sympathy, that I believe she would know what I wanted before asking me. I gave her a lot of minute instructions about people I wanted helped and about my things in the house, if there are any things left!

She asked his help in locating Christmas cards she had designed and to send on her false teeth: 'I expect they would make no difference here, as I can duly eat slops.'[120]

She urged him to make contact with Casimir and Stasko in Russia and advised sending a vague message in a registered letter. 'I believe very few of my letters ever got to him,' she wrote and told him to send a lot of postcards, but to say on one that she was 'all right but unable to write and send my love.' Maeve and Stasko had corresponded and she wrote to Josslyn on 4 July with Stasko's address in Archangel.

It is difficult to imagine the shock that must have run through the Gore-Booth family with the news that Constance had taken a leading role in the insurrection, an act of treason against the King. While no one could hold them responsible for her politics or actions they well knew that her notoriety would change how 'society' viewed the family name. For years afterwards Maeve was known in England as the daughter of 'that woman.'

With the exception of Eva the rest of the family supported the British war effort. Josslyn established an ammunition factory at Lissadell while

Constance's mother and daughter organized fundraising events for the British Army.

Although she took a different path Constance never tried to implicate or embarrass the Gore-Booths; any criticisms of the family were in the historical context. She is often condemned for neglecting Maeve by leaving the child with her grandmother in Sligo, but she protected her from the opprobrium that came to the families of those involved in the rebellion. Casimir and Stasko were likewise far out of danger and Constance was free to dispose of her life as she pleased.

Maeve in war work fete in 1916

Susan Mitchell took on the task of supervising affairs for Josslyn in Dublin. She wrote to him on 28 June that Surrey House had 'literally been sacked, furniture thrown smashed and flung about.' Crozier wrote to Herbert Samuel, the British Home Secretary, on 3 July as the Irish authorities no longer had the power to appoint an administrator in a legal vacuum:

> Re: Countess Constance deMarkievicz, a Convict...
>
> Sir Josslyn Augustus Richard Gore-Booth, Baronet, of Lissadell, Sligo, is the convict's elder brother. Her husband is in the Russian Army, and his address is unknown, but he is believed to be invalided from wounds. Her only child, a girl, is a minor under 15 years of age, and is residing with her grandmother, Lady Georgina Gore-Booth, in Sligo.
>
> The convict's property is at the moment badly in need of administration, and is subject to much loss, and it is essential that certain surrenders should be made forthwith. In the absence of a regular Government in Ireland we are therefore forced to apply to you to appoint Sir Josslyn Augustus Richard Gore-Booth.[121]

The Irish Attorney General, James Campbell, made an order appointing Josslyn to deal with her affairs on 18 July.

Sorting Out

Susan Mitchell became indispensable to helping Josslyn in his dealings over the properties. She cleared up the mess left by the military in Surrey House and helped to secure the contents. The removals firm Strahan & Co. were employed in early July to take away the contents and put them into storage. Four vans were needed – one just for the pictures. Susan wrote to Josslyn on 15 July about Balally Cottage on which two and half years rent was due, amounting to £9.15.00. Constance wanted to keep renting it for the Fianna on the understanding they would not run wild in the area. The woman in the adjoining cottage was looking after some of Constance's pictures.

The £10 rent owing on the Camden Street hall was paid on 17 July. Susan was unsure how much to value for insurance the pictures in storage:

> ... there are four paintings worth much more than £17 but I do not know how much they are worth. The two large portraits [probably Casimir's *The Artist's Wife* and Szankowski's portrait of Constance] and Casi's *Bread* I could not tell the value of at all.

George Russell estimated *Bread* as worth £50 and valued the rest at £4 each.

According to Hannah Sheehy-Skeffington, Constance was not attached to her belongings:

Strahan bill for removals

> I never knew a person with less sense of property or less attached to possessions.... I have seen her when someone admired a vase, a picture, say: 'Do you like it? Take it,' and literally force the thing upon an embarrassed acquaintance.[122]

When Constance wrote from Paris in 1899 to inform the family that she was engaged to marry a poor Polish artist, Casimir Dunin-Markievicz, she threw the Gore-Booths into a panic. They suspected Casimir was an unsuitable match for many reasons. Josslyn wrote to the Foreign Office, resulting in the dispatch of the Russian secret police to investigate Casimir in Paris. Seventeen years later Constance was again at the forefront of Josslyn's concerns. He remained in the estate office in Lissadell and wrote to his contacts in the military and administration; he especially wanted to get to the bottom of the story that she had shot a policeman.

The British Government set up a Commission of Enquiry into the Rising in May which considered the causes and events of Easter Week. One would imagine that the shooting of a policeman by a member of the aristocracy would have received prominence, but there was no mention of any such occurrence. The report contained a remark by Superintendent Dunne of Dublin Castle on night-time manoeuvres of the Citizen Army:

> It is a serious state of affairs to have the peace of the city endangered by a gang of roughs with rifles and bayonets at large at that time of night, with a female like the Countess Markievicz in charge.[123]

Dr de Burgh Daly wrote to Josslyn confirming that Constance shot at him as he stood in the window of the University Club, but he took a philosophical stance on the affair:

> She released doctors ... and wounded officers when captured on Monday night and mixed up kindness and killing in accordance with her convictions on the rebellion and how to conduct it. I bear her no ill-will, and hope one of these days she may use her talents for the real benefit of the country.[124]

Lady Gore-Booth wrote to Arthur Sandbach, the new Chief Secretary for Ireland, enquiring about the charges at the court-martial. He replied to Josslyn and sympathized with the family as though they had suffered a bereavement and reminisced about the happy times he and his wife spent at Lissadell before the war. One gets the impression that official correspondents were careful not to give their opinions on paper. There must have been the suspicion that family requests for information were part of an attempt to have Constance released. Sandbach continued:

> I have been making enquiries that you asked about in your letter of 24 July.... There is no direct evidence of the Countess shooting policemen or soldiers in cold blood herself.[125]

A letter from a military source, G. Ball, of 1 August, 1916, repeated the de Burgh Daly incident:

> At the court martial the case was so clear we did not go into evidence of the Countess's acts but a boy gave evidence that he saw her fire at an officer in a window ... she missed. A policeman was shot and the crowd yelled 'that is the Countess again' but there is no one who saw her fire. A person at Phillipsburgh Avenue, Fairview says he personally saw the Countess order a wounded man to be shot and saw this shooting carried out on the Countess's orders in her presence. There is no more than this available at present.[126]

Despite such reassurances Josslyn would continue his search for definitive answers for the rest of the year and into the next. As well as dealing with Constance's finances and the allegations about her conduct during the Rising a further issue arose in July. The Governor of Mountjoy Prison wrote on 11 July to inform him that if Constance wished to have new teeth fitted she would have to apply to the General Prisons Board.

10

'Paying the Price...'

Constance was alone and confined to a cell. It was the most drastic change she had ever experienced; from early childhood her strongest impulse was to enjoy freedom without constraint. One of the earliest photographs shows her seated on a pony at Lissadell. As soon as she could escape the restriction of a minder she went galloping across the fields. In her adolescent years she loved riding with the Sligo Harriers or sailing in the coves along the Atlantic coast. In Paris her nickname was 'Velo', from her habit of arriving breathless on a bicycle. When she moved to Dublin she would cycle five miles from Belcamp into the city for Sinn Féin meetings. Involvement with the Irish Citizen Army meant a change to foot-slogging, but she kept herself fit with route marches of up to forty miles in a day.

The thirteen years with Casimir were characterised by movement and action – a continuous whirl of activity in art, drama and politics. Now she found herself in solitary confinement in Mountjoy; many of her closest friends were dead. Others such as Hanna Sheehy-Skeffington were denied access. For the first time in her life she was entirely alone. However the passage of time changed her opinion of Mountjoy as an ordeal: a letter to Eva from Aylesbury Women's Prison on 8 August painted a nostalgic view of the Dublin prison:

'The Scout' by Constance from prison journal

> There was so much life in Mountjoy. There were seagulls and pigeons which I had quite tame, there were 'Stop Press' cries, and little boys splashing in the canal and singing Irish songs, shrill and discordant, but with such vigour. There was a black spaniel, too, with long silky ears, and a most attractive convict-baby with a squint and soft Irish voices everywhere. There were the trains, 'Broadstone' and 'Northwall' trams, and even an old melodeon, and a man trying to play an Irish tune on a bugle over the wall.[127]

She had no reason to believe that her fate would be much different from Tom Clarke who spent long periods in solitary confinement and whose health was permanently damaged by prison conditions. Her friends wondered if her fast-moving life had prepared her for the privations of a long prison sentence. She was kept in solitary confinement where she wrote poetry to sustain her morale. 'In Mountjoy' attempted to depict her surroundings in a poem free from political rhetoric:

In Mountjoy

There's sunlight in the world outside,
The happy pigeons coo,
I know the summer's warmth has come,
I know the sky is blue.

There's twilight in my dreary cell,
So ugly cold and bare;
A chilly twilight – towards the north
The opaque windows stare.

I press my face against the pane
A great grey wall appears,
Riddled with windows just like mine,
Entombing hopes and tears.

The verses would be more memorable if she had revised some of the weaker rhymes and shifts in rhythm, but they are remarkable considering the circumstances in which they were written. The line about the wall riddled with barred windows reflects her sense of prison as a living death.

> I know the living sunlight shines
> On all the world outside,
> And sunshine gilds my heart in dreams
> Though walled and locked inside.
>
> The dead white of a prison cell,
> The jangling keys, the loveless hours,
> The broken hopes, the stunted powers,
> And tolling of a passing bell outside.
>
> The white light of a rising sun,
> The pink of spring in apple trees,
> The purring wings of waking bees,
> With work and hope the day's begun.

While Constance and Eva lived separate lives in the years leading up to 1916 the trauma of the Rebellion renewed the bond between them. In the years to come Constance would serve more prison terms and would develop ways to deal with confinement; she would also have the support and sense of being part of a burgeoning national movement. The period of isolation after the crushing of the Easter Rebellion was the most difficult ordeal she would experience. Eva became concerned about her sister's well-being and devised a project that would keep her occupied.

Constance told R.M. Fox that she found a copy of Eva's *The Three Resurrections and the Triumph of Maeve* and began drawing in the margins. 'There is nothing so happy in this old Kosmos as trying to draw and paint, and such a rest to tired nerves,' she wrote from prison. At one stage she illustrated by hand a copy of Eva's poetry collection, *The One and the Many*. It may have given Eva the idea to occupy Constance with a collaboration on her verse play, *The Death of Fionavar*.

The story of Fionavar, daughter of Queen Maeve, was originally part of the longer drama, *The Triumph of Maeve*, published with a selection of poems in *The Three Resurrections and The Triumph of Maeve* in 1905. Eva extracted three scenes from the play concerning Fionavar and added 'An Interpretation' to explain why she changed the myth to highlight a hitherto minor character:

> As I have been accused of taking liberties with an ancient myth, I would say in defence that all myths have many meanings, perhaps as many as the minds of those who know them.... The meaning I got

out of the story of Maeve is a symbol of the world-old struggle in the human mind between the forces of domination and pity, of peace and war.¹²⁸

Eva connected the tension between Maeve and Fionavar with the contemporary struggle between the pacifists and dissenters with the British military machine. Her fusion of Celtic legend with Christian lore enabled her to contrast the violence of the ancient world with the new message of peace and love. In the play Maeve has a vision of the death of Christ and Fionavar dies when she sees heaps of dead bodies on the battlefield: 'For very pity she lay down and died.'

Winged horses from Fionavar

The play can be read as a protest against the Great War, but the pacifist argument could also be directed at her sister:

> For force is a useless and futile weapon against the soul and its mysterious powers, and the ambitious fighter is for ever an outcast from the country of the mind, which can only be entered by a pilgrim who has cast aside anger and power and worldly possessions.

Constance trained to be an artist in the Slade School of Art in London and Academie Julien in Paris; she was skilled at sketching and drawing – she drew illustrations for the Fianna Handbook, created their banner and designed the masthead for the Daughters of Erin paper. To illustrate a book in the confines of a prison cell was a fresh challenge that delighted her.

> I made quills out of rook's feathers that I found in the garden. They are much nicer than most pens: you can get such a fine, soft line.¹²⁹

The images express a longing for freedom with winged horses and wild birds above waves dashing against rocky shores in romantic landscapes that evoke the wild Atlantic coast. She filled the margins with roses, shells and seagulls, swords and crowns. Many of the images are Rosicrucian symbols, another link with Yeats who told her about the Theosophists. While she was engaged in producing the drawings the authorities received an unusual request from a government supporter, Mr. J.F. Cunningham, Barrister-at-Law, writing from the Irish Literary Society, 20 Hanover Square, London:

> The Countess Markievicz is of the Gore-Booth family and really you gain nothing by keeping her in prison. Mr. Asquith has announced a policy of leniency, so that you may now do one more gracious act for this influential family. I ask it especially on the grounds of recruiting.... I know she has been tried and sentenced and all that, but the idea of her being a bloodthirsty revolutionist is preposterous. See how she apologized to those she inconvenienced at St. Stephen's Green. All the other women have been released. What is the use of pretending that these women are a danger to the Empire? The Countess is not a bit more crazy than Annie Kenny, or Mrs Pankhurst. If you think it necessary I will go security for her future good behaviour. She will be a little noisy for a while, but it will be nothing serious...[130]

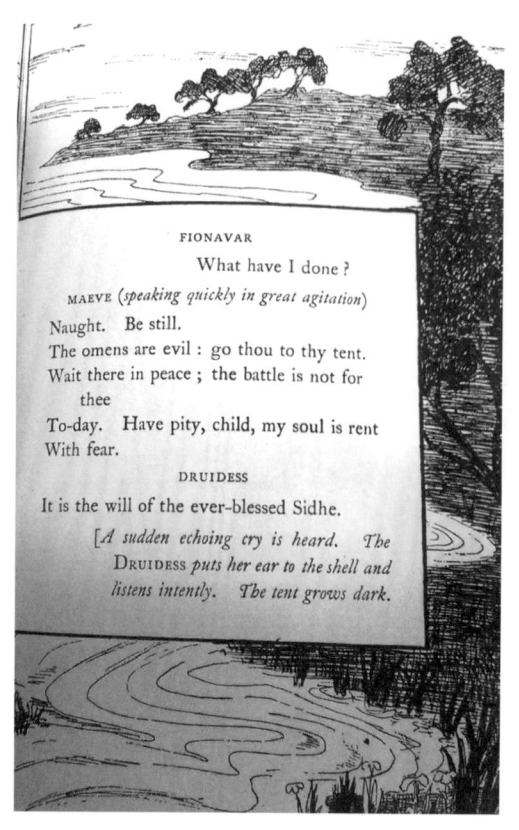

Page from Fionavar

No official reply has survived. Constance wrote to Josslyn on 22 June and asked him to write to Casimir and to send him her love – 'He might get it into his head that I've eloped or something.' Casimir was recovering from battle wounds sustained in the Carpathians in 1915 when he was wounded by an exploding shell. By mid-1916 he was back in Kiev, determined to live life to the full – writing plays, painting pictures and drinking like a fish.

He wrote to Josslyn on 16 August: 'I hardly could find what to say about the sad events of the spring.' Despite his disapproval of the Rising he was anxious to contact Constance in prison and requested details. He gave information on his own war experiences:

> Typhus and effects of a shell bursting at very close distance have done their work and I am suffering from very severe headache and haven't quite recovered the use of my left arm. I am writing and working with Polish theatre.[131]

Stasko was a conscripted translator with the Russian fleet at Archangel from which he wrote to Josslyn on 16 August in terms that echoed the sentiments of his father:

Casimir photographed by Constance

> I was delighted to have news of poor mother. What a sad stupid business it has been.... Father was very worried & we were most anxious on her account.... It's a blessing she can't get into more trouble.[132]

Despite the breezy tone in her letters and notes Constance was traumatised by the executions of her closest friends, James Connolly in particular. In July she wrote a poem to express her sorrow and anger:

My 1916 Lover

You died for your country my Hero-love
In the first grey dawn of spring;
On your lips was a prayer to God above
That your death will have helped to bring
Freedom and peace to the land you love,
Love above everything.

> You died for your country and left me here
> To weep – No, my eyes are dry
> For the woman you found so sweet and dear
> Has a sterner destiny –
> She will fight as you fought while you were here
> For freedom I'll live and die.
>
> On your murdered body I'll pledge my life
> With its passionate love and hate
> To secret plotting and open strife
> For vengeance early and late
> To Ireland and you I have pledged my life
> Revenge for your memory's sake.

The poem was entrusted to a wardress and, decades later, was given to Stasko who donated it to the National Museum. He was uneasy about some of the passionate expressions, concerned that people might interpret them as evidence of a sexual liaison. Connolly's home was in Belfast, but he worked in Dublin and lived as a lodger in Surrey House; he was close to Constance and would hear no criticism of her, according to William O'Brien, but there is no proof that the relationship was other than platonic. The poem expressed her dedication to Connolly's vision of a Workers Republic and her inability to compromise with half-way measures.

The popular view of the Rising began to change after the executions. George Bernard Shaw condemned the military policy in the *Daily News*:

> The shot Irishmen will now take their places beside Emmet and the Manchester Martyrs in Ireland and beside the heroes of Poland and Serbia and Belgium in Europe; and nothing in Heaven or earth can prevent it...[133]

The refrain from Yeats' play, *Cathleen Ni Houlihan*, became a mantra for the executed leaders:

> They shall be remembered for ever
> They shall be alive for ever ...

Yeats wrote to Lady Gregory on 11 May: 'I had no idea that any public event could so deeply move me.' He began writing a poem, 'Easter 1916', almost immediately in which he declared that everything was:

'Paying the Price...'

> All changed, changed utterly:
> A terrible beauty is born.

Constance was among the participants who were transformed, but not in a positive sense:

> That woman's days were spent
> In ignorant good-will,
> Her nights in argument
> Until her voice grew shrill.

By criticizing Constance he was also attacking Maud Gonne as he admitted to Ezra Pound: 'When Madame Gonne quarrelled with me I felt it necessary to denounce Madame Markievicz.'[134] The aftermath of the rebellion excited him in other ways. The execution of Major John MacBride had turned Maud Gonne into a widow and he made his way to France where he renewed his courtship.

In Ireland the shift in sympathy to the rebels was noted by the writer Kathleen Tynan:

> The shootings, the deportations ... were with me all day, going on at the back of my mind as I wrote, lying down with me, rising up with me, treading the daily round with me: I was rebellion-ridden.[135]

During the summer of 1916 military repression intensified – army officers scanned newspapers for hints of sedition; soldiers raided corner shops for cards with images of the executed rebels. The police seized song-sheets and compiled reports of subversive behaviour such as singing in the street or speaking Irish at home. Maxwell fretted about having Constance in Ireland and wrote to the Home Office on 16 July:

1916 Memorial cards – Constance & Connolly

It appears to be desirable that Countess Markievicz should be removed from Mountjoy Prison, Dublin, to some prison in England. From censored letters it appears that sympathizers know how she is getting on in prison and that in some way information is leaking out.[136]

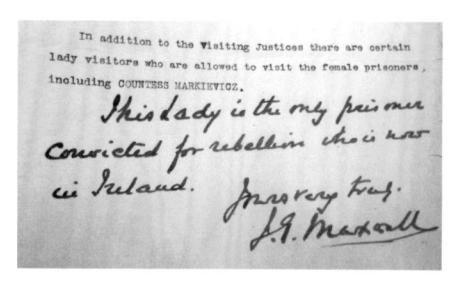

Note from General Maxwell

The military were concerned to maintain control over public opinion by handling information. They were anxious about a possible plot to rescue Constance from Mountjoy. Maxwell saw traitors in the Visiting Justices of the Peace elected by Dublin Corporation, a body with Sinn Féin sympathies. He regarded Constance as a symbolic figure around which the defeated rebels could reorganize. 'This lady is the only prisoner convicted of rebellion who is now in Ireland,' he wrote in heavy black letters across the end of his report.

The sympathetic wardress from County Wexford smuggled notes and letters written in tiny script on pieces of toilet paper. The disjointed messages shows Constance's determination to rebuild the shattered republican and socialist organizations. She was attempting to recreate a network through Father Albert Bibby and Fianna and Citizen Army people – Eamon Martin, Garry Holohan & Padraig O'Rian:

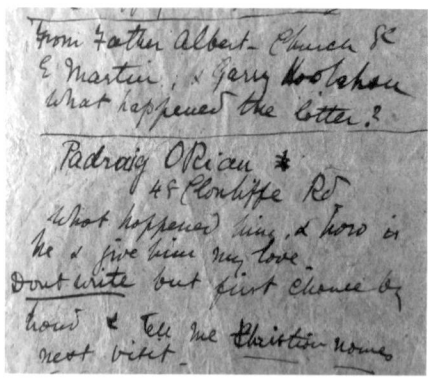

Note smuggled from Mountjoy

Find out news & give code to Joe Connolly, Christie Poole etc... What happened the letter.... What happened Jim, how is he and give him my love. <u>Don't write</u> but first chance by hand & tell me Christian <u>names</u> next visit.[137]

She also sent a brief note to James Connolly's wife, Lillie: 'I want Miss French Mullen to have Poppet.'

She refers to the wardress in an undated letter to Eva:

You see, the gap has been thrown and I have found a real friend, and it makes the whole difference: both mentally and bodily. She is taking awful risks for me.... I want you to give her a copy of our book, with your autograph.... Trust her absolutely and let not your left hand know what your right hand doeth (Esther of course excepted). None of the crew or the family must even guess, for people *will* talk....You had probably better not try and see her again as you are both probably under watchful and protective eyes. At present anyhow, I see my friend a lot. I am sending you also some things to do for me.[138]

A letter of support came Sir John Leslie, an old family friend, whose estate at Glaslough in County Monaghan the sisters visited in the past. John Leslie studied art in Academie Julien and followed a career in the British Army. In 1916 he was based with the 18th Reserve Battalion, Inniskilling Fusiliers, in Enniskillen when he responded to a letter from Eva.

Dear Miss Eva,

Your letter is painfully interesting. I do hope my letter gave your sister a ray of pleasure. It is dreadful to think of the charming high-spirited girl I used to know being a prisoner. It is wonderful her keeping up her spirits. Perhaps they will find her some kind of work that might suit her clever artistic fingers.

An enormous Army doctor was in here yesterday who described being captured by the Countess in person, who deprived him of his belt and allowed him to look after wounded Sinn Feiners.

Her pistol was enormous and he was terrified of its going off. I don't know what the dear child would say if she knew I was commanding the garrison here, defending bridges and controlling the district.

Shall we ever have peace and quiet? Anyway, we cannot manage without belonging to an Empire. Small states seem to be demolished.[139]

After her transfer to Mountjoy Constance began taking religious instruction from the prison chaplain, Father McMahon. One day Hannah met him at the prison gate and the exasperated cleric complained:

I don't understand Countess Markievicz at all. She wants to be received into the Church, but she won't attend to me when I try to explain Transubstantiation and other doctrines. She says: 'Please don't trouble to explain. I believe all the Church teaches. Now, Father, please tell me about the boys.'[140]

The 'boys' were her dead comrades of 1916 with whom she wished to be reunited, a desire that remained until her death in 1927. She alarmed the priest by advocating a Miltonic interpretation of Lucifer as a 'good rebel'. Hannah told Esther the literal-minded cleric could not understand that Constance loved to pull the leg of people in authority: she belonged more to the Church of St. Francis of Assisi than that of St. Paul. She was sincere about wanting to become a Catholic, but did not wish the ceremony to take place in prison.

11

ROGER CASEMENT

Eva was busy in London all through July where she attended the treason trial of Sir Roger Casement at the Old Bailey. She found time to carry out many of the tasks for Constance and wrote to Father O'Ryan thanking him for making ten shilling weekly payments to Mrs. Mallin. While the attitude of the Irish public towards the Rising began to change the response of the British Establishment was tested in the trial of Sir Roger Casement, which began in the Old Bailey on 26 June. Casement was an associate of Constance, had helped her with funding for the Fianna and was now charged with high treason. He was represented by George Gavan Duffy who could not find an English counsel to take the case and invited his brother-in-law from Ireland, A.M. Sullivan, who turned out to be a weak advocate.

The trial lasted four days and was over when the great offensive at the Somme began on 1 July. Eva was reluctant at first to attend because she had never met Casement, but she allowed Esther to persuade her. Sir John Lavery composed an epic canvas of the courtroom with the judicial bench looming over solicitors, witnesses and the frail figure in the dock. He included a tiny distant spectator, considered to be Eva, high up at the corner of the public gallery.

There was sympathy for Casement among humanitarians because of his work in the Congo and South America. The British Government attempted to destroy any support for a reprieve by spreading details of homosexual encounters in the 'Black Diaries.' Eva and Esther had low expectations of the intrigues by the powerful and expected a black propaganda campaign. Nearly twenty years later Esther still considered the 'Diaries' to be government-inspired forgeries:

Relentless foes sat in seats of power and they poisoned the public mind by circulating lying stories (that had nothing to do with the case) against the personal character of Roger Casement. Only those who did not know him believed them and it was a vile way of hounding a man to death.[141]

Casement was condemned to death and lodged an appeal. His cousin, Gertrude Bannister, began a campaign for clemency, claiming that he came to Ireland to stop the rebellion as he knew it had no hope of success. Eva and Esther joined in the campaign by writing to many of their prominent contacts, including Yeats and Shaw. Gavan Duffy, secured permission for them to attend a sitting at the Court of Criminal Appeal which began on 17 July before five judges. 'The judges, coming into Court, were received by the assembly standing up, as is the custom,' Esther wrote.

> When they had taken their seats Roger Casement was led by two warders up the steps into the dock. He courteously bowed to the Judges who, following the inhuman practise of such places, took no notice. Then he caught sight of Eva, who had risen to her feet when he appeared. His face lighted up with a rare and beautiful smile.

> 'Give my love to Eva,' Casement wrote that night. 'I thought she looked so tired in Court today.'

The appeal was summarily dismissed and an appeal for clemency met with no response from the British Government. Eva plunged into the campaign and wrote letters to anyone with any possible influence, such as Lord Sumner, a member of the Privy Council:

> Dear Lord Sumner,
>
> May I beg you to read the enclosed papers? I don't think it's generally known what was Casement's object in his mad seeming expedition & it does seem the most ghastly thing that he should be in danger of hanging because of his frantic attempt to stop the rising ... the enclosed interview clearly shows that he made an attempt at Lisduff to get the priest to try and stop the rising. Please forgive me bothering [you] but it's such a miserable tragic business & the personal side is so awful ... poor Miss Bannister & agonized suspense is quite heartbreaking...[142]

She received a letter dated 23 July from Yeats in response to her petition against Casement's death sentence:

> Dear Miss Gore-Booth, I thank you very much for your most interesting account of Casement's purpose. I had already written to the HomeSec and sent a copy of my letter to Mr. Asquith.... Will you permit me to say how much I sorrow over the misfortune that has fallen on your family? Your sister and yourself, two beautiful figures among the great trees of Lissadell, are among the dear memories of my youth.[143]

He avoided any apportionment of blame while expressing sympathy with the Gore-Booth family. It would be another eleven years before he would write *In Memoriam,* but the image of the sisters as symbols of a lost order had taken shape in his mind.

Eva accompanied Gertrude Bannister on a last minute mission to King George V in Buckingham Place. They pleaded for him to use the royal prerogative of mercy. He replied that the exercise of mercy was no longer the King's Right, but resided in his ministers. It is uncertain if Eva was among a small number of sympathisers who stood vigil outside the prison on the day of Casement's execution. From early morning of Thursday, 3 August, a crowd of Londoners gathered outside the prison on the Caledonian Road. As the prison bell struck nine a man shouted: 'He is on his way'. The joke caught on and the great crowd of well-dressed men and women broke into a laugh and gave a horrible cheer that chilled sympathisers to the bone.

According to Esther the crowd went silent when a small group went on their knees and prayed for Casement with tears falling down their faces. Other accounts claim that they were abused by the crowd. Casement became an iconic figure for Eva and the ending of the death penalty an urgent cause. She supported the

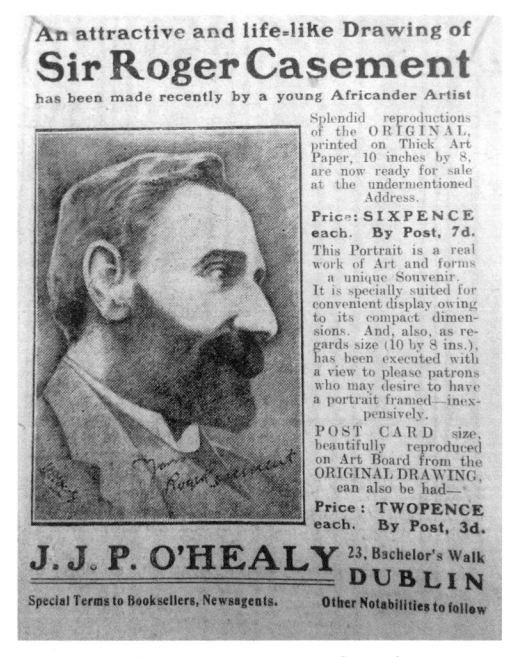

Casement memorial card

London crowd outside courthouse awaiting Casement verdict

campaign to have his body returned to Ireland, a request that would not be granted until 1965. She wrote an article on Casement published in the *Catholic Bulletin* praising his international work for the oppressed in terms that recalled her appreciation of Frank Sheehy-Skeffington:

> Roger Casement was one of the world's great champions of the weak against the strong, of goodwill and freedom against militarism and empire, of life against death, and thus he takes his places among seers and prophets of all ages.[144]

She wrote several poems about him, notably 'Roger Casement', in the volume, *Broken Glory*:

> I dream of one who is dead
> As the forms of green trees float and form in the water
> The dreams float and fall in my mind.

Meanwhile, Home Office chiefs were considering Maxwell's demand to move Constance to England. Their comments were recorded on her prison file on 20 July:

> Samuel to Sir E. Troup: 'Will you arrange this transfer as General Maxwell desires.'

Troup to Dryhurst: 'I suppose we must take her. The reasons seem conclusive. Shall she go to Aylesbury?'

Dryhurst to Troup: 'Yes, she should go to Aylesbury. I wd. like to have the prison record before she actually gets there.'[145]

When Constance discovered she was leaving Mountjoy she wrote to Eva:

Darling, I am, alas! going into exile. Make a point to try & get in to see me. I believe you could by influence… Remember I don't mind being in jail and if it's better for the cause I'm prepared to remain here. My only desire is to be of use to those outside. Nothing else matters really to me.

I believe that by rights I am entitled to receive and write one letter on moving, so that if you get no letter in a few weeks, write and say that previously, at your visit, I arranged to write to you always. Quote this rule and ask why you have not heard. They would do a good deal to avoid any fuss and to combat the idea that we are being ill-treated.

This is d'être (unofficial) paper! and written under huge difficulties![146]

She was concerned that Eva would be too mild in her approach and lack persistence in dealing with the prison authorities.

Remember it is only by pushing & by sort of discreet threats & making yourself disagreeable that you will be able to do anything for us.

I am going to Aylesbury. Shall be quite amiable – am not going to hungerstrike, as am advised by comrades not to. It would suit the Government very well to let me die quietly. I want to work for the Army, that's all. I look forward to seeing you the whole time. Put on your prettiest hat when you come! Give Esther my best love. I shall never forget her coming. My family must be quite amusing about my latest crimes.

She rarely mentions her family in the letters from prison; she knew the censor would read everything and she was careful not to bring private matters to the attention of the authorities. The remark about the family being 'quite amusing' shows a high degree of complicity between the sisters.

> I told you to write to Casi & try to get the news through. It would have to be diplomatically done to evade censor. You might try. Now I must stop. Very very best love. Am going to Aylesbury. Let friends there know.

In the House of Commons on 3 August Herbert Samuel announced that Irish prisoners had been moved to England and it was proposed to move Countess Markievicz also.

> She registered herself in Mountjoy Prison as a Roman Catholic, and will, therefore, be treated as a Roman Catholic prisoner in England. There is a Roman Catholic priest attached to the prison where she is going. I am informed that her husband is serving with the Russian Army. No communication has been received from either the Russian or the American Government.
>
> Mr. Byrne MP: 'Where is she to be transferred to?'
>
> Mr. Samuel: 'I am not quite sure.'[147]

The transfer was no simple matter as can be seen from the paperwork on her prison file. Dublin Castle issued an order to 'the Governor of His Majesty's Prison, Mountjoy,' J. Wylie:

> We, the Lords Justices and General Governors of Ireland do hereby, under and in pursuance of the Statutes in such cases made and provided, order you to cause the prisoner named in the margin to be removed from the above named Prison to His Majesty's Prison at Aylesbury and there delivered to the Governor of the said last named prison provided that the prisoner is in fit state to be removed. Given at his Majesty's Castle of Dublin, this 26th of July, 1916. E. O'Farrell.

Sir Edward O'Farrell informed London in a letter to the Under Secretary of State at the British Home Office on 31 July:

> I am directed by the Lords Justice to inform you that the necessary warrant under directing her removal thence to Aylesbury Prison has now issued (copy enclosed), and to request that you will be good enough to take the necessary steps for issue of the corresponding warrant directing her reception at the last named prison.[148]

The transfer took place on Monday, 7 August. The standard procedure was to send the prisoner with a plainclothes police escort and a female wardress. Constance did not leave Dublin without a final dramatic gesture. She scribbled a quick note to Eva on the back of an envelope and concealed it inside a glove.

> Darling. Got yours. Ever so much love. If it's better for the cause to leave me in just leave me – being sent to Aylesbury! You can probably get in *back door* influence. Duchess of Bedford is a 'visitor' there. I want to get my teeth done, two ought to be stopped. I am glad that M [Maeve or Mabel?] was amused & not shocked! Best love & kisses and hoping we may someday meet again.[149]

The police escort brought her by taxi through the main gate of Mountjoy and onto the North Circular Road. She saw three friends on the footpath, leaned out the window and, before the astonished escort could stop her, threw away one of her gloves. The episode would later become the subject of a police enquiry. Superintendent Lewes of 'G' Division was in charge of the transfer:

> I beg to state that on the 7th August, '16, accompanied by Constable Hoey and a Matron from Mountjoy Prison, I was handed over the above named to be conveyed to H.M.P. Aylesbury.
>
> Immediately after leaving the Prison in a Taxi Cab, the prisoner recognised three women standing at the corner of Berkeley Road and she threw out one of her gloves to them.
>
> I understand the gloves were only given to her immediately before starting and it would be impossible for her to have such a thing as a 'Message to the Rebels' in her glove or on her person when she was handed over to me, and it was only about one minute afterwards the incident occurred. I am of the opinion it was merely bravado on her part to make such a statement, as she is much given in that way.[150]

Supt. Lewes does not seem to have considered she might have hidden the message up her sleeve. The bravado was on his side and Constance showed again her ability to outwit the efforts of the authorities to curb her. At Kingston (Dun Laoghaire) other friends, including the faithful Poppet, were present to see her off. When he saw his mistress the dog broke free and raced on to the boat. Faced with this unexpected manoeuvre the escort made no attempt to remove him.

Constance wrote to Eva about the voyage:

> I had the loveliest journey over here. My escort had never been on the sea before and kept thinking she was going to be ill. I lay down and enjoyed a sunny porthole and a fresh breeze. There was a big airship (like the picture of a Zeppelin) cruising about when we arrived. I was awfully pleased, as I had never seen one. I do so long to fly! Also I'd love to dive in a submarine.[151]

Meanwhile in their top-floor apartment on Fitzroy Square, Eva and Esther were discussing how to counter some of the lurid stories about Constance. They found it impossible to defend her without knowing the exact nature of the charges, but the official sources refused any information. Esther remembered:

> ... we were sitting in the flat thinking and talking of Constance. We knew that at the end of a month in a local prison, long-term prisoners are sent to a convict prison. We also knew that Irish men prisoners had been sent to Lewes Gaol, but we had no news whatever as to her movements. Suddenly, for no reason whatever, I felt I must go to Euston Station to meet the Irish Mail. I was reluctant to say so, for Eva was tired out. However, I did so.
>
> She asked 'Why?'
>
> I was obliged to reply, 'I have no reason whatever, only I feel I must.'
>
> She looked very much astonished, but said, 'Very well, then, I will come with you.'
>
> 'No, don't,' I begged, 'it will all be for nothing, I expect.'
>
> 'Oh no, if you go, I will go with you,' she said.
>
> Mercifully she kept to that. In the late afternoon we went wearily enough. The station was hot and quiet when we got to the arrival platform and I felt exceedingly silly.
>
> 'You go to one end of the platform and I to another,' suggested Eva, and she chose the furthest end.
>
> I waited alone, watching idly while various policemen and detectives came along and someone I took to be a staff-officer from the War Office. Then the train came in, a number of passengers emerged, none

of whom I knew. I got more and more depressed, when suddenly looking up, I beheld coming towards me the strangest little procession ever seen by my astonished eyes. First a brown cocker spaniel, well known in Dublin as 'The Poppet', then a couple of soldiers with rifles, then Eva and Constance together, smiling and talking hard. Lastly an officer with drawn sword, looking very agitated.[152]

When Eva had walked to the end of the platform she glanced at the carriage opposite and saw Constance at the window. As soon as the group emerged on the platform she raced to her sister and threw her arms around her. The soldiers stood around helplessly as the sisters embraced and kissed. Constance used the confusion to push some papers into her sister's pocket. The embarrassed officer urged them to stop and move quietly along the platform. Esther continued:

Stasko and Poppet

> This they did at once, but much conversation must have been got in on the way. I, of course, shouted a greeting as I tried to get near. A detective opened the door of a taxi and Constance got in accompanied by an escort. All information as to her destination was refused. The dog jumped in too, no one apparently venturing to touch him. As the car drove off Eva called out,

'Send Poppet back to the flat if they won't let him in.'

Then as she turned away, she added quietly,

'I heard the detective tell the chauffeur to go to Holloway Prison.'

They waited until they were well away from the station before they examined the paper Constance brought.

> It gave the names of the Court-Martial Judges, the charge against her, and the verdict, in fact all the information which had been denied to Eva or her legal representative.

About an hour after they returned to the flat the doorbell rang. It was a military escort with the unrepentant Poppet.

Esther continued:

> I am not in the least psychic, nor have I ever had a similar experience. I can only suggest by way of explanation the fact that as Constance told us later, when she had suddenly been taken from Mountjoy and put on the steamer and realized she was going to England, she was filled with an intense longing to see Eva, and a deep regret that she had not been able to tell her beforehand of her journey.

Esther Roper

Did the telepathic message fail to reach Eva because of her exhaustion and transfer to Esther instead? We will never know if the women had other intelligence that a move was afoot. The Irish authorities hoped that exile to England would remove Constance from the public mind. She was following the other Irish prisoners into exile in England. Kathleen Lynn had escaped a court-martial, but was deported to Bath. The majority of the women prisoners had been released in June 1916 with the exception of a few internees such as Helena Molony and Winifred Carney who were detained in the Borstal section of Aylesbury Women's Prison. Marie Perolz had been detained in England and held in Aylesbury, but released in June.

12

Aylesbury: 'It's Queer and Lonely Here...'

Constance was a Londoner, born at 7 Buckingham Gate on 4 February 1868 in a terraced mansion close to the entrance to Buckingham Palace. Before she lived in Paris and Dublin her childhood years alternated between Sligo and London. The city was her second home with the family in residence each year for the season when mothers showed off their daughters and sought wealthy husbands among the eligible bachelors. Constance was presented to Queen Victoria on St. Patrick's Day, 1887.

She lived in London for long periods during the 1880s and the 1890s when she studied at the Slade on Gower Street. Along with Willie Yeats she visited fortune-tellers and attended séances in darkened rooms and even took up smoking with fellow art students. Her marriage to Casimir in September 1900 was held in St. Marylebone's Church. London had been a haven over the years, even if she now viewed it as the centre of the malignant Empire. Like Oscar Wilde she was a felon on the stage where once she shone as a celebrity.

She was admitted to Aylesbury Women's Prison on the same day. Aylesbury is the county town of Buckinghamshire on the north side of the Chiltern Hills, thirty-six miles from London. Among the inmates was May Sharpe, born in Leitrim but known as 'Chicago May,' serving a sentence for trying to kill a former boyfriend. The first thing that struck her were the double entrance doors where the escort halted like a boat in a canal lock as the transfer took place. Constance might have thought of the porte cochere in Lissadell with its great doors protecting visitors from the Atlantic storms. 'Then we were entered on the prison rolls, and our clothes were

Aylesbury Women's Prison

taken from us, in exchange for the prison garb, marked with the government's broad arrow.'[153]

On admittance Constance weighed 128 pounds, a loss of 8 pounds over three months in Mountjoy. Her new abode was a rambling building with a high stone wall, opened as a prison in 1847. It became a women's prison in 1890 and had a Borstal section for young women as well as the convict section. According to May Sharpe the building was not cold, but the limestone floors and walls were damp. It held over 300 cells with one woman to a cell.

Constance's reputation as a rebel preceded her and stiffened the resolve of Governor G.W. Winder and his Deputy, Dr Selina Fitzherbert Fox, not to indulge any demands for political status but to treat her as an ordinary criminal. However from the beginning she was treated as an exception. She was initially put into a punishment cell with a gate instead of a door. The Woman Superintendent in Aylesbury, soon to take over as governor, was another strong woman. In an age when women struggled for equality Dr S.F. Fox forged a career in the medical section of the public services. She was three years younger than Constance and qualified as a medical doctor from the London School of Medicine in 1899. Like the Gore-Booth sisters, she held the idealistic view that one should strive to improve society. She went to India with the Church Missionary Society in 1900, but could not bear the hot climate and returned to found a voluntary hospital, the Bermondsey Medical Mission, in one of the poorest areas of London. The

Aylesbury: 'It's Queer and Lonely Here...'

Mission was her life's work where a client remembered her as being 'kind but very strict.'[154]

> Aylesbury was under the control of a Doctor Fox when I arrived,' Constance wrote. 'Besides holding the position of Medical Officer she was also Deputy Governor. A more unsuitable person to run a gaol it has never been my misfortune to come across ...[155]

As a result of the social upheaval of the Great War women were appointed to public service positions normally reserved for men. Ms Fox was no suffragist, but she created a strong precedent for women when she accepted the post of Woman Superintendent in Aylesbury Prison in 1914; the authorities thought her experience of the criminals in London's inner city suited her for dealing with women of the same class. It was ironic that she should be suitable to serve as prison governor, but was ineligible to vote in Westminster elections. She was deeply loyal and patriotic and lectured the prisoners on the treachery of the Irish rebels. As a result Constance got a cool reception when she arrived, but the effect was somewhat mitigated by the rule of silence.

When she was moved to a 'normal' cell she was upset by the large eyeball painted over the peep-hole in the door. Prisoners could be observed at any hour of day or night. The eye was the symbol of authority, taking the place of the all-seeing eye of God. She found being spied upon hard to bear and told May Sharpe that she walked the cell for hours at night 'trying to exorcise the devilish spyhole.'

In the eyes of the authorities prisoners had broken the moral as well as the criminal code. The focus of the penal system was to bring an end to a perverse or malignant way of thinking and behaviour. A programme of hard labour would bring about transformation in the prisoner's character and lead to rehabilitation into civilized society. In the early twentieth century the British penal system was believed the most progressive in the world, replacing the former system with the cruel punishments suffered by the Fenians.

> Imprisonment is a contest for moral domination ... there is a determination to use the well-tried tools – silence, isolation, personal contamination and association with criminals: a regime crafted and thoughtfully modified over the years to compel submission, and so bewilder, belittle and demoralise.[156]

Constance took a different view:

> Prison might aptly be described as a scheme in which many unfortunates were initiated into every form of vice, and from whence they were launched into the underworld of criminals.

Dr Fox at work in her study

Prisoners were sorted into three categories: Star Class, first time offenders with a red star under a number on their sleeve; Intermediates, who wore bars on the sleeve; and Recidivists, who had no marks at all. Constance was Star Class and was determined to survive the prison system by means of agitation, passive resistance and by keeping her sense of humour. When she arrived in Aylesbury there were four other female rebel prisoners – Helena Molony, Winifred Carney, Breda Foley and Ellen Ryan – who were kept in a separate section as they were internees. Constance alone among the Irish prisoners had no opportunity to associate with her comrades. In Dublin, Hannah Sheehy-Skeffington looked with alarm on the transfer of her friends to England: 'It was as if the tomb closed on them.'[157]

The prison day began at 6.30 followed by a meal of cold tea and bread in the cell at 7.30. Lunch came at noon and consisted of two ounces of meat, a potato, two ounces of cabbage and six ounces of bread. There was never enough to eat. The menu was fish on Thursday, bully-beef on Sunday, and on other days 'a couple of small slices of meat floating in greasy water ... twelve ounces of vegetables, mostly potatoes with slices of carrots or dried beans or onions, rarely leeks or cabbage.'[158] Rations were cut during the war to match the food given to soldiers at the front. The last meal was supper at 4.30 consisting of a pint of cocoa or tea and four ounces of bread. The inadequate and inferior nourishment, added to the loss of liberty, was enough to wear down the strongest spirit. May Sharpe wrote:

> At first the food they gave me turned my stomach. But after the first revolt of my stomach I never knew a day when I was not hungry. I could have stolen and devoured more than was given me, of that awful, noisome, prison fare.[159]

Constance complained that her mattress was 'so dirty that I cannot describe it.' Her clothes with the prison arrow were passed on from a released prisoner and the shoes were 'full of holes which let in wet and snow.' The rough conditions were the lot of the ordinary convict, but they were material for the political prisoner in her war against the system. You could attempt to wear down the authorities by a persistent campaign of complaining, demanding and protesting. The prison protocols on letter writing were laid down:

- Prisoners could only write to a respectable friend;
- Prisoners should watch the language used;
- Write only about personal business or domestic affairs;
- No politics, complaints, or subversive opinions.

Star Class prisoners were on probation for the first six months with a restricted allowance of letters. (William Partridge was sent to Dartmoor where he could receive and send one letter every four months.) Constance's first letter to Eva on prison notepaper was dated 8 August, the day after arrival. She appeared to be familiar with prison routine and the carrot patch in the garden which prisoners passed every day:

> Dearest Old Darling – The one thing I have gained by my exile is the privilege of writing a letter, but there's very little to say, as I do not suppose that an 'essay on prison life' would pass the Censor, however interesting and amusing it might be!

During her spells of freedom she would write freely about the prison system, pointing up the irony in the remark on the 'interesting and amusing aspects.'

> What you call my 'misplaced sense of humour' still remains to me and I am quite well and cheerful.

> I saw myself – for the first time in over 3 months the other day. It is quite amusing to meet yourself as a stranger. We bowed & grinned & I thought my teeth very dirty & very much wanting a dentist & I'd got very thin & very sunburnt. In 6 months I shall not recognize myself at all my memory of faces is so bad! I remember a fairy tale of a Princess who banished mirrors when she began to grow old. I think it showed a great want of interest in life. The less I see my face the more curious I grow about it, & I don't resent it getting old.[160]

She compared the atmosphere in Aylesbury with the familiar sights and sounds of Mountjoy.

> It's queer and lonely here, there was so much life in Mountjoy.... Here it is so still & I find it awfully difficult to understand what anyone says to me & they seem to find the same trouble with me. 'English as she is spoke' can be very puzzling. One thing nice here is the Holy hocks in the garden, they seem to understand gardening. There is a great crop of carrots too that we pass every day, going to 'exercise' round & round in a ring – like so many old hunters in the summer.

A glimpse of nature could lift her mood; she gave a breezy account of the journey across the Irish Sea already quoted.

> I dreamt of you the other night. You had on a soft looking small blue (dark) hat & it was crooked. You had bought tickets & 3 donkeys & were going to take Esther & I to Egypt of all places. When I woke up I had to laugh, but it was wonderfully vivid. Look it up in a 'dream book.' I dream a great deal since I was in jail & never hardly did before.

It is more probable she was too busy to take note of her dreams before prison.

> I'd love to show you all the dogrel (sic) I wrote in Mountjoy, though I know you'd only jeer in a kindly way. I love writing it so, & I've not lost it - it's in my head all right!

> When is your next book coming out, and the one with my pictures, if it ever does? They were very bad. I can do much better now. I was just beginning to get some feeling into my black and white when I left Ireland.

Aylesbury: 'It's Queer and Lonely Here…'

After *The Death of Fionavar* Eva would not publish another book until 1918 – a collection of poems inspired by the events of 1916, *Broken Glory*, and a short play, *The Sword of Justice*.

> Now, darling again I repeat don't worry about me. I am quite cheerful & content & would really have felt very small & useless if I had been ignored. I am quite patient & believe that everything will happen for the best. One thing I would enjoy getting out for, & that would be to see the faces of respectable people when I met them! I don't like to send anyone my love for fear that most valuable offering would be spurned. I expect though Molly has a soft spot for me somewhere. Very best love to Esther & Susan & to all of the 'rebelly crew' if ever you come across them.
>
> Do go to the Transport Union headquarters if ever you go to Dublin, they'd all think you were me & love to see you & you could tell them about me. Now best love, old darling & send me a budget of news & gossip, when you can write, about all my pals, & my family & any things amusing as well.
>
> I laugh when I think of Mordaunt! & Mabel –
>
> Yrs. Con(Vict G.12)

Molly Gore-Booth was married to Josslyn; it appears from the references to the Gore-Booths that Constance was shielding herself from the family's disapproval. The reference to Mabel and Mordaunt, both married and with families in England, was omitted by Esther Roper from the published version. Josslyn received a note from Eva on 19 August, asking if he had any message for Con. His reply was to the point: 'I don't think I have anything of interest to Constance but you can tell her that I am doing my best to straighten her things out.'[161]

Constance made up her own list of prison protocols in another smuggled letter with the emphasis on prison work:

> These questions should be asked me and all political prisoners on a visit:
>
> What do you weigh? What was your normal weight?
>
> What do you get to eat? Can you eat it?
>
> How much exercise do you get per day?
>
> How often do you get clean underclothes?

Are you constipated? Can you get medicine?

What temperature is the room you work in?

What is your task? How much do you do in a week?

If they won't let me or any of the others answer, push to get answers by every possible means.[162]

Star Class prisoners were given a coveted place in the sewing room. Constance later described her first encounter with the governor:

> The first morning I was sent to the workroom and given some rough sewing to do with eight others. We carried on a whispered conversation whenever it was possible. Every now and then the warder in charge ejaculated 'Stop that talking' and there was a lull.
>
> Presently the door was flung open and 'the governor' was announced. Each woman humbly rose to her feet with the exception of myself. When she was gone the warders took me aside and told me I had to stand up when 'the governor' inspected us. Firmly, but politely, I refused to show respect to any British official.
>
> The warders coaxed and threatened, but I remained stubborn and explained the attitude of an Irish rebel. The next morning the warder announced the governor had told her the women were not to rise to their feet as it wasted time and she liked to see them working so diligently. So the first morning I won a victory for the unfortunate people. This episode put me on good terms with my fellow convicts in the workroom.[163]

The authorities were well aware of the publicity implications of a high-profile prisoner and were careful to document their dealings with Constance. She was skilled at embroidery, but she was unhappy with the workshop tasks and longed for creative work. She stole a needle and pulled coloured threads from cleaning rags. Rising each morning before 6.30 she carried out surreptitious embroidery in her cell. She soon completed a pincushion on which she embroidered 'Easter 1916' with strands of her hair.

Sometime later a wardress discovered a picture of a Madonna and Child in one of Constance's books from the prison library. Dr Fox had her cell searched and the materials confiscated.

There was another occupant in the cell which she revealed in an offhand manner to Eva almost a year later:

Aylesbury: 'It's Queer and Lonely Here...'

> I forgot did I ever tell you that the first cell I had here was haunted. It was haunted by a man. I always wondered if he was Irish but he never spoke tho' he often kept me company.[164]

When she edited the prison letters in the 1930s Esther Roper deleted all reference to the phantom visitor.

Some of her biographers describe her making aprons, nightgowns and underwear from unbleached calico in the workshop. One of these garments, a prison apron, can be seen in Sligo County Museum. It was officially government property, but Constance decided to keep it as a souvenir. On her release she wore it as an undergarment and smuggled it out of the prison.

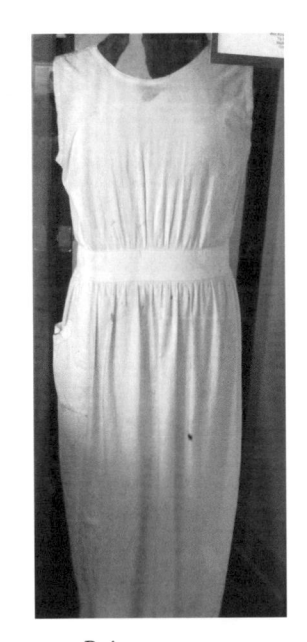

Pin cushion made in prison

After some weeks she became ill from the long hours of enforced sitting in the sewing room. 'Then she was transferred to the kitchen, where her work was washing and cutting up vegetables and scrubbing stone floors, and hard work it was,' Esther wrote.

> The food was very poor [it was wartime]. Once she lost weight alarmingly. She could not eat the red, coarse meat provided and the brown bread made her ill. Eva begged that she should have one glass of milk a day instead of meat, but I don't think she would ever have succeeded in her efforts but that Mr. Healy came to the rescue, and in some way got the home office to agree to it.[165]

Prison apron

Work in the kitchen gave her an outlet for her energy, but she was not impressed with the food:

> The dinner is always inspected after it is cooked by the Governor or Deputy-Governor. A table of 'samples' is neatly laid out. The bits are

carefully selected by warders in charge, and are always the best bits the Governor looks at and says 'excellent' while we grin ironically.[166]

She hated the prison food, quickly lost weight and became drawn and haggard.

> The dinners were served in two storey cans, used indiscriminately among 200 women, and, more, some of the cans were very old and musty. A great many of the women were known to be suffering from venereal disease, and at the time an attempt was made to keep their tins separate. This was dropped after a while.
>
> There was no proper accommodation for washing these 400 tins. I used to do 200 with another convict. We did our best to get them clean in a big terra-cotta bowl on the kitchen table and to dry them on two towels. Sometimes the water would not be hot, sometimes there was no soap or soda, and then you could neither dry nor clean the tins. Many of the tins were red with rust inside.
>
> I could give you endless examples of English cleanliness. It may be summed up as follows: Brasses, floors, doorknobs, all that jumps to the eye immaculate, but dirt and carelessness behind the scenes. I have seen vermin found in the baths.

We know very little about the other women in the Star Class except their names and offences. B. Lingard & M. Nash were sentenced to death for 'murder of an illegitimate child' and had the sentences commuted to penal servitude for life. F. Bush got three years for manslaughter and A. Griffiths the same for embezzlement. Two ladies in Aylesbury not in the Star Class were L. Wertheim and E. De Bournonville, serving sentences for spying on behalf of Germany.

While she developed sympathy for their circumstances Constance was initially repulsed by the majority of her new associates:

> The only variety in their lives is the advent of a new criminal or the return of an old offender with a new sentence.... Their long lonely hours are spent in going over the carelessness or indiscretion that led to their arrest and conviction, and planning all sorts of schemes to revenge themselves on false friends, to get the better of law and order, and to live the rest of their lives wildly, luxuriously and idly.

It was a far cry from evenings in Surrey House when Hannah would come around and they would sit in the front bay window surrounded by candles and talk for hours. She noted how prison life was dominated by rigid rules: 'Everything is done by rule, and there are endless rules, and endless red tape, and endless inspections.'

The most difficult rule was silence. Most humans are gregarious by nature and the enforcement of silence goes against one of the deepest human instincts – it was a form of torture, the most difficult rule to enforce and put the warders in difficult situations where they could be blackmailed by prisoners if they failed to carry it out. Constance had sympathy for the double game they were obliged to pay to avoid censure. As one who loved conversation she was irked by the rule of silence:

> Even the miserable little grain of comfort you get from a few minutes talk with another prisoner can only be procured by endless trickery and deceit. The silence rule merely gives people an incentive to underhand intercourse. The old hands are experts at this, and their conversation is often filthy. A few words exchanged are worth any risks that may be run, especially to a newcomer, and it is the worst of their comrades that they find it easiest to talk with.

The exception to the rule was on Sunday afternoon when certain prisoners were allowed to sit outside the cells and converse. The question of association became an issue in the campaign to have her relocated with other Irish prisoners. She believed the strategy of the British authorities was to destroy the morale of political offenders:

> ... to try and break them morally and physically by herding them with the worst criminals, depriving them of books, writing materials and decent companionship and confining them in unsanitary and disused prisons.

Her own companions included some refined and educated women, but also the 'lowest of the low' whose talk was mainly of 'the *gay life* and how to *put away* a baby without being caught were always being discussed, disgusting jokes were passed around.' Despite her breezy tone in the letters she was feeling the strain of talk that was 'a torment to some of the prisoners and a training in vice to others.'

Constance was suddenly in daily association with women she had no contact with up to now and her early comments reveal an instinctive aversion. Her supporters were keen to appeal to class prejudice against the 'lower orders'. Her attitude to her fellow prisoners changed over time as she came to appreciate the social causes of criminality. Chicago May considered herself a close friend, in as much as that was possible in Aylesbury, although Constance did not mention her in letters. 'I always took her part,' May wrote, 'when the Englishers tried to ride her.'

Agnes Mallin gave birth to a baby girl in Dublin's Coombe Hospital on 19 August. Constance asked to be the godmother and had a miraculous medal sent from England. The baby's godfather was William Partridge, then in Dartmoor. The baby was christened Maura Constance Connolly Mallin with James Connolly's wife Lillie standing in for the absent godparents.

Agnes Mallin and children in 1916

13

SEPTEMBER 1916

The Death of Fionavar was published by Erskine Macdonald, London, in late August or early September. The imprint was transitory, set up by a poet, William Galloway Kyle, who published Eva's *The Perilous Light* in 1915 and was a publishing scam according to Eva's biographer Sonja Tiernan. Her usual publisher was Longmans Green & Co since 1898. The book was a tribute to the memory of Francis Sheehy-Skeffington with the dedication:

> To the Memory of the Dead
> The Many who died for Freedom
> and the One who died for Peace.

It began with her tribute to the 1916 leaders:

> Poets, Utopians, bravest of the brave,
> Pearse and MacDonagh, Plunkett, Connolly,
> Dreamers turned fighters, but to find a grave,
> Glad for the dream's austerity to die.

She praised the:

> Dreamers turned fighters but to find a grave
> Too great for victory, too brave for war

But wished that they:

> Had dreamed the gentler dream of Maeve
> Peace be with you, and love for evermore.

In Eva's version Maeve fights the Ulstermen to seek revenge for the death of Deirdre of the Sorrows. She tries to shield her daughter from the horrors of battle, but Fionavar visits the battlefield where she witness wounded and dying men. In a melodramatic turn she is overcome by grief and dies. Maeve is stricken by remorse and abandons her kingdom and possessions, going to live in a hazel wood on an island in the River Shannon.

> Thus without force or sovereignty, in loneliness and poverty, she finds the way into faery land, the way to her own soul.[167]

In Eva's view the use of violence had failed, but Constance could still triumph by turning to the pilgrim's path of non-violence and creativity. The charting of a route into her soul would enable Constance to endure her term in prison.

Water decoration from Fionavar

The book was reviewed in the *New York Times* on 10 September under the heading 'Irish Rebel Illustrates Non-Resistance Play':

> There will soon be published a poetic drama destined to receive an amount of attention seldom bestowed on this important but unpopular sort of writing. The book is profusely illustrated, every page having its elaborate decoration of landscapes and cabalistic designs...[168]

The writer went on to do his part in the creation of the Constance myth, depicting her for the readers of the *New York Times* as a modern Joan of Arc:

> The play is a plea for a peace, a glorification of non-resistance, a Goethe-like defence of thought against action. There is something ironical about the fact that the pages of this most passionately pa-

September 1916

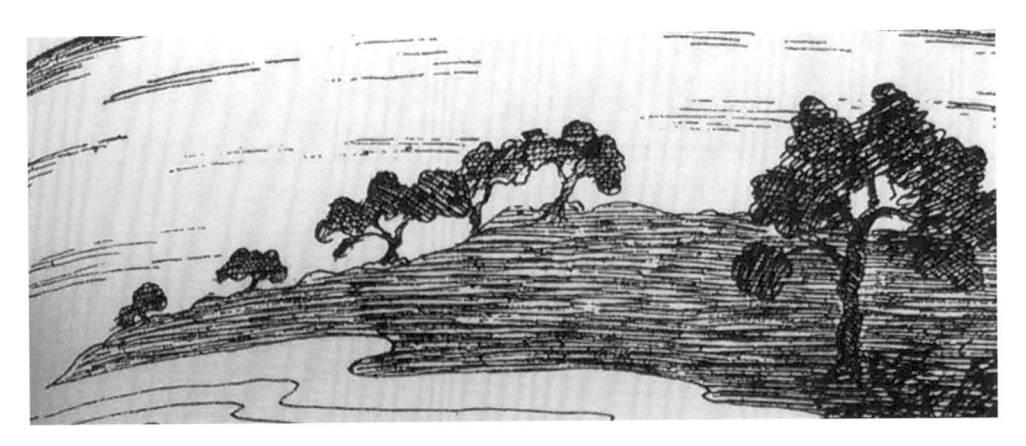

Tress decoration from Fionavar

cific work should be made by so convinced and practical a direct actionist as Countess Markievicz, the woman with the sword, who with her little band of fighting men helped hold the streets of Dublin for days and nights against British machine guns.

Constance wrote an undated letter on unofficial paper to Eva. It appears to have been smuggled out of Aylesbury and dates from August or September to judge by the comments on *Fionavar* which she studied carefully, noting a printer's error on page 15 where the printer changed the position of a rose inside a Star of David.

> Darling, this will go tomorrow, with my love. For God's sake, be discreet.
>
> I am alright and not a bit unhappy. I love the book, it is a real joy. They have put the Rose in the triangle on its side, didn't I put it upright?
>
> Ask me all the questions you can think of.
>
> It makes all the difference having a friend here.
>
> Don't count on my getting out for ever so long, unless a real fuss is made (home and America). I don't see why they should let me go.[169]

The rose

Britain was eager for the USA to join the Allied Powers in the Great War and was wary of the Irish-American influence, considered a factor in the ending of the executions and the commuting of the death penalty on de Valera.

> You should get 'questions' asked on – anything you can think of – the company one is in, starvation etc., and try to make them publish the trials.
>
> You've probably done all this. I am so in the dark. They don't want a continuous fuss.

The reference to company can only refer to the criminal prisoners in Aylesbury, but she was understandingly aggrieved at being treated differently from the other Irish prisoners. Eva and Esther were well used to harassing the authorities during their long campaigns for suffrage and women's trade union rights. Constance was writing to an expert in the field.

> Let me know the Trade Unions conditions for workrooms *temperatures*. The Trades Unions should have a visitor or inspector here. They should start jail reform. The people are all poor people, and they should see to them.

The letter ends on a different note with a reference to her inclusion in Eva's poem in *Fionavar*: 'I love being in poetry and feel so important.' She would feature in many other poems on 1916, much of it sentimental, but some had substance like Yeats' 'On a Political Prisoner', written in 1919, which depicts her in Aylesbury:

> A grey gull lost its fear and flew
> Down to her cell and there alit,
> And there endured her finger's touch
> And from her fingers ate its bit.

Eva and Esther came to visit on 4 September and they chatted with the prison matron, E.W. Sharp, in attendance. It was a strange reunion in the dingy room with the matron writing down the conversation in shorthand. Ms Sharp wrote a two-page report on the visit for Governor Winder. It was hardly the kind of attention accorded to an ordinary criminal. The half-hour conversation was almost totally taken up, not with her current well-being and surroundings, but with events before the Rising:

> Sir, I beg to state that for your information that on the 4th inst. when q.12 C.G. Markievicz was being visited by Miss Gore Booth and Miss Roper the following statements were made by Markievicz. She mentions the episode of the letter in the glove which Eva said had 'been cut up and distributed among her friends'.[170]

Sharp captured the details, but struggled with unfamiliar names:

> During the conversation a woman named Proles (?) was named as being of very great assistance to Markievicz. A short time before the Revolution Markievicz had promised to attend a meeting. When the date of the meeting arrived the leaders would not allow Markievicz to go as it was too near the time of the Revolution. She thereupon wrote a seditious speech, dressed Prole in some of her clothing and sent her to deliver the speech, and explain the reason for her absence.

This can only be the meeting in Kerry in early April. It is not clear why Constance should go into the details of this particular story at this time.

> She asked Miss Gore Booth to give Prole a certain dress of hers, Markievicz's, and to tell her that she was to wear it, it was 'Elijah's Mantle'. Prole was to be sure to keep things going and 'to keep the clique together'.

The injunction 'to keep things going' could only refer to maintaining the morale of the revolutionary circles. At times one wishes for Eva and Esther's responses but the transcript focussed on one side of the conversation. The authorities were only interested in what Constance had to say. From the account one would think the visitors said nothing at all.

> Markievicz said all the business transactions were done by messenger, they were afraid to trust to letters. One of the chief messengers was Lucy Kenstone or Kempstone who was her 'right hand'. She gave her sister instructions to find this girl Kenstone who lives in Pyles Buildings, and she is to let Markievicz know if she is alright, I think she meant financially.

> She also told her sister that Conolly (sic) went away for a fortnight, and it was feared that he did not intend to come back, but if he had not returned, Markievicz was quite ready and would have started the Revolution herself. Markievicz said she was quite happy to see

the old crowd and told her sister to bring one at a time when she visited. She also wants to see her daughter May (sic), but fears that obstacles will be put in the way due to the girl's age, but her sister is to remove these obstacles at any cost.

Constance has often been condemned for being cold and indifferent to Maeve, but this request suggests her daughter was uppermost in her mind. Children between one and fifteen were not allowed into the prison. Nothing came of the wish for a visit. Ms Sharp kept her attention focussed on everything Constance said, ignoring the messages Eva read from well-wishers.

She said the girls must have played a very deep game, for all 'those who mattered' were released a day or two after they were arrested. She said if any assistance were needed, her sister should send a message to a man named Devoy, America, mentioning her name. Miss Gore-Booth read extracts from letters, messages from various people. The conversation throughout the visit was principally relative to the Revolution.

I am, Sir, yours obediently, E.W. Sharp, P1.Matron.

Governor Winder sent the report to the Home Office and the Under-Secretary for Ireland, Robert Chambers. 'Instructions are requested as to whether the Irish Rebellion question is to be discussed at future visits,' he added. The report crossed the Irish Sea to Dublin Castle and the office of Sir Edward O'Farrell, assistant to the new Chief Secretary for Ireland, Henry Duke. It appears that Constance was not due another visit for four months, but O'Farrell urged that Constance and Eva be allowed regular meetings in the hope they would reveal more about the Rising. O'Farrell sent Troup a memo on 16 September:

It might be that useful information may be obtained on the lines suggested by the conversations, and in the case of future visits to this lady the Irish Government would be glad that no obstacles be placed in the way of discussion of the Rebellion...[171]

The Special Branch of the Royal Irish Constabulary opened a 'personality file' on Constance and Eva. A detective went looking for Lily Kempson and reported she lived in Golden Lane, but was now in the US. Eva wrote regularly to her sister and filled the letters with jokes, poems and illustrations to lift her spirits. Esther described them in the Editor's Introduction to the *Prison Letters* as her most charming writing:

> Eva, being a writer of exquisite prose, looked upon the allowed space of one sheet of paper as the limits within which to create a little work of art, supplying her sister's need of beauty and joy and laughter. These gems, which Constance loved so much, can never now be read by anyone.[172]

She diplomatically claimed the letters were destroyed 'by a tragic error'; in fact they were torn up by Maeve in a tantrum at a family gathering after Constance's funeral in 1927. We can guess at the contents of some letters by the responses from Constance and by cross-references with other correspondents, but we unfortunately have to progress with one side of the correspondence.

Esther was well-used to visiting prisons after many visits to suffrage activists:

> I ask myself how in Heaven's name shutting out the sun, the wind and the sight of the trees could make a rebel loyal or a thief honest – or indeed do anything but fill the heart with bitterness and hatred of all mankind.[173]

She went on to describe a prison hospital in 1916 which suggests she visited Constance in Aylesbury infirmary:

> The place was clean, there was an iron bedstead and a window, but the glass was frosted three-quarters of the way up and it opened upwards only, at the top. So even the sick were deprived of the joy of trees and flowers, for there were both outside.

When she passed a group of women working a warder blew a whistle and the prisoners turned their faces to the wall. She was astonished that such a thing could happen in the twentieth century.

> Some upright citizen will say this is all sentimentalism on my part, but it is not, it is merely common sense. I marvel at the patience and courage with which a fiery soul like Constance went through the ordeal and learned from life before the end, as she did, the lesson of love and of pity. But how many of us could say as she said to her sister, 'Don't worry about me. Remember no one has it in his power

Picture by Eva

to make me unhappy,' and this when she was being banished from all that makes life lovely.

Esther and Eva followed Constance's advice on wearing colourful clothes and borrowed from their friends before visiting Aylesbury. Esther described a typical visit:

> No prisoner is allowed to talk in the passages, but the first sounds we heard while we waited in the dreary 15th-class waiting room, was always her gay ringing laugh as she came along the corridor from the cells, talking to the wardress in charge of her.

For Constance the prison food and lack of hygiene were subjects of annoyance:

> The black bread did not agree with me and they put me into hospital when my weight dropped to about 98 pounds. It had been 136 pounds when I left Mountjoy gaol, and even that was a good deal below my normal weight.

September 1916

When she worked in the kitchen the food trays were returned 'in a state too disgusting to be described.' Some of the Borstal girls had venereal disease and these had their mess-tins marked with 'D' – for diseased. They were supposed to be kept separate from the others, but this proved impossible. The baths were filthy with 'vermin ... constantly crawling over one.' Constance and the prisoners refused to use them until they were cleaned. She claimed the porridge ladle was stored 'in a dirty pail with the brush which was used to sweep out the lavatory.'[174]

Some of the Borstal girls had syphilis and the fear of contagion was strong among convicts. When Constance came to write about her experiences she wrote with sympathy of conditions faced by her fellow prisoners:

> All the convicts lived with their nerves on edge, the horror of catching syphilis, the struggle to keep your health so that when eventually you were released you could work, occupied everybody. It was their horror of breaking down, much more than gluttony that made women risk severe punishment in their efforts to steal margarine or dripping, or a raw onion, or a bit of bread.[175]

Constance lost weight rapidly during August and early September – the record has her at 120 pounds on 7 September, a drop of two pounds a week. In early 1917 Dr Fox prepared a report on Constance's diet and health:

> She has not been in Hospital, or had her diet altered in any way other than that mentioned above (mincing her meat), as her health has been good and her weight retained on the whole. In September when she lost a few pounds it was arranged to take her into hospital for extra food, etc., but she particularly asked that she be allowed to continue her kitchen-work. This was granted on the understanding that unless she was better in a few days she would have to go into hospital. After this she steadily gained weight up to the end of January.[176]

Despite Dr Fox's assurances many of Constance's friends remarked on her loss of weight. She appears much more gaunt and frail in photographs after June 1917 than in those taken before Easter 1916. She wrote a long letter to Eva on 21 September.

> Dearest Old Darling, – I wonder if you expect this. I was always a rotten correspondent and hated writing and now it is such a joy.

> I could go on babbling for ever, though there is nothing to write about. I did love seeing you and Esther so. By the way, I hope she got her hat all right. Yours was very nice. You don't know what a picture the two of you made, all soft dreamy colours.
>
> (Moral: always visit criminals in your best clothes, blue and grey for choice, if it's me!)
>
> I am now going to see if anything arises out of the minutes – i.e. your last letter.[177]

Much of the letter reads like light chatter as if keeping her spirits up by enquiring after friends.

> First, tell O. Morrell not to get into my boat, unless she has the health of an ostrich. I often think how lucky it is that I am here rather than you! Give her my love. I would so much have liked to see her, and have since found out that I may have *three* visitors! But I *must* give their names.
>
> Puzzle – how find out for next time, so as to give their names? *You* may answer this, but it's very hard to tell now who will be able to come here in January.

Lady Ottoline Morrell, the society hostess and pacifist who lived in Bedford Square, was acquainted with Eva and Constance. Lady Morrell patronized the arts and featured in many paintings and novels – she is reputed to be the inspiration for Lawrence's Lady Chatterley. At this stage Constance expected she will have no more visitors until January 1917.

> I have been dreaming again. A school of village boys, perched on high, high stool at enormous desks. You the schoolmarm, in blue. Boy turns round, in a blue Holland pinny with shorts, bare legs and socks and Esther's head *and a beard!* It seemed quite natural! He had been writing x's on a paper divided into squares, two on the top line and three on the bottom thus:
>
> x x
> x x x

The dreams may have held deeper meanings for Eva. What is significant is that Constance was looking inward and recording her inner life, something she rarely did in her hectic days of freedom.

September 1916

> Thank Susan and Violet [Russell] a thousand times for settling the house. It must have been an awful job. I'd love to write to Susan. Tell her how I am and that I often think of her the right side of the bars in Dublin.
>
> I wish that for your next visit you would try and get a statement of accounts from Joss. I want to know what bills are paid. Some easily get left out otherwise, as people would not know where to send bills. Find out if he did anything about Christmas cards. I wrote him about some drawings I had done.

Her visitors must have told her Susan Mitchell was helping Josslyn to sort out her finances. Margaret Skinnider was a witness to the Christmas card project:

> She realized one day that the Christmas cards usually sold in Ireland were 'Made in Germany' and since the war was on, had been supplanted by cards 'Made in England'. She sat down at once to design Irish Christmas cards for the holiday season of 1916. But when Christmas came around she was in prison, and the cards were – who can say where?

Constance went on to write:

> I hope Mrs. Mallin is getting her £1 a week all right. Give all the crew my love. Tell Andy Dunn to go on singing. Perolz will know where to find him. I often think of the 'click' and the refugees and our kitchen teas. Tell Andy too that later we'll try to get someone to teach him, and ask him to give my love to Mr. N-, if he will accept such a gift from a felon.

Andy Dunn was one of the 'Surrey Clique' of Fianna Scouts who surrounded Constance in Surrey House. He was in the College of Surgeons and was imprisoned in Frongoch. Others in the 'clique' included Harry Walpole, Jack Shallow, Louis Marie, Ed 'Eamon' Murray and Patsy O'Connor.

> By the way, convicts can have photos, so send me yours. I always forget to tell you this – and Maev's. Talking of dreams *fix* five minutes in the day and think of me. I will think of you at the same time and we'll do it as often as we can. Tell me what hour when you write.

After Eva's death Constance wrote to Esther:

> When I was in Aylesbury, we agreed to try and get in touch for a few minutes every day, and I used to sit at about 6.o'clock and think of her and concentrate and try to leave my mind a blank – a sort of dark, still pool – and I got to her and could tell how she sat in the window and I seemed to know what she was thinking. It was a great joy and comfort to me.

'Don't hurry to answer this,' she writes wistfully, 'as news may come of Casi.'

Despite the physical distance between Constance and her husband the pair still had great affection for each other; it had simply become impossible for them to live together. Esther wrote to Josslyn on 28 September that the censors were preventing letters between Constance and Casimir from reaching each other. After 1913 the people closest to her were engaged in the social and national struggles, the ones she remembered most fondly in prison.

> I send my love to all my friends in the Transport Union and the Co-op. Tell them I am often with them in spirit, and that I have nothing but happy, pleasant, busy memories of them. Mr Forbes is a friend there, of course he may be in jail! So many of my friends I know nothing about. Mr. Bill O'Brien, too, I'd like to be remembered to, and oh! so many more! – and I don't even know if they're alive.
>
> Where is Bessie Lynch stopped? Give her my love. I think she would be very wise to go to America. Give her a letter to 'John Brennan' (Sidney Gifford, one of the Gifford sisters) if she goes. 'John' would remember her, and would, I am sure, like to see her, and she would be something from home for Bessie.
>
> Do you know what the other Gifford girls are doing? Tell Perolz to give them my love and to M. Cavanagh. She and Perolz are great pals.

The names are a cross-section of Republican and Socialist activists in the period before the Rising. Some, like Nora Connolly, Sidney Gifford, Lily Kempson and Margaret Skinnider, were safely in America. We see Constance clutching at the world of normality in the way she tries to locate lost belongings.

September 1916

> By the way, did you remember about the blue serge dress? Perolz has the trunk. The key, a small one, was in a red leather bag left in Liberty Hall. The second key was left in a house that was burnt. My lace, with a lot of household gods are in the trunk. The dress is at the bottom.

One wonders if she ever did recover her household gods. More enquiries about friends follow as they come to mind and then an announcement:

> I am now going to lapse into verse! I want you to criticise. Tell me something about metre and what to aim at. I am quite humble and I know I'm not a poet, but I do love trying.

> High walls hang round on every side
> A cage of cruel red,
> The sickly grass is bleached and dried,
> As brick the flower bed.

> The fierce rays of the sun down beat,
> The burning flagstones scorch our feet,
> As in the noonday's blighting heat
> We walk with weary tread.

There are echoes of Wilde's 'The Ballad of Reading Gaol' from 1897.

> I walked with other souls in pain
> within a smaller ring.

Constance's prison poem is less intense and shares with Eva a deep love of nature. 'Of course it's only jingle,' she writes, a self-protective ploy most poets will recognize, but she went on to include it in her prison journal.

> I loved the metre of the dedication you read me out. Trying to do a thing oneself makes one appreciate anything good much more. Write me a verse or two in your next letter and tell me how to get to work! Don't tell me to wait till I am blest by the 'gift'!'

She did not have the patience for sustained literary work and the ballad format suited her needs. Her imprisonment meant she had time to focus on arranging words and images as a personal as well as a political act in a form of mental reorganization and resistance. 'Don't worry about me,' she continues, 'I am quite happy.'

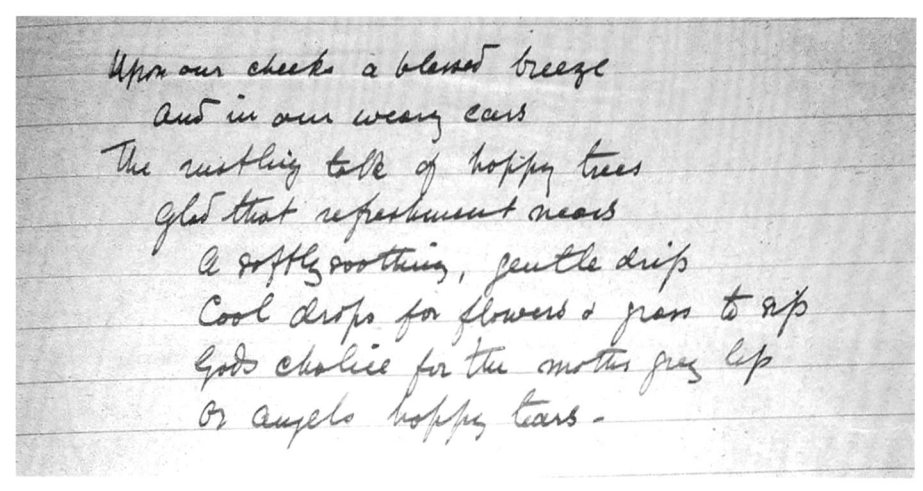

> Upon our cheeks a blessed breeze
> And in our weary ears
> The rustling talk of hoppy trees
> Glad that refreshment nears
> A softly soothing, gentle drip
> Cool drops for flowers & grass to sip
> God's chalice for the mother grey lip
> Or angels hoppy tears –

'Upon our cheeks' from prison journal

> It is in nobody's power to make me unhappy. I am not afraid, either of the future or of myself. You know well how little comforts or luxuries ever meant to me. So at worst I'm only bored. With so many thought-waves of love and kindliness coming over to me, how *could* I be unhappy? Indeed I feel very privileged.

The phrase about nobody having the power to make her unhappy became a mantra to reassure her friends. Despite the brave face she put on things she could be despondent. It is hard to know if she seriously believed that friends in Ireland were giving her telepathic support, but it would have helped to boost her morale. It must have been puzzling to the censor and very different from the usual letters that passed over his desk. She was able to use a literary discussion to make sharp political comments.

> You remember, 'They shall be remembered for ever?' What we stood for, and even poor me will not be forgotten, and 'the people shall hear them for ever?' That play of W.B.'s was a sort of gospel to me. If any man would help me, he must give me himself, give me all.

Yeats' play from 1899, *Cathleen ni Houlihan*, was one of the key texts of the national revival, the play over which he would agonize in case it inspired 'certain men the English shot.'

From her comments we can infer that Eva's previous letter had included some gossip about society ladies:

September 1916

> I love hearing about all the people you write about. I remember Clare Annesley's mother so well. She was very beautiful and I used to love looking at her. I hope some day to meet C.A. and Ottoline Morrell. I remember her so well, though I never got to know her. I'm longing to see her.
>
> Tell Miss Reddish I often think of her and of Mrs. Dickinson and all the others and of the great election we fought and won. Tell Mabel that her sick soldier never came to Dublin. I wrote to him to (I think) Tipperary. I remember Mr. McNeil now quite well; he is awfully nice.

There is something poignant about this list of names, for the most part forgotten today who flicker briefly in her reflections. Some are people who campaigned alongside the sisters in the Manchester by-election of 1908. The list of tasks on Eva might seem excessive, but she was trying to compress a few months into one letter. It was important to her to maintain connections with the world outside the prison, even if only by listing the names of people she had not seen for years.

> Fancy GaGa doing the Grand Tour again! Please give Maeve £1 of my money for her birthday and ditto for Christmas.

Her mother was visiting relatives in England, probably to get away from Ireland. Maeve was born at Lissadell on 13 November, 1901, making her fifteen in the winter of 1916. After the family business Constance mentions *The Death of Fionavar*:

Maeve and Gaga

I am so glad about the book. I hope that it will go well and it is a great joy to me to think I may help to sell it, and that my little gift of drawings may be worth something to my old darling.

There are the most beautiful cloud effects here, East and South over big old elms. They are really wonderful. Did not know that England produced anything so heavenly! Oh! for the Dublin Mountains and the soft twilights and the harvest moon on cornfields! I must write a poem about cornfields.

Love to you and Esther, all rebels and felons, comrades and friends!

We do not have another letter to Eva until 29 December 1916; in the meantime, Constance was allowed to write to Josslyn about her business affairs.

Lissadell in the early 1900s

14

'Life's Secret Forces...'

Eva and Esther were occupied with their various campaigns in the autumn of 1916.

'We continued to work in the Women's Peace Crusade and regularly visited the prisons to comfort conscientious objectors or Irish men and women who had taken part in the Rebellion,' Esther wrote. She played down her role in these affairs, leaving Eva in the limelight:

> Unshakable in her own deep convictions she could always respect the convictions of others and admire their sincerity and courage.[178]

They worked in the No Conscription Fellowship set up in 1914 by Fenner Brockway, editor of *The Labour Leader* and member of the Independent Labour Party, to protect men who refused to fight on moral, religious or political grounds. Conscription was introduced in Britain on 2 March 1916 and a network of tribunals established to hear objections to military service. Many tried to avoid being conscripted for economic reasons, but a large number were conscientious objectors or 'conchies'. Eva became a 'watcher', one of a group who travelled around England to study the work of tribunals and reported on the biased decisions in a weekly publication, *Tribunal*.

She wrote a pamphlet based on her experiences, *The Tribunal*, published by the National Labour Press, undated but possibly in 1916. Her response to the board members was expressed in her poem 'Conscientious Objectors':

> ... six ignorant men and blind
> Reckless they rent aside
> The veil of Isis in the mind.[179]

The boards generally treated objectors in an arrogant manner, refused most grounds of appeal and harassed applicants into military service.

> The ugly airless room with its hot-looking glass roof seemed to be strewn with wreckage and haunted with memories of vain appeals and helpless protest. It was just 3.30. The watcher in the gallery, whose head was beginning to ache from the bad air, was engaged in counting up from notes ... 'Would you rather kill a German or allow a German to kill your mother?' the clergyman on the tribunal asked a conscientious objector. Over and over again the clergyman repeated his question, doubtless convinced that his foe was utterly defeated, not knowing, as indeed men of his kind never do know, the difference between silence and defeat.

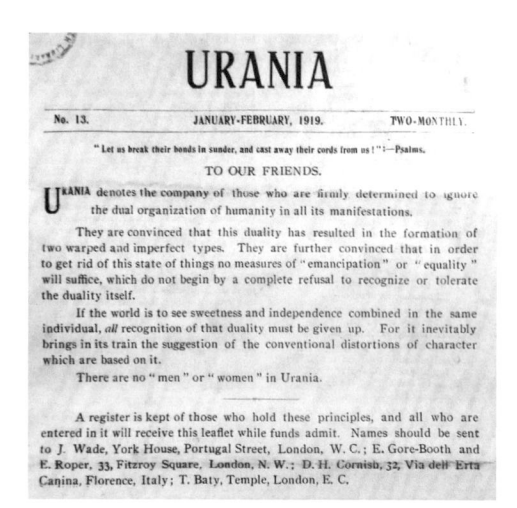

Eva and Esther were also involved in founding and editing a journal *Urania* from the first issue in October, 1916. They were part of a group of people interested in social and cultural change – feminists, vegetarians, animal rights activists, some of whom first came together in a short-lived Aethnic Union. *Urania* preached that gender differences were socially conditioned and freedom would only be achieved when men and women rejected sexual stereotypes.

Urania

The journal was distributed to those who subscribed to its ethos. It preached a message that was very much marginal in the debates of the day but would become more relevant in the gender controversies of the twenty-first century. At the same time they continued to campaign for improved conditions for Irish prisoners with a special emphasis on Constance. Eva maintained a wide network or contacts including Constance's comrades in the Irish Citizen Army, some of whom were confined a short distance from her cell. Helena Molony, Winifred Carney and Nell Ryan were in the Borstal Section and complained of the constant supervision, dirty conditions, brawling and filthy language. In compensation they had their own company for support and encouragement.

Helena Molony remembered Constance:

> We caught a glimpse of her now and again at Mass. There was a very nice priest there – a Scot. He would bring us verbal messages from her, and we would send messages to her.[180]

The chaplain, Father Scott, became a confidante and instructed Constance in the doctrines of the Catholic Church. 'Her great consolation was the visits of the Roman Catholic chaplain, who was a saintly man, full of human understanding,' Esther wrote.

> Now that Father Scott is dead, perhaps I may tell a little story that appealed to me greatly. Knowing that the smells of prison were to her particularly hard to bear, once when she was ill and he came to give her instruction, his first act was to produce from his pocket a large bottle of eau-de-Cologne, and sprinkle it about.

> What made the deepest impression on her was his gracious courtesy to what the world would call the most degraded of women.... We knew him well, for we used to visit him often in the Presbytery and shared her feeling for him.[181]

Father Scott brought news from outside the prison which he would share when Constance was arranging the flowers in the chapel, although she noted that even there they were not safe from informers. 'An appalling system of spying called supervision pursues you even when you kneel at God's altar...'[182]

Eva wrote to Helena Molony on 15 September:

> My dear Miss Moloney (sic), I don't know if you will get this letter, because I don't know what the rules are for interned people, but I thought I would chance writing you a line to say I have seen my sister since she came to England and she is well and cheerful.... I hope you are all right and not having a bad time. My sister says 'man never made a wall but God threw a gap in it' as an old woman used to say at home.[183]

When the Germans launched an offensive the prisoners were instructed to gather in the chapel to pray for a British victory. Some of the convicts like May Sharpe were hoping for a German victory which might bring their release.

I knew the rules and I knew they could not force me to go. I slammed my door shut. The Irish Countess and the German spy Bertha (Wertheim) would not go. For spite, they (the guards) made the three of us woman carry enough gruel around the prison to feed the entire two hundred convicts. We had to carry immense, heavy cans, up winding stairs. While we were doing this the Countess recited long passages in Italian, from Dante's Inferno.[184]

Constance knew Italian from her six months in Florence with Eva and a governess in 1886. 'The place looked like Hell all right,' May wrote, 'with the lights dimmed and musty-smelling bags tacked across the windows, as a precaution against bombing.'

Nuala O'Faolain wrote:

> It is one of the most bizarre images from the long struggle for Irish freedom – the prostitute and the lady clattering along the corridors of an English jail, inefficiently ladling out gruel at each hatch, while Constance intoned lines from the *Inferno* in her Anglo-Irish accent.[185]

The Prisoner by Constance

Dr Fox noted that Constance kept herself clean, but was not very tidy. As she grew thinner the prison uniform hung loose on her tall frame. The blouse was usually sticking out of her skirt band, the skirt hitched up to show a grey petticoat. One could view her untidiness as a lack of concern for appearances or a low-level protest. Prison did not diminish her sense of mischief. She told Esther about an encounter with Adeline, Duchess of Bedford and Lady Battersea, on an official visit. It was especially difficult for Lady Adeline who had known Constance in her childhood. Sean O'Faolain gives a dramatized version of the meeting:

Madame Markievicz was brought in the usual way to the waiting-room, and as usual her dress was hitched up and crooked, and an inch or two of underskirt showed beneath; and as usual, also, the prisoner stood (on one leg) and the visitors sat. Perhaps it was this that ruffled her.

'What are you doing now, Constance?' asked the duchess, and she told her, with a gay smile, that she had been scrubbing when they called.

'Oh?'

There was a slight pause.

'That is rather hard work,' sympathised the duchess.

'No!' protested Constance quite seriously.

'Well – eh – you don't *like* scrubbing out your cell?' smiled the duchess.

'Why not?' asked the countess in genuine surprise. 'Wouldn't you?'

Presently the duchess asked, perhaps probing about the rumoured change to Catholicism. 'Do you say your prayers at night, Constance?'

'I really felt a bit insulted,' Constance told Esther, 'but I thought I would get my own back, without showing my feelings, so I opened my eyes wide and replied:

'Of course: why? Don't you?'

The dowager was not fluent. She looked to her friend for help, but Lady Battersea was silent.

After a few more awkward words they rose. 'Well, good-bye, Constance.... I suppose you wish you were out of this place.'

'Why, yes,' admitted Constance. And then she produced a little smile as they fumbled for the door-handle. 'Wouldn't you?'[186]

There is no record of any further visit from the ladies.

Despite her annoyance with the conversation of some of her fellow convicts Constance could not withhold her sympathy from their desperate circumstances. Esther wrote:

> Each person in the prison became an individual to Constance, not a number, as in the regulations. Nothing that anyone had done made a barrier between them.[187]

Among the convicts was a woman who shot and wounded her lover after he boasted he was leaving her and their baby for another woman. 'He was, I believe, practically unharmed,' Esther declared. The woman had served about three years of a seven year sentence and was desperate to see the son taken from her when he was a year old.

> Constance begged Eva to try and get her out. Mrs. Cobden-Sanderson, a wonderful friend to all in trouble, undertook the difficult task, and so successful was she that presently the woman was released...

Esther and Eva had a visit from the woman and son in Fitzroy Square. The mother was delighted with her freedom and the boy read an art magazine, *Colour*, while the women talked.

A short review of *Fionavar* in *The Irish Times* of 28 October may have brought some cheer. The writer made an oblique compliment to 'the Countess Markievicz, sister of the author, who displays all the wild imagination which we might expect from her stormy career.' The reviewer highlighted the lyrical beauty of the poetry:

> Out of the depths of the crystal sphere
> To the wind-blown world a spirit came,
> And from the joy of her shining years
> She brought but a little waving flame.

The 1916 Rising made a deep impression on Irish-Americans and one of the first books was published in the autumn of 1916. *The Irish Rebellion of 1916 and Its Martyrs* edited by Maurice Joy, published by Devin Adair, contained articles by writers with nationalist sympathies – Padraig and Mary Colum and Sidney Gifford. The latter provided material for the growing legend of 'The Rebel Countess' who:

> ... became famous throughout the West as a daring horse-woman and crack shot. She stored up a treasure-house of the most perfect health and abundant energy, so that later on in life the frail-appearing, slender Countess was able to do more than a man's share of work for the cause she had at heart.[188]

After the Rising Tim Healy joined a group of Irish MPs in Westminster in a successful campaign for improved conditions for Irish political prisoners. After concessions for male prisoners were announced by Home Secretary, Herbert Samuel, on 14 November, the focus of the campaign shifted to extend the right of association to Constance. An open letter was circulated in Ireland, England and the United States by the Dublin MP with the Irish Parliamentary Party Alfred (Alfie) Byrne:

> Constance deMarkievicz is the only one of the Irish rebel prisoners not to receive the benefit of the late Home Secretary's concessions, and this, notwithstanding that she was on the list published by the Home Secretary of those who would benefit by these privileges...[189]

Irish male prisoners would be gathered together in Lewes Prison where they would have freedom of association. It was a tacit admission that they were to be considered political prisoners. The male prisoners were able to organise and created the military structures for the War of Independence three years later, but there was no provision for Constance:

> She is not to have the chief and most valuable privilege of association and conversation at stated intervals with other Irish prisoners ... because she is a woman and it is too much trouble for the Home Office to arrange a woman's side to the new prison specially arranged for Irish convict rebels...
>
> The company she has been restricted to ever since the day of her arrest have been that of the dregs of the population. She has had no one to speak to except prostitutes who have been convicted of murder or violence, and the atmosphere and conversation in which she has lived all this time has been 'the atmosphere and conversation of a brothel'.

Constance wanted to be treated the same as the male prisoners and to enjoy the company and stimulation of people who felt and thought as she did. The opposite prevailed in Aylesbury:

> Also it is part of the system that if you are seen trying to avoid one you are probably put to work with her, for in jail every human affection, every attempt at discrimination, is remorselessly stepped on ... if you show any preference for a wardress she is at once an object of suspicion to the other wardresses and to higher authority.[190]

Constance told Esther on a visit:

> The only thing prison does for people, as far as I can see, is to teach them to use bad language and how to steal. I was so hungry yesterday that I stole a raw carrot and ate it.[191]

The impassive wardress sat and made no comment. Esther was always generous, ready to distinguish between individuals and the system: 'Constance never grumbled at conditions, and she received great kindness from some of the officials in prison.'

It fell to Dr Fox to draw up a response to the allegations with a document dated 21 December in her usual direct manner:

> I enclose a list of the Star Prisoners, giving their names and offences as requested. There is no direct evidence of any one of them having been a prostitute – though eight of them have had illegitimate children. Many of the women in the Star Class cannot by any means be classed as 'the dregs of the population'. Several have had no charge of murder or violence and are quite decent well-behaved women. The charge that 'the atmosphere and conversation is that of a brothel' is a gross exaggeration.[192]

Handkerchief made by Constance in prison

15

SETTLING ACCOUNTS

Constance wrote to Josslyn on 17 October. From the tone of the letter it appears there was earlier correspondence concerning the court-martial:

> I have signed enclosed document but I am afraid it will be very little interest to you to see my court-martial. They went into no particulars. I have nothing I wish to conceal and anyone may see it.[193]

Josslyn had been 'confined to his room this few days with a severe cold' when J.A. Cooper, the Lissadell land agent, wrote to Cochrane & Co. on 21 October in connection with the letting of St. Mary's:

> I am sure however he has not yet received a reply from Countess Markievicz, or he would have let me have same at once. I agree that the reply ought to have been here before this, but it is quite probable that her facilities for writing, even on business matters, are not what they ought to be.[194]

Cooper was not far wide of the mark, but Constance managed to write to Josslyn on 17 October. It is clear from the letter that she had received information of monies outstanding. After some preliminaries on bills she discusses the leasing of St. Mary's:

> £50 is very little for St. Mary's – it would be all right but 8 years would mean over £100 loss to me, but you can judge better than me and have possibly done so by now. Anyhow I am quite content to leave it to you & in any case with Eva who is like my second self.

It is hard to remember if I owe anything more. Casi owed a bill of about 15/- to 'Ceppie,' a framemaker & and cast maker on the Keys (Quays). It might be paid. I am afraid that I am writing very badly, but I am beginning to forget how & my hand won't work properly from want of practice.

Lyons is the only bill to question – it might be an Xmas gift either for Casi or I. Eva will tell you. This is all rather like living to see yourself dead & your business all being wound up & 'Amen' being said.

<u>Income tax refund</u> I had the papers for two years refund. The full papers for both (W. Coopers & the dividend ones) If they were not in the drawer of the desk they may be in the box I left at Miss Perolz, when I heard that the house was going to be occupied. Eva thinks the police opened the box & took papers. Try to get them back if so – there was not a scrap of writing that has anything to say to the rebellion in it or even political. Some of Casi's letters & the unfinished act of a Society play, a few poems – nothing except personal things, some photos, lace & scarves I valued – I believe all my clothes were looted. However they would not be of use to me here – Eva thinks they were anyhow.

I am very sorry you are having so much bother and selfishly thankful that I have not got to do it for myself – I always wished Casi had been a financial expert who would have seen to house and given me so much a week pocket money – Anyhow here I have no expenses.

Eva gave me messages from Mr. & Mrs. Cooper. Please tell them how glad I was to get them & give her my love. Eva had so much that she will never remember all!

Let me again repeat that with regard to St. Mary's, I cannot possibly judge, shut away here & I know you will do the best you can & that it is really a gamble & I am very grateful & know that you will act for the best & will be content whatever you decide.

I should just like to know about my 'business affairs' now & then. But shall always be pleased and grateful.

Yrs., Constance de Markievicz

PS. I have signed enclosed document, but I am afraid it will be very little interest to you to see my courtmartial. They went into no particularities – I have nothing I wish to conceal & anybody may see it (I mean the record of proceedings.) I gave Eva a full account of all that occurred at the C.M. Don't bother about rumours. My enemies will make a monster of me; my friends a heroine & both will be equally wide of the truth. I really did very little, I was not in the thick of it at all. Yrs., Con

Her concern about the income from St. Mary's would give the impression she was thinking of a life beyond prison, but other remarks about settling accounts hint at a creeping acceptance that Aylesbury would be her abode for the foreseeable future. The letter belies the impression that she was cut off from the Gore-Booth family after the Rising. She remained connected to them in many ways including financial matters, but there were many more connections.

Lady Gore-Booth wrote to Josslyn around this time:

Dearest Joss,

I am so glad you have had a satisfactory letter from Con & look forward much to seeing her handwriting again – it is so much better for you to get direct communication with her, is never very satisfactory to go through 2 or 3 people. Everything gets wrong and misunderstood. Of course, Con has much more common sense than Eva – who is all sentimental – her whole heart is with Con & she would do anything to help her, but seems to go about it in a foolish way.

The old man will be very interested at knowing his dream came true – it's rather odd. Love, Mother.[195]

There is no trace of any exchange of letters between mother and daughter as though the gulf was too great to bridge. Lady Gore-Booth displayed concern for her eldest daughter, but was happy to leave all contact to Josslyn and Eva. Despite her remark on the effectiveness of Eva's intervention, her second daughter provided the support and encouragement that was lacking in the mother.

Matters relating to Constance appeared to take up a large amount of Dr Fox's time. On 31 October she sent Eva an invoice for Constance's dental work. The work had been done by Frank Chilton, 67 High Street, Aylesbury, for the sum of £7/02/06, which Eva forwarded to Josslyn with a note asking if he had seen the account of the court-martial. She added: 'I heard privately that her technical offence is 'felony'.'

She wrote to Kathleen Lynn in early November to pass on messages from Constance, sending:

... her love to a number of friends and hopes Andy Dunn and Mr. Nugent win something at the Feis or anywhere for their music. She is also anxious to receive any relics of Easter Week.... Could you tell 'the boys' this, especially she wants a stamp if possible kept for her.[196]

There was a message for Marie Perolz, urging her to look in the box for income tax papers:

> ... would she send them to me at once as they should be seen about directly. She also sends her love to the 'clique' and wishes she was going to be there to kiss them under the mistletoe.

At times Eva confuses the many unfamiliar names: 'we have so little time together & she is very vague about surnames and addresses.' The sisters were thinking ahead to Constance's first Christmas in prison:

> She is allowed a few cards at Xmas. Those that are sent she is allowed to see and choose two or three to keep.

She mentions that she got to see Constance without a pass and that she looked much better despite working in the kitchens:

> ... she got awfully tired and rather seedy with all that sitting still sewing. The governor remarked that 'she's very energetic!!'

This is a rare comment from the taciturn Dr Fox. The letter refers to a visit in late October or early November. The reference to making the visit without a pass may indicate Dr Fox was flexible where Constance was involved. Or the authorities may have hoped for further nuggets of information. By this stage Dr Fox had moved to a house in Aylesbury which she shared with her faithful companion, a widow named Mrs Graham. When time allowed she would make visits to the Church Mission in Bermondsey.

Dr Selina F. Fox in 1938

Josslyn received a letter from Eva on 7 November with the news that Constance considered the letting of St. Mary's a mistake. She included a snippet on the court-martial, saying Constance was advised to plead not guilty as she had no communication with the king's enemies. His sister 'was looking better & is working very hard in the kitchen.'[197] She mentioned Stasko's letter which Constance wanted her to bring on her next visit on 2 January, 1917.

The letting of St. Mary's was still not settled. Josslyn received another letter from Eva on 11 November:

> I could not get anything definite out of Con about her house as she said the lease was for eight years and before this time was up it might be possible to let it to better advantage.[198]

This appears to contradict Constance's assurance of 17 October that she was happy with the arrangement, although that letter may have been delayed. Eva sent another note to Josslyn, received on 18 November. It seems to refer to the visit in the Kathleen Lynn letter. The script is unusually crabbed as if written at speed to catch the post:

> My dear Joss, I have just seen Mr. Gavan Duffy. Con would like to see him (if the Home Office allows) as he has had advice from Counsel that there are certain illegalities in her case & he wants to discuss it with her at first hand.
>
> As I had not got any further with her about the house and you seemed to want her to understand and give her opinion. I suggested at the same time he should talk to her about it. I thought it would be better to do this because even if you have already acted it can't do any harm and she was so keen about other things when I was there that I didn't get much out of her I'm afraid.
>
> Things anyway are beginning to look <u>much</u> better. I'm beginning to have great hopes of amnesty & anyway these new concessions ought to make a lot of difference. Hope you are better. I have been having an awful cold. Going to Manchester for a couple of days tomorrow. Yrs., Eva GB[199]

Even though Casimir had been absent from Ireland since 1913 he was still Constance's husband for income tax purposes; Josslyn attempted to get his permission to receive income tax refunds due to Constance. The completed tax form finally arrived from Casimir in Zywotowka in September 1917. He made a droll entry on the form by writing 'none' in the space for occupation. Despite the turmoil of the Great War his debt to an Irish bank was quietly gathering interest. The Bank of Ireland wrote to J.A. Cooper on 22 November to state that Count Markievicz owed the bank £22/06/09, including interest, on a loan taken out on the lease of St. Mary's.

Meanwhile Casi was still trying to send letters to Constance from Kiev. He wrote to Josslyn on 9 November, who was staying in Bundoran for health reasons: 'I am extremely anxious to know how is Constance and is there any chance of my letters to her reaching their destination.'[200]

He was enjoying the Bohemian life among the artists and writers, unaware that his carefree days in Ukraine were soon to end. His letter crossed with a short note from Josslyn to Stasko on 16 November: 'I heard from your father once. Give him my love if you see him.' He was vague about Constance, urging him to write to Eva who was due to visit the prison on 2 January.

Josslyn continued in his efforts to establish the truth about Constance in the Rebellion and to try and quash the rumours. Immediately after her return from Manchester Eva sent him a letter received on 23 November:

> My dear Joss, Con was anxious Lyons bill should be done with. She said that she was afraid they might put down to her by mistake the Christmas present (last year) as hat and coat. That is all she says of Lyons bill as far I know. So glad house problem is solved.
>
> I know they said horrible things against her, but they were absolutely certain to do that. Of course she fought like anyone else in that I cannot see that she did anything different to what soldiers get praised for & called heroes for.
>
> I don't believe any of the other stories & I don't think people do here, there are always so many wild stories. I did not ask her, but she volunteered how she held a revolver at a policeman's chest but <u>could</u> not shoot when it came to the point as she recognized him & had known him before.
>
> She also said she thought she hit one in the arm as he <u>jumped</u>. She is not the least inclined to minimize her own actions or make little of them nor does she in the least mind saying anything she had done. I expect those two stories, embroidered on, account for all the myths. Anyway the courtmartial did not condemn her on anything of this

kind but on rebellion & sedition & helping the King's enemies & Sir J
Leslie's story was that she was quite <u>charming</u> to the enormous army
Doctor – whom she captured with her enormous revolver, which
made him nervous as she thought it would go off! Yrs., Eva GB.[201]

This was followed by a note in pencil: 'The new regulations are a great improvement don't you think –'

The comments from Constance raise more questions than answers: Who was the policeman she held at gunpoint? Where and when did it happen? Was this the same policeman she shot in the arm? And why did he jump? After the Rising newspaper reports mentioned a policeman among the prisoners in St. Stephen's Green, a Sergeant Hughes, who had been shot in the arm. Could he have been the one she shot when he jumped? We will probably never know for sure all that happened on Easter Monday and conflicting versions will continue to circulate.

Stories of Constance's bloodthirsty nature persisted despite Eva's effort to give a more rounded view of her sister. She wrote to Kathleen Tynan:

> Others have been strangely unsympathetic and misunderstanding about her, putting down the absurd sentiments such as a mad desire to kill soldiers, which makes me laugh when I think of her universally friendly nature … the accounts of her hob-nobbing with her prisoners in Stephen's Green are much more like her. She is incapable of thinking of individuals as enemies, anyone who knows her knows that.[202]

Josslyn and his agent continued to deal with a mountain of paperwork. He had also taken on the responsibility of finding secure employment for Bessie Lynch. Susan Mitchell wrote on 25 November to say that Bessie had a job in a hospital washing and ironing every day from 10.00 o'clock to 6.00 for eight shillings a week. As the pay was so low Susan would continue to pay her five shillings a week on Josslyn's behalf:

> Food is so dear here and dearer for the poor. Half these girls live on tea & fill the hospitals. Bessie is a gentle pretty creature. Madam took such a great interest in her.[203]

Maria Perolz reported to Josslyn from 10 Nth. Great Georges Street on 30 November:

I have searched Box & the only papers in it are some mss of plays & Books etc. She told me when packing the box that she was only putting in things of sentimental value.[204]

Eva had her own problems with money flow and sent an undated note to Josslyn:

I fear I have been a bad steward of your money. I lodged it to a no.2 account in bank & have kept accounts, but can't find details.[205]

Susan wrote to Josslyn about the Christmas cards Constance wanted to produce. The print blocks were set up but there was a muddle about the printing: 'I hope it will come all right as I know Madam was looking forward to them.' It appears the cards were never printed, but a sample of what might have been survives in a card drawn by Constance with a verse by Susan.

Susan sent a note to Josslyn on 20 December to relieve him of one burden while another returned. The Fianna did not need the Camden Street hall – they had an alternative venue which they would rent themselves. The bad news was that Bessie was now working part-time and still needed help. Josslyn noted that he paid Bessie £1.17.00 in total during the month of December 1916.

Christmas card by Constance

Of the five Irish women internees sent to England only Winifred Carney and Helena Molony remained in Aylesbury Prison. On 1 December Winifred petitioned the Home Secretary to transfer her into the convict section where she could associate with Constance, who was:

> ... debarred from enjoying the greatest of these privileges which is free association. From experience I know that the other concessions will make comparatively little difference to her comfort if she is cut off from companionship.[206]

She offered to give up all privileges and come under the criminal regime. The Secretary of State replied on 11 December that he could not accede to her request. Eva wrote to Helena Molony:

> I am not under any delusions as to C's condition nor ever have been. I am sure it's a mistake about Mr. G. D. [Gavan Duffy] who has been working night and day as also has Mrs. G.D. for all the prisoners and whose splendid work with several others got the interned people out.... I get a pass once a month, anything else is extra ... you might perhaps give as a special reason that she is the only Irish prisoner not allowed to see the other Irish prisoners and entirely isolated...[207]

The Battle of the Somme finally spluttered out in November with over 400,000 British casualties. In early December Asquith was replaced as Prime Minister by David Lloyd George, who decided to conciliate Irish and Irish-American public opinion. He ordered the release of Irish internees just before Christmas. As a convicted prisoner Constance had no possibility of early release. Helena Molony and Winifred Carney left Aylesbury on 21 December and departed for home, leaving her more isolated than before. Her supporters kept up the pressure on the Government; Alfred Byrne asked the Government to consider opening a separate section for her in Lewes Prison.

William Partridge was delighted with his move to Lewes and the more congenial air near Brighton on 11 December. He wrote to his wife:

> We are permitted to converse while at exercise, have, I understand a visit once a month, and the most cherished concession of all – to be allowed to write and receive a letter <u>each month</u>.[208]

He did not forget his old comrade:

> If any of them are writing to Madame, I would like if they said greetings from the 'two' at Lewes.

In Ireland Constance's name was rarely heard in public. Cumann na mBan held a conference in Dublin in December and elected her President. She had been a member, but was not on the Executive. Her election was seen as a connection with the leadership of the rebellion and was a reminder to Constance that she was not forgotten.

Eva became ill towards the end of the year and was confined to bed where she worked on the poems published in *Broken Glory* in 1918. She began to illustrate the myth play, *The Buried Life of Deirdre*, which she wrote around 1908. There is some doubt it was ever performed. It is similar in tone to her play *Unseen Kings* with a pacifist theme – the possessiveness and violence of King Conor is contrasted with Deirdre's purity of heart.

She began to illustrate the text with sketches 'as a consolation while recovering from an illness,' but it was never finished. Esther edited and arranged for publication of the partly illustrated work in 1930.

> This play was written about 1908. In the winter of 1916-17 Eva Gore-Booth, while recovering from an illness, began to make pen and ink drawings of various scenes, writing the words of the play on each

Images from Buried Life of Deirdre

sheet. She had never had any lessons and drew for her own pleasure only.[209]

The play is a retelling of the story of Deirdre who rejects the love of an elderly and cruel king; her action brings death to Naoise, her young lover, and divides the kingdom. Deirdre claims her suffering is the result of actions she committed a thousand years previously. The theme of inherited karma reflects the Aryan origin of the Celtic myth. Deirdre tells the druidess Lavarcam:

> Behold, the soul of man is a wanderer, journeying again and again through many lives.... It is part of the secret knowledge buried in the stream.

Humanity is burdened by the evils committed in the past, but there is hope of transcendence where Deirdre tells her lover: 'Naisi, we have lived together, and died together, and I know that after many years we too shall stand together again.' We can wonder if the theme reflects the buried life of Eva and Esther which was a close-guarded secret between them. As the world moved into the fourth year of war with no end in sight, her mind full of anxiety about Constance's well-being, the idealized figures in a pre-industrial Arcadian landscape could evoke the innocent world of childhood.

Deirdre by Constance from her prison journal

16

CHRISTMAS 1916 – 'WHAT I WAS BORN TO DO'

Constance had still to endure her version of the buried life, but the December gloom was brightened by a visit from Captain J.R. White, DSO. We can imagine her excitement as she hurried along the corridor with the wardress to meet 'Jimmy'. White's second wife told his son, Alan, that she believed the relationship between Con and the flamboyant Jimmy was 'too intimate'.

After the visit White wrote to Henry Duke, the Irish Chief Secretary:

> Countess Markievicz is one of my very greatest friends and in many ways one of the finest women that ever breathed. It's horrible to think of her in the surroundings she now is when but for her sex she would immediately have the privilege of associating with decent and sympathetic people granted to the men...
>
> She does not want the 'privilege' of free association with her present fellow-prisoners in case the authorities think that would cover the mitigation now supposed to be extended to her.[210]

Captain Jack White

He suggested a transfer to Lewes Prison rather than concessions in Aylesbury and added: 'I am sure that Ireland would appreciate her being treated chivalrously.' Duke passed on the request to the Home Office. The Prison Commission considered her position on 22 December but refused to consider a move to Holloway

Christmas 1916 – 'What I Was Born to Do'

with more frequent visits or a women's wing at Lewes. They proposed extending the monthly visits to three-quarters of an hour.

Father Albert Bibby referred to Constance in roundabout terms in a letter to Eva on 23 December:

> I was delighted to have even a word about that dear friend of ours. Thank God, she is so well and in such splendid spirits. The ordeal she had to go through was terrible. I never can forget those awful days in Kilmainham. I was there as early every morning the executions took place & I was with 8 of the men who were shot [but it was not all gloom.] It was a time of awful strain on our friend but she bore up wonderfully. I was sure from statements in the Press that she had already benefited by the relaxations recently introduced for the men.[211]

Around this time the authorities allowed Constance to keep a prison journal for her poems and sketches. It is not clear how the concession came to be granted. Esther gives the credit to Eva's requests to the Prison Board while one of Constance's biographers, Van Voris, credits the intervention of Sir John Leslie. She was forbidden to write about prison conditions and the pages were numbered to make sure she complied.

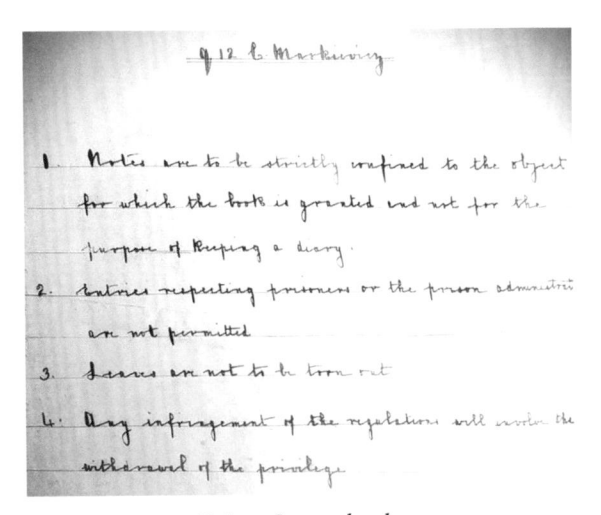

Prison Journal rules

The journal was a large hardback notebook with poor quality paper; the pages were lined and the prison pencils rough and difficult to use, but she set to work and soon filled 55 pages with poems and sketches. The first drawing was a bookplate for Eva on a mountain road following a dove encased in a globe. She followed it with the prison poem she wrote in August ('When my fancies wild white horses') with a self-portrait showing her behind bars grasping the tail of a winged horse.

Christmas 1916 found Constance in a buoyant mood. The possibility that her conviction might be overturned, however unlikely, gave her hope. The prison rules allowed the extra delivery of Christmas cards and she was

Constance behind bars

delighted to find so many of her friends remembered her. She received enough cards to cover the bed, but the authorities delayed the one she was expecting the most – a hand-made card from Eva. She began a long letter to Eva on 29 December:

> Dearest Old Darling – I was waiting and wondering who ought to write first, and now I've got St. Ursula from you and can contain myself no longer.[212]

This is possibly John Ruskin's biography of St. Ursula published in 1912.

> Mr Gavan Duffy interviewed me yesterday and we talked my trial up and down. Of course, I forgot to ask him about Casi and Staskow's things that were lifted by the police! But no matter. He seemed very capable and careful, and he took copious notes.
>
> Do the following lines fit into the poem I sent you before? – and do they improve it?
>
> > We're folded in a sheet of rain.
> > Clasped to the heart of things
> > My spirit slips the yoke of pain,
> > And one with nature sings.

Christmas 1916 – 'What I Was Born to Do'

> I am the cloud that floats so free
> The boundless space, the deep blue sea.
> Of Heaven and Peace I hold the key
> And poise on golden wings.

I am not quite sure if it's sense. Words are such odd things – they suddenly come alive and mean all sorts of things on their own and not what you meant at all. And they simply run away with me and I can't manage them at all.

I have begun another poem, but one is so hustled here one can't do much. But I love trying and trying to put things into verse. It seems to show one so much of the beauty and secret and symbolic side of life that one never dreamt of before.

All that has happened to me seems to have opened to me such wonderful new doors. I seem to pass through it all now as a dream. Day by day slips by and I am not unhappy. I just live in a sort of expectant peace and feel so very close to *you*.

Christmas day has come, and more and more beautiful cards. They seem to me to be symbols of the wonderful love and friendship that is waiting for me and fighting for me outside.

I am blest with such a number of warm-hearted, true friends. If I had not got to jail, perhaps I would not have found it out. You see, there is compensation in everything.

Your beloved letter has just come, such a joy. But still no card of your own design.

The card had arrived in Aylesbury, but the Home Office had to be consulted about the image of Dark Rosaleen playing the harp beneath Constance's barred window. It appears they were concerned the poem and picture might contain a coded message of a rescue attempt.

> Brownie is a darling and a dear friend. Give her my love and tell her I'm afraid her key was lost. Doesn't that sound mysterious? She is not one of the 'crew,' but just a dear friend of Casi's and mine, gay and warm-hearted.

'Brownie' was Mrs Rudnose-Browne, a friend from Dublin, who would visit her in early 1917.

Talking of keys, do write and ask Ella Young for mine. I lent her nearly all my keys and she never gave them back. She wanted to open something. On second thoughts, *don't.* I'd sooner lose the keys than fuss her, and in any case, they are probably lost, and I certainly don't want them!

Ella Young was another writer from a Unionist background who sought liberation in mysticism, Theosophy and the Celtic Renaissance. She published modern versions of Celtic stories with Maud Gonne supplying the illustrations.

My head is quite turned with the reviews you sent me! Those poor rough scribbles! If ever I get out I'll do a lot more. I've learnt such a lot since. This is a real jail pen, *vile,* and I couldn't make it do what I wanted in the drawing at all. Don't make yourself miserable, darling, about me. I am often afraid that you are much more unhappy than I am. I feel a quiet, peaceful, a 'nunc dimitis' sort of feeling.

All my life, in a funny way, seems to have led up to last year, and it's all been a hurry-scurry of a life. Now I feel that I have done what I was born to do. The great wave has crashed up against the rock, and now all the bubbles and ripples and little me slip back into the quiet pool of the sea.

Eva's Christmas card

I am getting even more sentimental than you – in spite of the Censor's cold and unpoetic eye! – but that's how I feel, quite peaceful and calm. Tell me about Willie if you think of it and Maud Gonne. Give my love to the doctor, Madeline and all of them. I *love* Susan's verse on my card. Wish her a very happy Christmas, with all my love. I got three copies of that one, but none of the others.

I had a really lovely dream the other night: try and interpret. A wonderful crimson sun rose in the corner of my cell, slowly passed up and along and stood over my head. It was followed by a gold one and that by a blue one, and they all gave such wonderful lights, and when they passed over my head l felt a wonderful opalescent glow of colours that mix and yet keep their own peculiar qualities. It is difficult to explain but it was wonderfully beautiful.

The sun was a motif in Constance's nationalist artwork, featuring in the masthead for the Bean na hEireann paper and on the Fianna flag and insignia.

> Still more cards came today. Such a joy. I enquired about yours, and it came, but I cannot have it until the Home Office has been consulted and approved! My curiosity is most vivid! What can you have put on it?
>
> Some of my 'army' sent me cards. I never had so many in all my life before. Mrs Murray Robertson sent me such a lovely one. Try and meet her. She paints lovely fans (New English Art Club) and knows Mrs Dryhurst. She is awfully nice.
>
> Now, darling, the limit is approaching and I must be bidding you goodbye. Give my love to Ireland and to all her children, my comrades, and to my 'Poppet' and to his foster-mother. I loved the card they sent. Just room enough to tell you how beautiful I think 'dew-pearled cobwebs.' Your words are like colours and lines – so restrained, vivid and pure. I love the end of 'Maeve' so. The peace she found was, I think, rather like mine. But I've gone a step further, I don't need hazel boughs and mystic streams. I've found it in jail.
>
> Don't say 'How conceited!'
>
> > The wandering winds of Christmas time,
> > The twinkling of the stars
> > Are messengers of hope and love,
> > Defying prison bars.
> > The birds that fly about my cage
> > Are vagrant thoughts that fly
> > To greet you all at Christmas time –
> > They wind the wintry sky.
>
> This is supposed to be a Christmas card! for you and all friends. I have already got 46 and love them, such beauties. But I have not got the one you said you were drawing yourself.

You, Esther, Reginald and Beatrice C- sent me a picture gallery. But who sent Mona Lisa? Thank GaGa for her two and Maeve. They were so pretty and such nice poems. Tell Mabel I wish I were on the boat (picture) with her! However I am quite cheerful, for Christmas has brought the world of Art and life and hope into my cell. I have all the cards arranged upon the bed and they are the greatest joy.

Constance: Live Dangerously

We might think she exaggerates her happiness to defy the prison authorities, but there is a genuine note of inner peace in the letters that is reflected in the drawings from the same period. Eva was the soul-mate in whom she could confide her deepest feelings. She did not wallow in self-pity during the enforced solitude of her cell, but took the opportunity to make a connection with the creative self which had been buried in the years of constant activity.

In childhood she shared with her sister a sense of the material world as a screen for the supernatural, but lost this sense in the 'hurry-scurry' years, as most people do. Eva wrote:

After one has made the great compromise, and the soul has adapted itself to the needs of the flesh, and learnt the language of material life, the way of the spirit becomes more difficult, and our minds, confused by the succession of events ... seem more easily to ... lose their grip of the abstract.[213]

Constance found the connection to the supernatural during prayer in the College of Surgeons and afterwards in the quiet of her prison cell. She was delighted with the verse and drawing on Eva's card when the authorities finally let it through:

Christmas 1916 – 'What I Was Born to Do'

> Do not be lonely, Dear, nor grieve,
> This Christmas Eve
> Is it so vain a thing
> That your Heart's Harper, dark Roseen,
> Crowned with all her sixteen stars,
> A wandering singer, yet a Queen,
> Outside your prison bars,
> Stands carolling.

On 27 December, John O'Dowd, MP for Sligo, pressed her case for association with the Home Secretary: 'The Countess is a native of Sligo and belongs to one of the leading aristocratic Conservative families of this country.'[214] He was told she had all the privileges of the male prisoners, but association had to be ruled out because she was the only female convict among the Irish rebels.

Meanwhile she was filling the pages of the lined journal with poems and drawings:

> When twilight comes with
> its drift of dreams
> Floating down to my lonely soul
> And peace smiles soft on
> the last faint beams
> Of the tired soul who
> crawls to his goal.

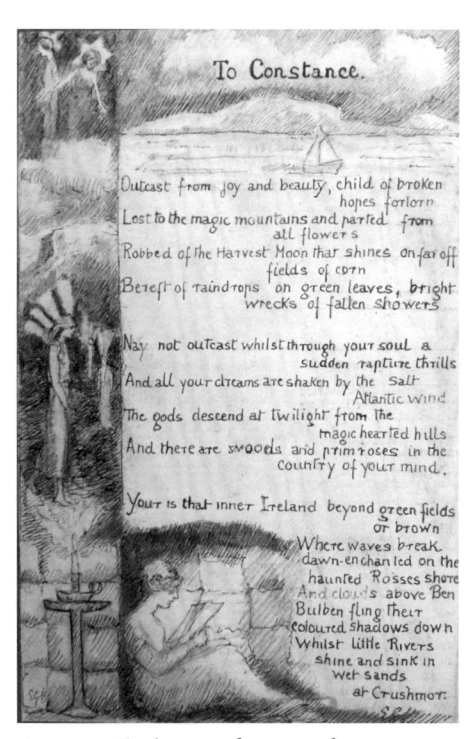

Eva's verse from card

In the poems and sketches she escaped from the confines of the cell and wandered in a spirit land 'where the world's wild rebels are'. The landscapes in the poem are from the wild shores of the West of Ireland, especially Rosses Point, Drumcliffe Harbour and Mullaghmore, the beautiful and stormy Atlantic coastline Constance and Eva explored in childhood. The initial emphasis in the journal was on poetry; she copied in carefully crafted letters Eva's poem, 'Survival', from the collection, *The Three Resurrections and the Triumph of Maeve*:

> In the darkness I planted a rose
> And it withered and died
> Now a poisonous fungus lives and grows
> By the dead rose's side.

There are echoes of Blake's 'Garden of Love' and Yeats' 1916 poem, 'The Rose Tree'. Jacqueline Van Voris believed the poem was inspired by a failed attempt to grow a rose in her cell.[215] The final verse is a passionate response to her condition:

> There is nothing good, there is nothing fair,
> Grows in the darkness thick and blind –
> Pull down your high walls everywhere,
> Let in the sun, let in the wind.

She followed 'Survival' with a recent poem by Eva, 'Pinehurst', written in *1916*:

> Deep in the high-built
> fortress of the pines,
> Lost to her stars dark
> night imprisoned lies,
> Near my hushed soul in peace
> a white rose shines…

Even among the most beautiful natural scenes Eva cannot blot out thoughts of war and carnage. She cast herself in the role of a grief-stricken conscience of the world. Constance absorbed these poems and reproduced them with beautiful illustrations. They were doors into the inner world that had been locked in the busy world, but which, in her long hours of enforced leisure, she could now explore. She followed these with a sketch of a Christmas crib, a tranquil image at the end of a

Constance, Tending the Rose

Christmas 1916 – 'What I Was Born to Do'

year of turmoil. The poem, 'Magi', is illustrated with Constance at her cell window grasping the tail of a winged horse climbing into the sky.

> When my fancies wild white horses
> Go galloping out apace,
> To play with life's secret forces,
> And conquer all time and space.
> They float on the waves with the Sunbeams
> And scorning all prison bars,
> Live free with the morning breezes,
> And die with the deathless stars.

Magi poem

17

1917 – 'Dim Sunshine and Pearly Waves...'

On 1 January 1917 the Great War, which had been expected to last a few months in 1914, was now entering its fourth year. Despite attempts on both sides there was no sign of a breakthrough on the Western Front. In the East the Brusilov Offensive of 1916 made initial gains before ending in a great loss of Russian men and materials. Throughout the upheavals Casimir was living in an apartment in central Kiev, living each day as if it might be his last. Stasko described his father in a letter to Eva:

> ... he is either painting pictures (for which he is never paid – or never finishes) or writing plays – in which also, if he is successful, he gets well done in. One understands him very well, it's just his character – he cannot tie himself down to anything and likes to be free and his own master...[216]

C.P. Scott, the influential editor of the *Manchester Guardian*, wrote to Eva on 2 January to say he could not advise her on a public campaign on Constance's behalf. He had written to Lloyd George, but got no answer: '– as you know he never does answer letters.' He expected to meet Lloyd George the following week and was hopeful of a sympathetic response as he was 'on the line of reconciliation towards Ireland.'[217]

Josslyn's year began with a request from Eva that placed him in a dilemma: could he publicly declare support for Constance and avoid being associated with her politics? She met the Irish Parliamentary Party MP for North Sligo, Thomas Scanlan, who wanted to launch a petition in Sligo to free Constance, but thought Josslyn was against Constance. Eva assured him it was not the case, even though her letter suggests a vague doubt.

1917 – 'Dim Sunshine and Pearly Waves...'

Would he sign a petition, she asked, to show that the Gore-Booths were standing beside Constance?

> And really the worst crime they seemed to have against her was that she shot a brick in the Shelbourne. And I don't suppose the brick is much the worse for it. I hope I wasn't wrong in saying I felt sure you would sign it...

> She looks ill but says she wouldn't for anything say her throat was bad as they'd given her medicine in a dirty glass & the people have such filthy diseases, the company she has is simply revolting, the conversation disgusting...[218]

Even from behind prison bars Constance was proving to be a major problem for Josslyn. Eva wrote again:

> My dear Joss, if I understand you right you think a petition for C's release would be a mistake as she has bitter enemies who would at once retaliate by circulating abusive stories against her. I am not keen myself to have a petition, because things are moving so quickly I think she will be out quite soon in any case. It's not me, it's W.S. who wants the petition. Have I your authority for assuring him that much as you naturally wish for her release you think a petition would be a mistake as it would rouse her enemies into activity and for thanking Mr. S for his wish to help?

> You ask me to ask C. what her orders were & what she did all through. My difficulty is this I never see her alone there is a wardress always present who writes down every word we say for the authorities. I have quoted to you things she said in her talk but I simply don't ask her for a long definite statement like that. Not that I am afraid of any awful revelations (because I feel sure there aren't any!) but because she talks in such a careless haphazard sort of way & anything she said might be twisted and used against her. I try on the other hand to keep her off as much as possible and on to harmless subjects. Surely you agree that this the only safe course? When she is safely out the stories can be squashed.

> For the present don't you think the court martial proceedings are what we should go on? They are quite clear and prove that the Government has not accused her of anything beyond participation in the rebellion & sedition. Her enemies were bound to invent stories against her. Think of the limits Major Price went to try and involve

Dillon. (I think you said you had the C.M proceedings didn't you) They seem to me to be an answer to any reasonable person - as to the stories I shall deny them through thick & thin as I believe them to be pure fabrication of those very bitter enemies who tried hard to get her shot.

I have a visit on the 4th or 5th (pass not come yet) & I will ask her anything you like, if you can think of roundabout ways, but you understand the difficulty of a public interview & the tremendous precautions that we might get a private word together. Colonel Moore says that he doesn't think the stories as harmful as they might be as everyone in authority knows such stories are always invented against anyone in her position & sworn to all over the place.

My real trouble is that Mr. S is going about saying that you are so bitter against her, not that you don't approve of the Rebellion because everyone of course realizes that, but that C's own family won't stick up for her personally which is <u>awfully</u> bad for her position, and of course quite another thing. I told him it wasn't true, but I would like your assurance to stop the gossip.

I do hope this letter isn't too muddled. I've got the Flu again & bronchitis in the awful Fog we have had. Yrs. Eva GB[219]

Constance and her affairs were a major concern for Josslyn as the year began. He wrote everywhere for confirmations and clarifications, but remained in a cloud of uncertainty. He was not a man to make public statements – in a rare departure he urged Irish people to support the war in 1914 and distributed recruiting leaflets at Lissadell in April 1916. He was careful not to make any gesture that could be interpreted as support for Constance's politics.

The Home Office responded to John O'Dowd M.P. on 11 January:

The Countess Markievicz about whom you wrote to me on the 29th December has the same privileges as the male Irish Convicts, except that of association with other Irish prisoners which is impossible in her case as there are no other female Irish prisoners for her to associate with, and as a special privilege the duration of her visits has been extended.[220]

While Constance languished in prison and Eva agitated the rest of the Gore-Booth family were steadfast in their support of the British war effort.

Constance, Woman at Seashore

The production of bombs continued in the local ammunition factory. Susan Mitchell wrote a number of letters to Josslyn in January, 1917. She informed him on 1 January that Cummins was owed £10 rent on the hall. 'I have the key which he will take over from me when the rent is paid.' She added that she hoped Constance would get the same privileges as the men.

She wrote on 5 January about the persistent rumours:

Dear Sir Josslyn,

If you could tell me particularly what you want to know I might be able to get the information you want, as I know at least 2 or 3 credible persons who had every opportunity of knowing all the events of that time. With regard to the scandalous stories I have heard some & I find the way to stop them is to ask the name of the 'friend' from whom they came, & to take it down remarking that you are doing so with a view to legal action on C's behalf. To tell such scandal mongers that they are putting themselves in danger from the law of libel is a good deterrent. Of course I needn't tell you that there is absolutely no foundation for any aspersion that has been cast on C...

She (Constance) was quite careless of opinion & quite frank about all she did, but there was very evidently a determined attempt made to slander her... Have you heard anything of Casi? C. was very <u>anxious</u> about him for some time...'[221]

Josslyn sent a note to Susan on 11 January that he was going to Dublin to stay in the Shelbourne for a few days, and presumably to meet with Susan although she wrote to him on 13 January: 'The only person who could truly answer your questions is C. herself, but there is one other person who might give some information, but I have so far failed to meet her, but I have tried. If I am more successful in a few days I will write to you. If you were here yourself I could put you in touch with these people. It is difficult to write. As to C's actions in obeying orders, one thing is certain, she did nothing in time of stress that was contrary to her character in normal times, & her character was always both fearless & chivalrous. There is more than a suspicion that the CM [court martial] was illegal.

Susan wrote with more suggestions for lines of enquiry on 30 January:

Dear Sir Josslyn,

I enclose this letter from Mrs Rudnose Browne, wife of a professor in Trinity. She saw Constance on the 4th of the month & I believe Eva was ill and unable to see her. She is coming to see me on Thursday, she should have come at once. She says that Constance is starving & treated with brutality, overworked and suffering. This Mrs Browne told to friends of mine, hence my letter to her to which this is her reply.

You will have seen by the papers that the whole subject of the Courtmartials is to become public now if possible, as it is believed they were illegally held with closed doors. I suppose Constance can have another visit on the 4th of February. I wish you could see her yourself. There is very bitter feeling here over this last news...

There is one returned prisoner I should like you to see, Miss Helena Moloney (sic). She was a great friend of Constance & lived in her house a good deal. She is a level-headed girl, with none of the bitterness or hysteria one may sometimes encounter amongst adherents of unpopular causes. She was in Aylesbury & what she can tell you will move you as it has moved me. I will write to you again on Thursday when I have seen Mrs. Browne & I then propose taking other steps to help Constance.

I do not like to distress you, but I believe you are the person who could see and help her. They dread publicity & would ameliorate her lot to save this. As to the questions you asked me, no one will give the information unless they know exactly how it will be used. The shooting of policemen in cold blood ascribed to her is an absurdity. She always acted up to her character, which was chivalrous to a degree.

She added a footnote in pencil:

Miss Moloney is of the opinion we should not go on helping Bessie Lynch indefinitely, but try & set her up as a laundress, getting about 8 or 10 people to promise her washing & then leaving her to do for herself...

She sent a note with Mrs Browne's report on 31 January:

Her actual words to me were – 'I'm starved, Brownie & slave driven. I have to mix with prostitutes & baby-killers – it is the atmosphere of a brothel –

She assured me she had <u>never</u> shot a policeman & she was not near the Castle when that much talked of policeman was shot.

Josslyn wrote to his brother Mordaunt in Sheffield on 5 February:

Will you please tell me by return of post what is the common gossip about Constance. Do you hear or have you heard stories about shooting police and soldiers in cold blood and generally what view people take? I want to know what I am up against.[222]

Mordaunt replied promptly on 7 February:

My dear Joss, I have no very precise information about Con. S tells me that he has it from Sir J. Maxwell, (now G.O.C. in C. York – Northern Command) that there is no doubt she did shoot a policeman.[223]

The letter went on to discuss ploughs and disc harrows for Lissadell.

> In the sheen of her radiant plumage
> They lose themselves in a maze
> That is Heaven and earth united
> By a misty azure haze;
> The purple blue of the heather
> The greeny blue of the sea
> Where the clouds and the waves cling together
> Ere they melt in eternity.

Constance: In the Sheen ...

Susan Mitchell continued to dig and reported from Hampshire on 11 February on the results of an enquiry with an unnamed military officer. The excessive caution in these letters are indicative of an atmosphere of secrecy due to wartime censorship of the postal service.

> Dear Joss, I have heard from the officer I said I could communicate with & he says – 'she undoubtedly took a very prominent part in the Rebellion. She was in command of the Rebels who took possession of St. Stephen's Green. She and her followers were responsible for the shooting and killing of several innocent people. She wore a rebel uniform, was armed with and seen to use a revolver. When she surrendered the revolver was taken from her. She was offered a taxi cab to take her to prison after her surrender but elected to march to Barracks at the head of her followers.
>
> The above are facts. There were all kinds of rumours current in Dublin none of which were substantiated – but the military authorities were not responsible for these rumours. The kindest thing is to look

on her as mad but dangerous. Personally I am profoundly sorry for her relatives.'

You will not of course mention this officer's <u>name</u> as having given this information, but you will now in knowing the facts be able to deal with the circumstances as they arise.

One thread through many of the letters was the reluctance of people with information to make it public or to be identified. Josslyn prevailed on his friend, the Revd. F.S. Le Fanu, in Sandymount, to speak to De Burgh Daly and received a reply from Mrs Daly dated 20 February:

I spoke to my husband about Countess Markievicz and he asked now to tell you that, after thinking out the matter, he prefers not to say anything to Sir Jocelyn about it. He knows nothing of the death of the policeman...[224]

Josslyn was becoming frustrated at the lack of clarity after so much correspondence. He must have derived comfort from a card posted from the Presbytery, Catholic University Church, St. Stephen's Green, on 21 February.

My dear Sir Jocilyn (sic) – I cannot spell your name but don't worry as I think I have – I am sure I have for fact what you want – an eye-witness of the death of Const. Lahiff – I write in haste tonight to ease your mind. It was not your sister who fired the shot. She has given me leave to state this fact.... Your friend, J.P. Sherwin.[225]

Father James Sherwin was the parish priest of University Church in 1916. We have no information as to the identity of the eye-witness. On the same day Josslyn wrote to the Revd. Le Fanu that he was certain Dr Daly was shot at between 1.00-1.15. He replied to Father Sherwin on 23 February:

I am much obliged to your letter for your letter of 21st. This information you give confirms what I had already received from another eye witness (a man)...[226]

Despite these assurances Josslyn persisted in his quest and requested a police report on the shooting. He lamented to Mordaunt on 27 February:

I have been trying for a long time to trace things down. I am quite clear she did not do in the Stephen's Green one although she has been accused of this, nor do I think she shot the Castle one. Please find out for me in what locality & at what time in what day she is said to have done this but do not write any hearsay.[227]

Mordaunt's patience with his brother's enquiries was exhausted. He reported on 1 March about problems in contacting General Maxwell and advised Josslyn to drop the issue:

In fact you might almost say that the whole sorry business is forgotten with the reservation that if it recurs again people hope that a Cromwell will appear from somewhere & fix this business once & for all. As I hear anything I will let you know, but it's no good my bothering busy people with letters.[228]

In Ireland her comrades continued to keep Constance's memory alive. The Irish Women Workers Union met in early 1917 and elected her Honorary President. Acting President was Marie Perolz. Constance continued to draw in her cell each night, leaving a number of blank pages listed in the Index as 'Crystal Pages.' The next page features an ink drawing of a woman holding a crystal at the entrance to a prehistoric tomb with decorations similar to Newgrange.

The poem 'In the West the Waves are Green' shows her experimenting with the length of the lines and their position on the page; she is learning how the visual presentation can add to the poem's impact:

> I have seen his yellow hair
> Through the darkness shining fair
> Leading on without a care
> Eyes aglow
> From the West the Brown wind brings
> Brown wind blow

The figure from the West is intriguing, especially when we compare it with the naked horseman with shining hair on page 48. Hope takes a human shape in many of the drawings and appears as the Celtic God Lu with the rays of the sun on his head.

We can imagine Constance in her cell during the long cold winter of 1916-17 softly chanting the lines, listening for the rhythm before she writes the words. She fills pages with rough sketches, grasping at images gestating in her unconscious.

A high window above the cell door allowed light from the corridor and in winter she could read and sketch with the light of a gas lamp. Constance worked at a small table secured to the wall, drawing patiently on the rough paper until the darkness became too strong. She complained that Dr Fox had her light turned off at eight o'clock when regulations allowed for it to be on until ten.

In January 1917 the Home Office again refused to transfer Constance to Lewes Prison where the Irish male prisoners were now enjoying their limited association. It has been suggested that the authorities were unwilling to facilitate her because of the possible cost – she would have been the only female prisoner in Lewes which would have required at least four wardresses.[229]

Woman with Crystal

January was an especially hard month for Constance to get through. Brownie gave a full account of a visit to Kathleen Lynn:

> On Saturday Jan 13 I saw Constance Markievicz for the first time since April last. I was horrified at her appearance. A similar look on the face of an ordinary citizen I should describe as due to starvation. Her actual words to me were – 'I'm starved. Tell all Ireland that. I'm slave driven and have to mix intimately daily with prostitutes and baby-murderers – in fact I'm living in a brothel.'.. To any who knew her in the old days as well as I did, her look of mental torture was terrifying and plainly indicated the kind of hell she was forced to live in.[230]

Meanwhile, the undaunted J.F. Cunningham made another appeal on 17 January with a letter to Henry Duke:

Bright Horseman

> Dear Mr Duke,
>
> Please let me see you for a few minutes, when you have a spare moment, with regard to the release of the Countess Markievicz, a Sinn Feiner, now serving a Life Sentence. There is a particular reason I wish to submit to you personally that I cannot put on paper...
>
> Her family, the Gore-Booths are prominent people in the West, and now that you have released all those who were interned – all nationalists, I am begging this as a concession to a family of Unionists...
>
> You must have seen the Kaiser's latest note that he plays Ireland as a trump card against the Allies: 'Look at the fate of the Irish people' he exclaims before Europe – before the world, and when a Peace Conference assembles you may be sure Ireland will be the one great shot in his locker...
>
> For goodness sake have an end to it. Your predecessors could not do it, being declared Party men, but you can settle Ireland once and for all. Take that shot out of the Kaiser's locker...
>
> I am only a humble Barrister, but I have had 21 years service under the Colonial Office, and if you listen to the words I offer you will listen to the words of a man who has grown grey in the service of the Empire.[231]

It appears the authorities dismissed Cunningham as an eccentric voice. He made a last-ditch passionate plea to Duke on 23 January:

> ... the only thing that concerns <u>me</u> is to submit a humble prayer for the release of the Countess Markievicz on the grounds of ill-health. The Gore-Booths are no more rebels than I am, or than you are, or that Mrs Pankhurst is, or Annie Kenny. I may add that I am prepared to offer all my wealth and my <u>head to boot</u> as a guarantee for her good behaviour in the future.

The official response was a scrawled remark on the file: 'I hardly think it is necessary to take any further action on this.' J.F. Cunningham disappears from the story, leaving the question as to his motivation on such a quixotic enterprise. Was he simply a family friend or a former lover from the time before Constance met Casimir?

18

'In Prison All Her Life...'

Constance had an unexpected champion in Arthur Griffith of Sinn Féin, who had once thought her an English spy and opposed the strikers during the 1913 Lockout. But the Rising had changed allegiances utterly. In January 1917 he directed an open letter to the American newspaper magnate, William Randolph Hearst:

> It is less than a year since this woman [Constance], once the most beautiful woman in Ireland was clad in England's convict garb and now she is stooped and grey-haired.... Fear of America held back England's itching hand from shooting this Irish lady. Today, in secret, England tortures her with worse than death. American opinion is feared today by England. Madame Markievicz is being crucified daily because England thinks it can be done without the knowledge of America. Let America know.[232]

Esther Roper came to visit on 26 January accompanied by Lady Clare Annesley, a twenty-three-year-old feminist and pacifist from Castlewellan Castle, County Down. Eva was too sick to visit, but continued her letter-writing campaign. The dialogue was again transcribed by Matron Sharp. Some of Constance's remarks sound bizarre, but they caused a flurry in official circles when the report was circulated.

As with the September visit Ms Sharp focused on remarks and responses from Constance, giving the impression of a one-woman performance rather than a dialogue with visitors.

> Madam,
>
> I beg to state for your information that the following statements were made when q 12 C. Markievicz was visited by Miss Roper and

> Lady Clare Annisley (sic) on the 26th inst: - Markievicz asked Miss Roper to tell Mr. Gavan Duffey (sic) that when she was tried a sentry was placed at the door so that no witnesses in her favour could gain admittance. She also said that she was accused of being in command of the army that attacked Dublin Castle, but it was not true. The army was divided into sections, and each section was told off by Connelly (sic), to go different routes and her section did not go to Dublin Castle at all. Mr Duffey is to bring these points forward at the enquiry which is about to be held.
>
> Markievicz said the Citizen Army was the only place she knew where command was given according to merit, she Markievicz, was second in command the day after she joined the Army, with instructions to take charge if anything happened to the commander. Markievicz said that Inspector Quinn was a bitter enemy. When Captain White was arrested she went to the place and made a vow. Inspector Quinn ordered her to be turned out so she purchased some things from a chemist and got in again as a nurse.[233]

This refers to a Dublin demonstration in March 1914 when Captain White was beaten about the head with batons by the Dublin Metropolitan Police. Constance tried to help by attacking the police and attempting to trip them up.

> She went to a play called 'The English at Home' or 'The Englishman's Home,' went in the gallery and hissed the actors when they said anything favourable to England and clapped when the Germans were supposed to be entering England; causing such a disturbance that the play was stopped.
>
> Markievicz hopes that one result of the war will be that the British Empire is broken up. She spoke of an arch that has been erected to the memory of men who fought for England as 'The Traitor's Arch.' Miss Roper told Markievicz that people were continually going to the Home Office to worry them, as that was the only way to get anything out of the Government. Miss Roper said many people were longing to visit her, whereupon (sic) Markievicz told her to send them all to the Home Office to ask for permission to come; she said if she were asked if she knew them she would say yes, even if she had never heard of them.

> Markievicz said she would stay in Prison all her life rather than promise not to interfere in politics.

It seems hard to believe that Constance would have been so open about her plans, even urging people to apply for visits, including strangers that she would claim to know.

> Miss Roper said a man called Mr. Martin had asked her what he could do for Markievicz as he once did a good turn to a Member of Parliament and he will now go that man and say his reward is to take the form of concessions for Markievicz.
>
> Markievicz complained of the quality of paper of the notebook which has been supplied to her. She also said that she was practically living on dry bread, she said she only had a little rice for her dinner, fish was provided but it was big fish which lived off human bodies she could not eat it. Markievicz wants her sister to thank the people who sent her cards by means of one of the Nationalist newspapers.
>
> I am, Madam, Yours Respectfully, E.D. Sharp, Principal Matron

The report presents the visit in a strange light – it sounds as though Constance is rambling at times. Esther says little and Lady Clare appears to have kept silent all the way through. Constance seems preoccupied with the hope of an enquiry into her sentence and her mind casts around for reasons to overturn the verdict. The fish eating people could be a reference to the fate of bodies from ships torpedoed by German U-boats around England. Despite the bravado she was feeling the strain of the long winter nights in her cell. A few remarks by Eva suggest that Constance was in poor health in the early months of 1917. The Governor was alarmed and sent a report to the Prison Commissioners who forwarded it to the Home Office on 2 February.

'This is interesting as showing a conspiracy to worry the H.O. daily about visits to this woman,' an official noted.[234]

Eva sent a note to Helena Molony urging her to apply for a visit.

> I assure you C. isn't the least intimidated by anything & says everything out straight, but no amount of suffering touches her wonderful spirit of courage and gaiety.[235]

Maebhbh and Maca

Constance began her next letter to Eva on 29 January in a more measured and normal tone. It gives a different impression of the visit:

> Beloved Old Darling, – For goodness sake do take care of your dear old self and don't run any risks. This English climate is so awful that I wonder how you get along at all. Every day for months it seems to freeze. I long for our more considerate and gentle climate, that always gives you a peep at the blessed sun and a soft warm drizzle.[236]

The weather in the winter and spring of 1917 was unusually severe with snow on the ground until 1 May.

> I see the sunrise every morning, and it is most beautiful and quite worth the trouble of walking out to see it, though I need hardly tell you that it is not my will-power that guides my weary legs!

The last sentence indicates the support she draws from her religious faith. The reference to the sunrise might have reminded Eva of a day in 1892 when the sisters rose early in Lissadell to watch the sun rising.

> As I knew you were not coming, I was not disappointed at not seeing you. Esther and Clare were like a bottle of champagne to me, they brightened me up so. I thought Clare lovely and rather like her grandmother, who I knew quite well. It's such a joy to look at pretty things. I thought my 'Poppet' looked so fat and well; I longed to hug him!
>
> I *loved* your card. As you say, the idea at the back of yours and mine was somewhat the same, but yours was far superior. I loved the group of children round Roseen [Rosaleen]. You had a wonderful feeling in it all – movement, proportion and design were all excellent. The tone was very nice too. I feel so proud of it being done for me, and of being in three poems. My head is getting very swelled indeed! I like your new poem very much, especially verse three. Your poems have a magic effect on me. They transport me away to beautiful lands of dim sunshine and pearly waves, where beautiful, stately people drift gracefully about. They are all like you and have wild aureoles of golden hair and long white fingers!
>
> I'm awfully interested in astrology; do try to read Maeve's fate in the stars. Nobody seems to remember my birth-hour exactly, so you will have some trouble there! Couldn't you work back from some other date in my life, such as my wedding day? I was late and only just in time to get married that day. Or twelve o'clock, Monday of Easter Week? – which I think was the moment we started on our 'divine adventure'.

Clare Annesley sketch

She has become used to treating Eva as an unofficial secretary, dealing with enquires and sending messages. 'I don't understand from your letter whether the shop is still going in Liberty Hall.' She gives a list of people she wants thanked and messages delivered:

> Yours is that inner Ireland beyond green fields or brown
> Where waves break dawn-enchanted on the haunted Rosses shore
> And clouds above Ben Bulben fling their coloured shadows down
> Whilst little Rivers shine and sink in wet sands at Crushmor.

Extract from Eva's card

– 'old Miss Trevekes' who wanted to visit, Emer ... and Winifred Carney. 'I really did love my cards. I never enjoyed any Christmas presents half so much. I did enjoy seeing the photos of M. (Maeve) and the children that Esther brought...

I am getting off this letter as quick as I can as they have taken to reckoning your next from the date it goes, not from the date when you get your sheet of paper, which, if you delay writing, allows them to rob you of a certain number of letters in a year. I delayed a fortnight over the last, and that fortnight is lost to me in letters.

This explains the delay in writing the letter dated 29 December as she waited for Eva's Christmas card. The next 12 lines were cut from the letter by the censor.

I am still reading your 'Maeve.' I think Connaught should be spelt 'Connacht.' Someone else has probably told you this long ago! But you asked me. I do love Maeve's last speech, but it would be very difficult to make a stage success of. I long to give you a lecture on writing a verse play. It could be done and a success made of it.

Constance had experience of writing and producing plays with Casimir, but their productions were fast-moving farces or historical plays. Eva's style was more formal, closer to the work of Yeats and Lady Gregory.

I wish we could collaborate. Aren't I getting conceited? But I feel I understand audiences and stage-craft and play-producing: by this, I mean the whole process – from author to the meanest super. I include all these as material that goes to produce a dramatic performance, and they must all pull together. You can't play organ music on a Jew's harp, and *you* give your penny whistles organ music to play. Some day I may get a chance of trying to explain. I can feel it so well, but can't do it myself.

I am longing to know how you are, but am not anxious about you. I *was* for two days some time ago, but then got into my head that you were better, and now I feel confident that you are getting on alright, though it may be slow. But don't hurry to get up, as you love me.

I've been writing – [Unfortunately the following 12 lines were cut from the letter. Presumably they contained references to politics.]

With best love to all my darlings.

'Beyond earth's barred gates' every morning at 9.0 I seek you there.

The last sentence suggests the sisters also made a morning attempt at telepathy, maybe in connection with the sun rising. Friday, 4 February, was Constance's birthday – she was forty-eight. Eva wrote a poem and decorated a card to commemorate the occasion, 'To C.M. On her Prison Birthday, February 1917':

> What has time to do with thee,
> Who has found the victor's way
> To be rich in poverty,
> Without sunshine to be gay,
> To be free in a prison cell?

The Irish National Relief Fund kept up pressure on the British Government to grant her the right of association. On 23 February Art O'Brien protested to Home Secretary, George Cave, referring to Constance as 'this solitary woman':

> Among the outstanding feature of the new conditions was that which allowed one hour's communication. It was promised that these ameliorated conditions were to apply to <u>all</u> the prisoners. The male prisoners were moved to Lewes in December ... but in the case of Countess Markievicz this most precious of all the altered condi-

tions has not been accorded to her.... The Government has given a distinct pledge on this matter, and it is a callous breach of faith that no effort should be made to fulfil the promise in the case of the only woman prisoner.[237]

Louise Bennett, the suffrage and labour activist, also wrote on similar grounds appealing for the concessions to be extended to Constance. C.P. Scott raised her situation with Lloyd George, complaining that she had to choose between 'solitary confinement and association with the lowest female criminals and prostitutes.' Lloyd George replied that 'a little solitary confinement would do her no harm.'[238]

Dr Fox prepared a report dated 10 February to the Prison Commissioners:

> No complaints of any kind have been made to me, the Chief Matron, Principal Matrons, or any other officers about the food.[239]

She went on to list the treatment Constance received in Aylesbury and mentioned her dietary problems of the previous September:

> After this she steadily gained weight up to the end of January. No food has been returned by the prisoner at any time.

She quoted the comment on the large fish without comment and ended with a table of weights showing that Constance had fallen to 120 pounds in September. Her weight increased to 129.5 pounds on 21 January, but had slipped to 128.5 pounds on the date of the report.

Constance was the subject of a question by Alfie Byrne in the House of Commons on 14 February when he asked the Secretary of State for the Home Department:

> ... if his attention has been called to the treatment of Countess Markievicz; if he will cause instruction to be issued to improve the prison food and her general surroundings; and if he will say when she is likely to be released.[240]

Sir George Cave replied:

> I am informed that this person is in good health.... I am unable to say when she is likely to be released.

The political situation in Ireland was changing rapidly. A bye-election in Roscommon in February 1917 resulted in a Sinn Féin victory with Count Plunkett, father of the executed leader, Joseph Mary Plunkett, defeating the Irish Nationalist Party candidate. Even British politicians were forced to realize they could not continue to impose their will on a reluctant population. A British politician told the House of Commons on 7 March:

> Centuries of brutal and often ruthless injustice – and, what is worse when you are dealing with a high-spirited and sensitive people, centuries of insolence and insult, have driven hatred of British rule into the marrow of the Irish race.[241]

The speaker was not, as one might expect, a Sinn Féin sympathizer, but the new Prime Minister, David Lloyd George. Despite this public stance, C.P. Scott wrote to Eva on 11 March that Lloyd George was 'very hard to read,' but she was not to expect any further concessions: 'The wheels of Departments move with a terrible slowness.'

Constance found the journal difficult for drawing as the lines intruded on the pictures, and the rough pencil meant the images were crude and unfinished, and she began to experiment with ink wash. After pages of poems she completed a full-page picture – *Star of the Sea*, a powerful image of the Madonna appearing to a fisherman threatened by a wall of water. A dove flies towards Mary while a group of angels ride the crest of the surging wave. The depiction is conventional but the image could have made an impressive watercolour. The careful pencil-work depicts the coast of Sligo coast with its rocks, mountains and storm-cast sky.

The second picture, *The Watcher*, is confined to the kitchen of a traditional Irish cottage such as Constance and Eva knew from childhood days. A woman sits on a wooden bench beside a pot on the open hearth. Such scenes were often depicted in nostalgic pictures but the woman is watching the doorway and holding a rifle. Light streams from the open door, but the woman is clearly ready to fight. It could be a scene from the Land War or an allegory of Kathleen ni Houlihan resisting the invader.

Some of the early pictures are awkwardly finished where the splotches from the wash obliterate the details. When you turn the pages you can see an improvement in technique. The shading and cross-hatching is more effective in showing depth and shadow. Many pages are taken up with poetry including the long poem, 'The Thrush', on which she worked during February 1917 and included in a letter to Eva dated 27 February:

The Watcher

Dearest Old Darling, - The sun is shining, the sky is so blue and the horrid red walls make it look bluer still, and I seem to see it shining through your golden halo and touching up your blues and greys, and then I think 'perhaps she is in a murky English fog' and I grudge it being able to touch you and envelop you in its embrace. And then I think: 'perhaps the same fog will blow over here, and will have us both in the same grip' – and so I wander on, quite drivelling.

I loved your last poem and letter. If you can think of it, do bring Mrs. Meynell's poem next visit. I am burning with curiosity: I think I told you, but can't be sure.

Please tell 'Crew' not to publish any *unpublished* poems of mine without asking *me* (through you). Anything once published they can do what they like with, but there are one or two I don't want published yet awhile.[242]

This would suggest she knew some of the poems she wrote in Kilmainham were hurried and emotional.

I was so glad to hear of K____ the old darling. I'm sure he's a rebel in his heart. He's one of the people I should really love to see. He and I were so very sympathetic always. Tell him I was so glad to get a message from him and give him my love. He always feels like part of the family.

The greedy starlings are making such a row on the window-ledge, fighting most rudely over the remains of my dinner.

Birds at cell window

This morning a wedge-shaped flight of wild geese flew over us as we were exercising, making their weird cackling cry, and they brought me home at once. Do you remember the wonderful monster, supposed to be a cow, that Joss concocted, to stalk them from behind or within, and how they fled shrieking for miles at the sight, and how unapproachable they were for weeks owing to the fright they got? The Trojan horse was nothing to that beast.

I have just been reading your letter again and can't help wishing that I were Percy's cow or pig! … Give Father Albert my love and tell him I often think of him. Lord MacDonnell was an old friend, also his wife and nice daughter. He always impressed me as a very straight man, although he was a politician! I liked him very much.

Lord Anthony McDonnell, 'Tiger of Bengal,' was a senior British civil servant and Under-Secretary for Ireland 1902-08. He would have known Constance from the years 1903-08 when she attended balls in Dublin Castle.

Give Emmy (Mrs. Emmeline Pankhurst?) my love and tell her I would have sent her a gilt-edged invitation card, but the censor won't allow me! I'd love to see her, don't let her *not* come if she *says* she is coming. Once she gets a pass she must come.

Apart from her joy in receiving visitors the effect of multiple applications for visiting passes would have been a source of pressure on the authorities. Art O'Brien urged the Home Office to move her to Holloway where she could have a one-hour visit each day.

To place her in a prison close to the centre of London where access would have been infinitely easier for a range of friends, supporters and sympathetic politicians and journalists, and where she could hold court for an hour a day, was surely an attractive option for her.[243]

Constance was far from 'holding court' in her dismal waiting room in Aylesbury, but she could still present a cheerful face in her letters.

> I was glad to hear of Mrs Mallin, and so interested to hear that the boy is learning to draw. Perhaps I shall be able to help him, some day. Who knows? What a lot of letters I am letting you in for, you poor old darling. It would probably upset Mrs Mallin very much, seeing me. It would bring it all back to her. They were such a devoted pair. The last things he said to me were about her.
>
> If you are writing to any of the Hall crowd, tell them I got their cards. The Co-op girls sent a joint one, and the Norgroves sent me one each. Tell them to remember me to Mrs Norgrove and ask for news of her husband. Now I'm going to write out a poem, about another jail-bird – a thrush. It's true!

The poem is taken from pages 17-18 of the lined journal dated February 1917 and consists of nine stanzas that vary between five and six lines, running to a total of fifty lines:

> He sang the song of the waking Spring,
> The song of the budding tree,
> Of the chrysalis cradling the butterfly's wing
> And the waking to life of each earth-bound thing
> That the sun comes out to free.

The singing thrush is not prepared for the return of winter and the snowflakes that 'beat on his wings in a smothering pall;' he lies frozen on the ground:

> Was he right to rejoice or was he all wrong?
> Do hope and faith but to fools belong?
> Is courage all a mistake?

It would be easy to interpret the lines as a questioning on Constance's part. Is she the songbird? After nearly ten months in prison is she beginning

Sketch of thrush

to give up hope? Despite his death she concludes that the thrush's life was worthwhile because:

> He gave his best, and simple and strong
> Broke the darkness which lasted the winter long
> With Spring-time's triumphant melodious song…

It's very long, isn't it?' she suggests, 'and they say that "good things are done up in small parcels".'

In all probability she enjoyed composing the jaunty rhyming scheme, stretching some stanzas from five to six lines, filling the blank page with words.

> I love your birthday poem so much. You've missed your vocation. You should be a Poet Laureate. I will make you mine! I am sure no one had so much poetry written about them *spontaneously* before, while they were alive. Ordinary kings and queens have to pay for it, so they get rubbish. Pegasus, being thoroughbred, will not stand a spur – even a golden one.

The next passage showed that she had not forgotten the work of William Blake whose influence is visible on her prison drawings.

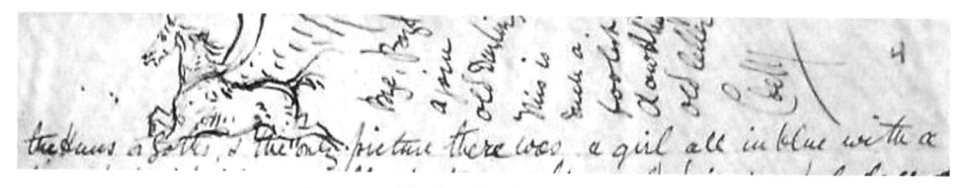

Letter with sketch of winged horse

> I wanted so to talk about Blake and about horoscopes the other day, but of course forgot about both! I wish I'd known Blake. I would love to argue about light and shade with him. He was all wrong – strange for such a great man. He took the superficial view that shadow is to soften and conceal. It never seemed to dawn on him that bad draughtsmen may use shadows for this: but a Master, such as Rembrandt, has as true an outline as Flaxman, and each shadow is a definite thing with a shape, as much so as an arm or a leg. But I must not write lectures on Art or Blake! I have no room and you no time to read.
>
> Take care of yourself, you blessed old dear. I am very well, and luckily for me escaped my usual bad cold, which generally gets hold of me in January. The frosty weather always agrees with me.
>
> Last night I dreamt I was walking on the cliffs beyond John's Port, with a ripe cornfield with poppies on my right, when a great khaki-coloured snake rushed out of the corn and slithered down the cliff!
>
> You didn't tell me if you found any meanings in the colours of the winds.

It should have been apparent to the Censor that the sisters had a code in the poems and dream images, impenetrable to anyone but themselves. After the dream she switches to enquiries about friends:

> Molly Byrne is a great girl. I wish I could write her some songs. She sings with such go and has such a nice voice. Give her my love and tell her I long to hear her sing again and I often think of the times we had together.
>
> Give Susan my love. It's awfully good of her to help Bessie. By the way, if Bessie marries, I promised her £10 to set up. If she married, it might help things, so ask Susan to let her know I have not forgotten. I don't even know if she wants to marry! – and remember, in setting

> her up, I don't mind a few pounds more or less, *but her mother must not live with her.* She's a devil.
>
> Please ask Joss to give Maeve £1 to buy an Easter egg.

She has been criticized for the scarcity of references to her family, especially Maeve, in these letters. Some view the absence as an indication of indifference. She knew the Gore-Booths disapproved of her politics and were embarrassed at her role in the rebellion and she avoided attracting attention to them. She has been often accused of abandoning her daughter, as though Maeve was flung out on the roadside and left to fend for herself. In fact Maeve was brought up in luxury among the Gore-Booths in Sligo and was sheltered from the dangers and hardships that attended her mother. She had musical talent and the family paid for a musical education, but she decided to become a gardener and was sent to a college in England.

After Constance's death Stasko would bemoan his step-sister's good fortune in comparison with his own struggles to earn a living. In later years Maeve considered an approach from a publisher to write a life of her mother. 'What I should aim at is to convey a true idea of her character,' she wrote to Josslyn, 'which, however much we disapproved of her actions, was really a very fine one.'

Constance continues:

> You are so encouraging about my poetry, and a little bird tells me all the time that it's twaddle, and I laugh at myself and so on and inflict it on you. Now I am arriving at the 'wall' and so must pull up. I hope you like being a 'respectable friend' (see preface to this letter).

It appears from a letter from Eva wrote to Father Albert, received on 6 March, that she was able to make her first visit to Aylesbury in 1917 at the end of February or the beginning of March.

19

'WHERE I WOULD LIKE TO BE...'

Although she found the lined paper difficult to draw on and the pencils rough Constance worked hard in the early months of 1917 to produce a series of evocative images. *Where I Would Like to Be* is a self-portrait sitting on a rock at the seashore like a figure in a Celtic romance with the peak of Knocknarea visible across Sligo Bay.

When we compare the pictures with Eva's poetry it is clear that the shared landscapes of childhood sustained the sisters all through their lives. *Where I Would Like to Be* could serve as an illustration for Eva's early poem, 'From the West Coast':

Where I Would Like to Be

> Fearless the sea-pink grows on the bare stone,
> Her wan face lifted to the wind and wave,
> Even as the Lonely turns to the Alone,
> And the brave soul is rooted in the Brave.

In a picture entitled *Hope* an androgynous angel with features resembling Eva holds a spear above the chest of a prostrate demon. Constance's angels are usually avengers of the robust type. Despite her disapproval of Blake's use of shadow there are similarities with his work in the postures of her mythic figures. She uses heavy plunging lines to add to the drama of the scene.

Some of the sketches she would later develop; others are half-finished images like scenes glimpsed in a dream. A female scout on horseback in a Sligo landscape is another recurring image. The more she draws the finer the detail and the hatched lines add to the solidity of the horse. She relished the image of a free woman on horseback. Yeats wrote to her in 1895 after a fall from a horse, referring to her as 'Sligo's wild huntswoman.'

Hope

Many drawings depict episodes from Irish stories and songs. *The Beggar Maid* is a carefree girl on the branch of a tree. She completes the sequence with an iconic image of St. Patrick on a rock in the sea. The Blue Bird appears as a symbol of freedom in pictures and poems:

> Floating on dream-bespangled wings
> My Blue Bird comes to me,
> One patterned locks shut Heaven and jail,
> She only holds the key.

'The Blue Bird' marks an end to poetry for the moment. The images on the following pages depict figures from Celtic mythology – Maeve and

Cuchulainn. She draws on the myth underlying *The Death of Fionavar* and combines it with Christianity in *The Death of Naoise*. Deirdre laments her dead lover as Jesus appears on the left of the picture. The emphasis is on strong female characters from Celtic mythology – *Medbh* is a sturdy warrior queen with spiked shield and staff, a strong face with hair in ringlets, her head radiating light. Deirdre and the Sons of Uisnu are featured and the lovers Diarmuid and Grainne who sought refuge from a jealous king on the slopes of Ben Bulben.

My blue bird

Despite the poor paper and the ruled lines the images are dramatic, moving and evocative. A rough sketch of a woman rising from a breach in a prison wall provides a template for a more polished version in the second journal. Some pages resemble sketches for a performance similar to the drawings she produced for Casimir's plays, but these dramas are performed inside the mind.

Dr S.F. Fox's initials

Dr Fox took a keen interest in the artistic activity of her famous prisoner and inspected the journal and its contents. The first appearance of her initials in tiny red ink on 16.02.1917 appears at the top of the page facing the drawing of *Deirdre*. She repeats the exercise on 21.02 near another image of *Deirdre* playing chess with her lover.

Perhaps she was busy as the next initial appears three weeks later on 13.03 opposite the *The Death of Naoise*. It would be naive to imagine that some empathy developed between the two strong women. Miss Fox must have been aware that many of the drawings had a deeper significance other than the merely decorative. Whatever her thoughts she dutifully inserted her initials in the journal at weekly and fortnightly intervals. The letters in tiny red ink are barely noticeable; she was complying with her duty to supervise her prisoner, but at least she tried to do it in an unobtrusive way.

'Where I Would Like to Be...'

On 6 March, George Cave wrote to inform Timothy Healy that Constance could enjoy an extra visit a month with her sister. Despite official denials the gradual pressure from family and allies was beginning to show results. Eva immediately passed on the news to her mother and Josslyn. Lady Gore-Booth wrote to her son on 12 March:

> Eva said yesterday that she has got a fortnightly visit thanks greatly to Mr. Healy who has been awfully 'kind and takes no end of trouble' to help, she says it doesn't sound much, but it will make a great difference to Con as she loves visits and counts the days to them, she says the ordinary convicts only get <u>one</u> visit in four months. Eva hoped to go yesterday if her pass came in time, she says Con is so extraordinary plucky but it's an awful life.[244]

The letter displays concern for her daughter with an air of detachment from the whole business. Eva sent a note to Josslyn on 13 March about the extra visit and suggested that he might visit his sister if he was coming to England in the spring. 'The weather is still appalling. Never remember such a bitter winter.'

On 23 March, Prison Commissioner Dryhurst visited Aylesbury and met Constance. She requested a journal with unlined paper for her drawings. Dryhurst reported to Troup:

> Countess Markievicz is allowed additional privileges as regards letters and visits to those given under the ordinary rules. She is allowed to write and receive a letter, and to have a visit, every month, and to have an additional special visit every month from her sister.
>
> She has been given special permission to engage in literary composition on the understanding that it does not relate to Prison life and conditions and to political matters, and she is furnished with a notebook for the purpose. At my visit to the prison on the 23rd instant she told me that she had made various pen and ink drawings in the book to illustrate her poems, and asked if she might have a book containing plain paper, - instead of the ordinary ruled paper, as it is easier to draw upon. This request will be granted.[245]

The new journal was of better paper than the first and the absence of lines allowed her to improve the quality of her work. She continues to use the old journal for experiments while starting the new book with improved versions of earlier pictures. She begins with the questing woman on Eva's bookplate and there is a second attempt to render Cuchulainn's duel with Ferdia. Many of the drawings are concerned with death, especially Fionavar and Deirdre, but there are also dramatic images of a giant female breaking open a prison wall and a slender woman alighting on Knocknarea from a winged horse. She illustrates many of Eva's poems, providing an especially ornate page for 'Survival'.

Her writing often strikes a similar mystical tone to Eva's, but at times she strikes out on her own. Page 22 begins a sequence of poems combined an elaborate imagery of winged horses and wild nature including a self-portrait of the artist at the seashore. The scenes are reminiscent of the work she produced for *The Death of Fionavar*, but her technique has much improved.

> They drink at the sacred fountain
> That wells from the storm-cloud's breast,
> Ere they scale the magical mountain
> And poise on the sun's bright crest.

The ocean and seabirds evoke a sense of space and freedom as she gazes through the stone walls to the landscape of her childhood. The magical atmosphere is redolent of the poetry of the Celtic Renaissance and AE's 'singing birds':

> The purple blue of the heather
> The greeny blue of the sea
> Where the clouds and the waves cling to
> Ere they melt in Eternity.

Some lines show signs of revision, but it was difficult to change words entangled with illustrations. The third page ends with a picture of Constance mounting a winged horse to fly away to the land of heart's desire.

> And thoughts that are
> winged and immortal
> Like moths round its radiance flit.

Not all the pages are as accomplished – many are sketches like the work produced

Prison breakout

in her art school years. Towards the end of the book she includes a sketch of Clare Annesley as St. Francis to illustrate a poem by Eva:

To C.A.

I know you for the Umbrian
monk you are,
Brother of Francis and
the sun and rain,
Brother of every silver pilgrim star,
And the white oxen on
the golden plain.

Clare Annesley is portrayed as a saint among flowers and stars while St. Francis has a panel to himself in a pastoral setting surrounded by animals with a seagull perched on his hand.

Stasko wrote a long letter to Eva on 4 March 1917. He was still at his desk in Archangel, engaged in translation work for the Russian Navy. Casimir was in Kiev and liable to be returned to military service:

They Drink at the Sacred Fountain

> Father is going to be taken again, but only for home service – it is very hard for him as he has never been himself again since the terrible four months in the Carpathians.[246]

Like his stepmother he could not mention politics in letters. After the war he intended to return to Ireland or England since his childhood in Ireland made him an outsider in Russia. Constance was always eager for news of her Polish family and we can be sure Eva passed on Stasko's news. As the letter made its passage from the north of Russia to London, soldiers in Petrograd refused to shoot demonstrators. The Russian Revolution was entering a critical phase that would destroy the foundations of the world on which the Markievicz family depended.

Eva was in communication with Father Albert in early March.

> I hope the Dublin Corp. [Corporation] will send the resolution to Sir
> G. Cave directly it's passed as he's still 'considering.' There is only one

slight inaccuracy which is 'but all convicts are entitled to these after a certain period.' I understand that ordinary convicts here never get monthly visits & letters and the association they get is not with their friends but with the chance one of prison.... I have also softened down my own statement as one imagines there might be a few others and one doesn't want to abuse unnecessarily any poor waifs, but my sister was <u>very</u> emphatic about the conversation.... I saw my sister last week & we were talking of you and she wanted especially to be remembered affectionately to you.[247]

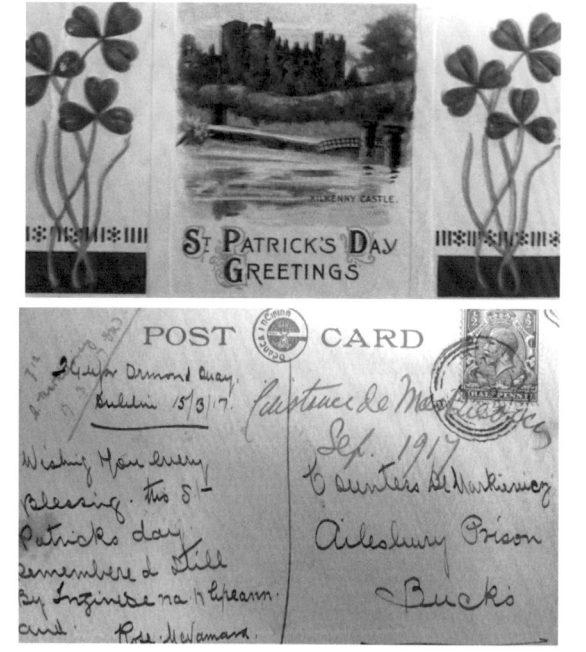

St Patrick Day cards

Father Albert wrote to Eva on 24 March with news that Dublin's Lord Mayor had called a public meeting in the Mansion House to decide on a resolution seeking an amnesty. He assured her that 'we are not forgetting the daily visit to Madam' – three resolutions from public bodies demanding a daily visit were needed before the Home Secretary could consider it.[248]

He mentioned sending a shamrock to Constance for St Patrick's Day, but this may be a reference to a postcard. She was allowed to receive cards for the national holiday.

Eva could now visit for forty-five minutes each fortnight. Susan Mitchell had some good news for Josslyn on 27 March. She found a permanent job for Bessie Lynch with a Miss Boland, sister of John Pius Boland MP for South Kerry, another old friend of Constance. Josslyn appears to have made another visit to Dublin to judge from Susan's note on 29 March:

I think your journey to Dublin has been useful. I hear no unpleasant stories now. I scotched one recently in Trinity told me by a poor person who was much troubled by feeling obliged to believe it.[249]

Father Albert was again in contact with Eva on 30 March – he was glad to hear that Constance's health was better and she was 'in splendid spirits'. The remark confirms that Constance had been feeling the effects of the severe winter and mental isolation. There is no mention in the official documents of her poor health in early 1917. 'I intend asking the Governor of the prison to allow her to receive a little book which I would like her to read,' Father Albert wrote. 'I am sure he won't object, it is called "Mysteries of the Mass in Reserved Prayers".' He was sure of the inevitability of Constance's release and hoped she would visit the Capuchin Friary on Church Street 'where she has such good friends. She knows it well as she often came here to assist personally the poor and destitute...'[250]

Around this time Constance encountered a new convict whom she recognized as Mrs Alice Wheeldon, convicted in March 1917 on a charge of attempting to assassinate the Prime Minister. Constance was delighted to meet a fellow rebel and immediately broke the rule of silence.

'Oh, I know you,' she called. 'You're in for trying to kill Lloyd George.'

'But I didn't,' protested the lady as the warders hustled her away. Mrs Wheeldon was telling the truth; she was a socialist who helped young men to escape conscription by providing a safe house. The charge of attempted murder was concocted by police spies on behalf of the British Government to damage the anti-war movement. Constance made no further mention of her so we must surmise they were kept apart. Mrs. Wheeldon later went on a hunger strike in Aylesbury and was moved to Holloway Prison.

The encounter gave Esther an insight into Constance's character:

> When she told me the story, with some lurid remarks on the politician concerned, I said to her: 'You know very well you wouldn't hurt a hair of his head yourself. Now what would you do to him if he was wounded and on your own doorstep?'
>
> 'Take him in and look after him, of course,' she said promptly, but not too pleased to have been made to admit the undramatic truth. Her hatred never went beyond words: they, I admit, were emphatic and bitter enough at times. But if I had the misfortune to be her enemy, I would have trusted myself personally, to her without hesitation.[251]

Esther's estimation can be interpreted as the generous remark of a friend, but she had a keen judge of character and was anxious to present an accurate view of Constance in contrast to what she saw as the condescending and demeaning approach of her first biographer, Sean O'Faolain. Her assessment of Constance as motivated by humanitarian concerns stands in contrast to the image of a bloodthirsty virago.

The campaign to allow Constance association was gaining support. Claims in the United States that she was ill-treated caused anxiety in British official circles. The issue gave ammunition to Irish-Americans who attempted to keep the United States out of the war. The Foreign Office was concerned to receive a deciphered message on 26 March from a Mr. Barclay, in charge of the British Embassy in Washington:

> Private. Information has been received by influential Irish here that Countess Markievicz is being ill-treated in Aylesbury prison. Complaint is that she is being made to do menial work and placed in cells with lowest criminals. An agitation will shortly be begun in the Press.
>
> If it were possible after investigation to afford her better treatment and I could be informed of the fact I think I might prevent agitation in the Press which would be undesirable at this moment.

Lord Hardinge in the Foreign Office wrote immediately to Troup:

> My dear Troup,
>
> I have no doubt that the idea that Countess Markievicz is being ill-treated is without foundation and I do not therefore see how we could authorize Barclay to say after investigation she is to be accorded better treatment. Perhaps, however, you might give me some facts which could be judiciously used by Barclay to avert the threatened agitation. It is most important just now that there should be no fly in the ointment.

Hardinge replied to Troup the following day with a letter rehearsing the line adopted by S.F. Fox in February:

> You may safely tell Barclay that there is no foundation for the statement that the Countess Markievicz is suffering any ill-treatment. She was employed at first in sewing, but, on her asking for more energetic work she was employed in the kitchen. She is not placed in a cell with other prisoners, but has a cell for her sole use.... She has the privilege of much more visits and letters than other prison-

ers, she also has facilities for literary composition, writes poetry and makes drawings.[252]

On 2 April, President Wilson made a speech before the joint houses of Congress urging the United States to go to war to make the world safe for democracy. The United States declared war on the Central Powers on 6 April, raising hopes among Irish nationalists that Britain would have to introduce Home Rule for Ireland. The campaign continued to remind the public of the remaining Irish prisoners and kept alive hopes that they would be released. But it was all far from Constance and the confined world of her cell.

Satyr

20

'The Brave Soul'

Father Albert wrote to Eva on 3 April informing her of communications from public bodies about Constance 'to tell her she is not forgotten.'[253] He was in regular contact with Tom Kelly, a Sinn Féin Alderman on Dublin Corporation. Constance continued to use the lined journal for occasional writing. Easter Sunday fell on 8 April in 1917 and she marked the anniversary of the Rising with a poem:

> **Easter Week (in jail) 1917**
> Dead hearts, dead dreams, dead days of ecstasy,
> > Can you not live again?
> > Nay, for we never died.
> > We thrilled the strings of time
> > And woke wild echo in the deathless hills
> > Lighting one star before we passed into
> > The golden circle of Eternity.

Despite the brave words of waking echoes 'in the deathless hills,' the poem has a resigned tone of one who longed to be in Eternity along with her friends. On the anniversary of the Rising the Irish Citizen Army held a defiant demonstration outside Liberty Hall and Helena Molony hoisted a banner from the roof. The banned tricolour was also displayed over the College of Surgeons, according to the *Irish Opinion* of 14 April, 'where Madame Markievicz was in command.' Eva wrote to Helena Molony:

> My sister was delighted with your photo, sent you her love & thanks. I saw her Saturday & gave her all news & I showed her picture post card and things & she was greatly pleased ... she is splendid, working better & in health too.... She is always frightfully interested in all

news of L. Hall & all its activities & is in splendid spirits and full of courage – I am very hopeful too...²⁵⁴

Cumann na mBan issued an appeal to the newspapers in April to keep before the public the Irish prisoners in England. The letter claimed the public were misinformed about conditions; their statement was based on letters, interviews and prison authorities:

> The prisoners wear Convict clothes stamped with the broad arrow. Their heads are cropped. They are not allowed to shake hands with relatives and a warder is always present during visits. They live on prison food, are allowed no supplies from outside, have only <u>one hour's</u> exercise and are kept in their cells after work. They have to rise at 5.30, are compelled to do monotonous work such as mailbag or mat making, and as lights are out at 8.00 in spite of promises they have practically no time for reading or literary work.²⁵⁵

The letter drew special attention to Constance 'only allowed association with the lowest criminals.'

Father Albert had news for Eva on 25 April of a Grand High Mass for the dead of Easter Week in Mount Argus. It went ahead despite the suppression of public commemorations by the military authorities:

> I suppose you have heard that Mr Partridge has been released on account of delicate health. We are hoping he may soon be able to return to Ireland, when he does, he will be able to help us do more for Madame.²⁵⁶

The next surviving letter from Constance to Eva is dated 14 May 1917 with no explanation for the gap of two and a half months. There are no further references to a review of the court-martial or an enquiry into her sentence; Constance appears to have become resigned to prison, although she must have hoped that she would one day be released. Prison life consisted of the predictable round of preparing food in the kitchen, scrubbing worktops and tables interspersed with walks in the courtyard. She had the refuge of her inner life and increased the number and quality of drawings. There was also the comfort of visits to the chapel and talks with Father Scott.

> Dearest Old Darling, - When I came up to my cell after seeing you I found this old blue sheet, the bird's own colours! so I begin at once.

Eva's drawing of an angel

I loved your drawings. They are quite wonderful. You have a wonderful gift for a line and a great imagination. All you need is the knack of wagging a pen and that is practice. You want to go on and *on* and *on*. Your figures have such grace and life. Do bring more next time.

Did I ever thank Reginald [Roper] for his Easter card with its tri-colour messages? I *loved* it and those cards of good pictures are such a help to look at.

I want you to send the following messages to Father Albert: he was such a wonderful friend.

[*eleven lines deleted by the Censor*]

I neglected this epistle to the 'Bird's Nest' all Sunday, for I suddenly got a craze to work out Clare's bookplate and it came out much nicer. I've started Esther's too, and I've got some more ideas for it and it is coming out better than I expected. I am going to do your birthday card all over again. I was really rather seedy and that is really why I went off into the wild smudging that you saw. I cannot wag a pen monotonously unless I am very fit, and I am feeling fine to-day.

I have some of Gertrude's primroses, some roses and carnations in my cell and I talk nonsense to them and they are great company.

Suddenly I heard you shouting at me this morning. I wondered so what you were trying to tell me, for I couldn't hear. One's imagination plays one such odd tricks.

Last night I dreamt too, such a strange beautiful dream. I was in an artist's house. He was a sculptor – German or Norwegian I think – and everything was very, very old, simple and massive. The windows were long, low slits with tiny panes, like some palaces in the times of the Huns and Goths, and the only picture there was of a girl, all in blue, with a mushroom hat of iridescent blue feathers, yellow-gold hair and a pale face. While I was looking at it, the figure suddenly looked down at a paper lying in its lap, and I realized that it was you! There were such lovely lilies growing in carved stone jars in that house and through the windows the sun shone on trees and a river.[257]

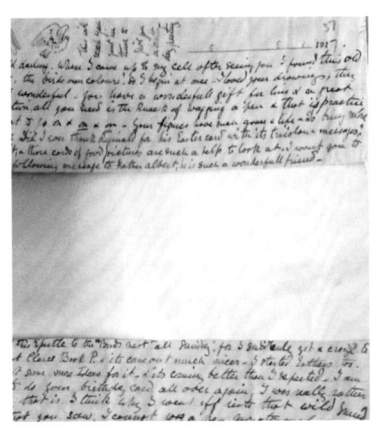

Mutilated prison letter

Constance's dreams often have the quality of pictures. If she had access to watercolours the dream would have made a striking image. She may have been dreaming a scene from Eva's unpublished historical novel, *On Bloodstained Wings*, set in northern Italy at the time of the Barbarian invasions.

> I am still reading Blake diligently and I like the two you quoted immensely and I too was struck by the prophecy. Do you know 'the Song of Liberty?' It ends with: - 'Empire is no more and now the lion and the wolf shall cease.' I wonder if that is a prophecy too? I don't understand anything else in it from beginning to end! Tiriel, Har and Heva etc. also puzzle me much. I suppose they are really only fancy names for quite commonplace articles.
>
> I have just been given F. Albert's gifts, so please say 'Thank you a thousand times' and tell him I love the beads in my own rebel colours! No one who has not been in jail can realise what a joy it is to get a coloured picture post-card! The *Life of S. Francis* too looks awfully interesting.
>
> I am already looking forward to your next visit in the flesh. They are like flashes of sunlight. Your letter still smells delicious. I have it here under my nose.

Constance treasured the letters from Eva and carried them with her through the years of turmoil until her death in 1927.

I wonder so who is acting 'tail' and who 'dog' in Dublin now. The younger generation of rebels will have a great chance now of building up and doing things for the country. I have great faith in the young.

These last few days the trees have simply flung out their green leaves. They did it at night, so that I should not learn their secret! The one thing I am learning here is to watch everything closely, whether it is trees or blackbeetles, birds or women.

The sparrows are delightful – like men at their best. Someone once said 'the more I know men, the more I love my dog,' and I think I rather agree. Dogs don't lie: I don't suppose birds do....

The letter drifts into inconsequential comments – she is rambling on paper. Apart from the intensity of her imaginative life she could find little to say about the monotonous routine of the prison. The lines show the numbing effect of the lack of stimulating conversation on her brain.

Dusk is coming on and the B.B. will have finished pecking at her evening meal by now and is probably preening her feathers and wondering what I am doing.

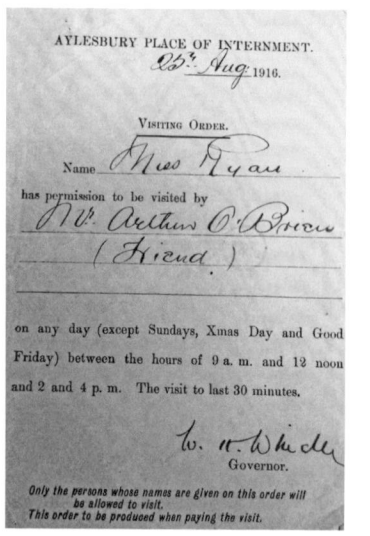

Aylesbury visitor pass

Again another day! And I don't know why I have delayed so long over this. Laziness and dullness I suppose, but really, if you come to think of it, I have nothing to talk about, only vague nonsense. The Chapel was a treat this morning, with the smell of the lilies. How I love the smell of them! I think they are your flower.

(Saturday) I have just seen the Governor. Miss Emily Norgrove wants to visit me. Of course I'd love to see her, but I don't want her visit to interfere with you. (I wish people would go to *you* about visiting me and let *you* arrange. I'm so afraid of someone getting your pass – by accident) It's so impossible for me to arrange and I only want what and who is convenient to you.

Naturally I am delighted to see any friends. There is only a week now till I see you. You probably won't get this till afterwards. I have written one more verse to the B.B. It ends in the middle of a sentence. Here it is. Next verse not done enough to send.

'The Brave Soul'

> Then my soul strikes the magical key-note
> And the circle of wonder is born
> When all beautiful thoughts that are free float
> In a vortex out to the dawn.

'I am sorry for the Censor,' she adds in a flash of mischief as if imagining the man poring over the lines for hidden meanings in his dusty office. The letter has a meandering quality as she searches for something new to write, but the monotony of prison life settles like ash on the soul. And then she rallies:

> By day I dream all sorts of vague ideas and theories about sounds, all sounds being musical notes. Echo will only call back to you when you pitch your voice on certain notes. Certain notes are re-echoed by dogs, who howl if you play to them on the violin or piano or sing them. There is a certain pitch that carries best in every different Hall. I think that there is a lot of natural magic in sounds.
>
> That's an awful nice photo of your drawing. I wish Esther were in the room too.
>
> The 'brown wind of Connaught' is blowing. He will kiss you for me and ruffle your curls at sundown. He passes here on his way from Ireland. There is a small sycamore here in the garden. It's not very 'paintable.' I am having an egg for breakfast! Alice Milligan's card was prophetic, only it's not a 'duck!' They say there was another air raid. I hope you were not alarmed or deafened.

Despite her attempts at cheerfulness the letter lapses into disjointed sentences and weariness. She puts her hopes in the younger generation of rebels as if consigning herself to the former generation. She does not seem aware of the Longford bye-election on 9 May, won by the Sinn Féin candidate, Joseph McGuinness, a prisoner in Lewes Gaol. Lloyd George needed to make it appear that England was making an effort to resolve the 'Irish Problem.' On 21 May he announced an Irish Convention of all interested parties in Dublin to make proposals on Home Rule. These stirrings had little influence on Constance as she entered her second year of imprisonment.

Casimir was now in Moscow, working with a Polish theatre company. He found some of his friends from Kiev and Petersburg were in the revolutionary government. Despite the distance he was still eager to help as he showed in a letter to Josslyn on 2 June:

I am very anxious to know how is Constance, is there any chance for her just now and could it be wise for me to try to do something through our new government? So let me know what you think...[258]

The fast-changing political events made little impression on Constance. She wrote on 9 June, a short time after Eva visited with flowers.

> Beloved Old Darling, - How short your visit always seems and how much must always remain unsaid, unless the powers that be provide me with a brand-new and absolutely clean and unwritten tablet for my poor old memory...
>
> Now don't work and worry yourself to death about me, you old blessing. I am wonderfully content and I know that all is going well with Kathleen and that there is nothing I can do in my own country that others can't do as well.
>
> The hours slip by, like rosary beads of dragons' teeth, with a big slowing opal bead to mark the rhythm – your visit. Don't I drivel?
>
> It is really very curious that you should write a poem on and give a lecture on S. Francis. For I have been thinking of him a great deal and thinking out pictures of him. I could find out very little about him here, then F.A. sent me his life – 'out of the blue' as they say – and then your letter came.
>
> I have copied your poem and decorated it already. It's very beautiful, the poem.

St Francis

The poem was 'The Sad Years', Eva's dedication to the poet Dora Sigerson Shorter who was deeply affected by the events of Easter Week.

> I am so interested in little Doyle's horoscope. You must make it out for Janey, his mother, for me to give her if ever I get out!
>
> What you poetically term my 'ascetic way of living' certainly has great compensations. I think that something I might call 'the subconscious self' develops only at the expense of your body – of course with the consent and desire of the will. To develop it, it is necessary to cut yourself off from a great deal of human intercourse, to work hard and eat little, and as your subconscious self emerges, it comes

more and more in tune with the subconscious soul of the world, in which lie all the beauties and subtleties you speak of...[259]

Constance was forced into learning the benefits of the ascetic life. When she was outside prison she was immersed in the day-to-day work of the political world with only her art as a tenuous link to the 'subconscious self'. Eva had mastered how to combine social activism with creative writing.

> I think too, that any friendships worth having have their roots on this plane: and, too, that this is the secret of the monastic orders and of the hermits and philosophers from the beginning of the world, especially of the Eastern mystics.
>
> It used to puzzle me so when I read of girls – like Maud's sisters – becoming Carmelite nuns, and I could never see either the sense or the use of it. Since I have been here I understand it absolutely, and I know that for people with a vocation the compensation far outweighs the things you give up.
>
> You ask me if the flowers last. They are wonderful. One lily – I threw it away on Monday – lasted one month and two days. I think it knew that I loved it. I am always going to keep a flower or leaf in water from one visit to another.
>
> I am glad that I am President of so many things! I should always advise societies to choose their presidents from among jail-birds, as presidents are always such a bore and so in the way on committees! I always rather liked taking the chair, for the fun of bursting through all the red tape: and when remonstrated with, I could always corner them by saying, 'ridiculous *English* conventions! Surely an *Irish* Committee is not going to be bound by them?' Now, they'll be able on all the committees in Ireland, to waste all their precious time tying up their minds and other people's in red tape. Notices of motion about rubbish taking the place of the divine inspiration of the moment, and then all that twaddle about amendments and addenda and procedure of every kind!
>
> I wonder whether you would get dignified and shocked? It is such years since we served on committees together: not since we went out to force a Suffrage Bill through Parliament.'

It was just twenty years since Eva and her sisters set up a Suffrage Committee in Sligo in 1897.

I have no ambition to have a vote for an English Parliament, and don't suppose I would use it. I don't think that Parliaments are much use anyhow. All authority in a country always seems to get into the hands of a clique and permanent officials. I think I am beginning to believe in anarchy. Laws work out as injustice, legalised by red tape.

You have such a lot of real good news and interesting gossip in your letter. You always manage to tell me about the things I most want to hear about. The Fianna news was very cheering, and isn't the Doctor [Kathleen Lynn] splendid? – when one considers that her paying patients must almost all be in the enemy's camp! I call it awfully plucky and fine of her to come out in public the way she does. It's wonderful too the amount she does for the poor. I feel so proud of having introduced her to the real Ireland. One has such wonderful luck sometimes. If another doctor hadn't suddenly lost her mother, I should never have met ours.

I think my handwriting is getting awful. I think the sort of work I do is bad for writing...

Do you ever hear of Mrs Connolly and her daughter, Ina, great friends of mine? Ask for news of them, next time you write to the doctor or any of them. Ina was a splendid girl. Ask too if the 'Feis' has come off yet.

Do you remember the verse labelled 'Introduction' at the head of Blake's *The Gates of Paradise?* Judges ought to take it to heart.

The verse from the prologue begins:

> Mutual Forgiveness of each Vice,
> Such are the Gates of Paradise.

The quote reminds us of the enduring influence of William Blake and the link with Yeats and Theosophy. The letter rambles in a stream of consciousness similar to the way that Constance sometimes chattered in daily life. The historian, Dorothy Macardle, recalled such conversations in her review of the *Prison Letters*: 'It is difficult to stop quoting, because to quote is to hear Madame's chatter again, to remember her refreshing, life-giving companionship, like that of a rapid brook by a dusty road.'[260]

I am already beginning to get excited over your next visit and to wonder whom you are going to bring. If wonder if any of my visitors will ever get into jail themselves? Take my advice, and *don't you*, for you are not strong enough. Some people it would be very good for. I am sure that six months of it would do P------- a lot of good!

I saw a lovely moon the other night, and in my mind's eye began to play billiards with it. I rolled my mind into a great ball and cannoned off the moon into the B.B.'s window. If you think of it, the moon is the apex of so many triangles.

I would have loved to hear your lecture on 'Peace of St. Francis.' You can tell me something about it, if you've room, in your next letter. It's so funny to me to realise that I never wrote letters until I got into jail! And it's really quite an amusing game! You're so awfully good. I sometimes find it on my conscience that I give you so much to do. I must be an awful nuisance. Don't wear yourself out, that's all.

Did you ever visit the catacombs in Rome? The old paintings must be so interesting. I have just been reading about them. I have always longed to go to Rome. That and the Pyramids and perhaps the Parthenon, which you would almost have to pass; I always feel I know these places quite well.

This morning, when the flutter of wings came, at nine o'clock, I was peeling Swedes. They, you may not know, are a kind of turnip largely eaten by sheep! We have been eating so many lately that I feel I shall soon begin to 'baa-baa.' But they are very good indeed. You should try them, though perhaps as a veg. (vegetarian) you already know them.

Now, darling, the limit is reached and there is no space for love which would require a very big one and remembrance to all friends. I hope Esther will be coming again soon. I long to show her the book. I know she would understand.

Things were to change dramatically during the following week and we will never know which book she was referring to in her last letter from Aylesbury Women's Prison.

21

'She Is the People's Countess'

There was no public expectation of the release of the prisoners in early June 1917. Irish members at Westminster were asking questions on prison conditions and the possibility of amnesty in parliament on an almost weekly basis. A meeting in Dublin's Mansion House on 21 May called for the release of the 122 Irish prisoners in England. The meeting supported a proposal by Kathleen Lynn: 'That we draw particular attention to the case of Countess Markievicz, who is in Aylesbury convict prison, England, and is denied all association except with criminals...'[261]

On the same day Lloyd George announced he was calling an Irish Convention where Unionists and Nationalists could sort out their differences. Laurence Ginnell reminded the Government that the 1916 rebels in prison should have a place in the convention. 'The time had not yet come to reopen the cases,' Henry Duke replied. Despite official discouragement it would appear that Constance sensed her time of liberation was coming closer. A picture from early June has a flame-haired woman striding along a prison corridor with sword in hand; a dove is perched in the other hand with outstretched wings. S.F. Fox dutifully inserted her initials and date on the opposite page.

On Friday, 15 June, Bonar Law, Chancellor of the Exchequer announced an amnesty 'without reservation of the prisoners now in confinement in connection with the rebellion of 1916.' They were officially pardoned on 16 June when the King remitted the balance of their

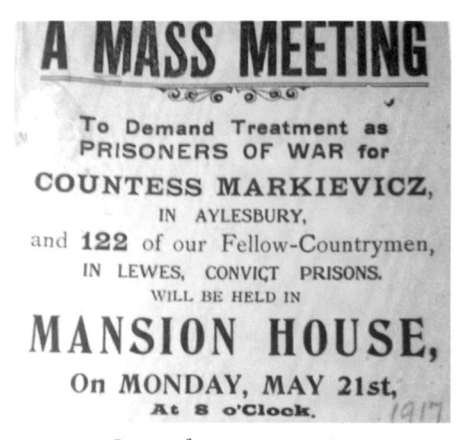

Poster for mass meeting

sentences. The men were moved by train on Sunday evening to Holyhead with the authorities attempting to keep their movements secret to avoid demonstrations. In spite of the lack of information thousands of people waited overnight at Kingstown ferry and Westland Row railway station.

Esther Roper recalled the events of the weekend:

> Next day all the men went home, and a courteous Home Office official arrived to say Eva would be allowed to go next day to Aylesbury and bring her sister away.[262]

We can imagine the disbelief, the delight and the laughter now that Constance was about to be free. During the long year since the Rising it must have seemed at times to Eva and Esther that Constance's incarceration was permanent and they would have to take the train from Euston Station year after year to the same dreary waiting room. They could expect to watch Constance lose heart as her spirit was whittled away by prison routine. And now, suddenly, at a stroke of a pen, all was reversed.

The male prisoners returned to Ireland on Sunday night and Monday morning while Constance had to wait one more day for release. Presumably there was no arrangement for release from Aylesbury on a Sunday, but the delay meant that she was the last prisoner of the 1916 Rising to be released, a symbolism many would remark on in the years ahead.

On Monday morning Eva and Esther set out:

> ... armed with all the gay clothes we could beg or borrow, we went and were admitted to help her to dress. Soon, Constance, herself again, thin and beautiful in a blue dress instead of that twice too large, hideously ugly cotton garment supplied by a paternalistic Government, left that prison for ever.

Esther neglected to mention that Constance smuggled out a white apron among her underclothes, a souvenir from her year in prison. She also brought a bundle of cards and letters, especially those from Eva, and the two precious journals with the images of her inner journey.

Did Dr Fox come to the reception area to say goodbye to the notorious prisoner who had taken up so much of her time? Esther has no mention of her presence so she probably left the procedure to one of the senior wardens. Most likely she breathed a sigh of relief as she signed the release forms. Selina Fox would remain in charge in Aylesbury until the end of the

Freedom by Constance

war when she returned to her former post at the Medical Mission in Bermondsey. She rarely spoke about her time in the prison service; she once remarked that Aylesbury was an interesting experience, but not a very congenial one which she left 'with great thankfulness.'[263] She bought a house in Leicestershire with her companion, Mrs. Ursula Graham. After the latter's death she returned to her beloved Bermondsey Mission where she died on 27 December 1958.

Helena Molony, Kathleen Lynn and Marie Perolz came from Dublin to add to the welcoming party. They travelled to a city recovering from a Zeppelin air-raid on East London the previous Thursday that left over a hundred dead. It must have seemed that the world was changing as they waited for Constance in the top floor flat with high windows on Fitzroy Square. Despite the loss of weight Constance was in good health and delighted to be free and amongst her friends.

As a released convict she had to deal with new challenges such as the freedom to open a door without asking permission, going outside for a walk and liberty to speak as often as one pleased. Crowds of well-wishers arrived at Fitzroy Square and reporters from Irish and English newspapers besieged the flat. She appeared intoxicated by her new freedom when she told a journalist:

> I shall keep the red flag flying to the end. I am as determined now as ever I was. I shake you by the hand, but my determination prevents me saying more than that I am quite well, and shall go to Ireland when I have had a rest in London and seen my comrades here.[264]

Constance stayed with Eva on Tuesday and Wednesday. She was on familiar territory; the Slade School of Art and her student haunts were only a few streets away. On Wednesday afternoon she and Eva had tea on the terrace of the House of Commons, accompanied by Alfred Byrne and Jimmy White in top hat and spats. She was celebrating victory over the govern-

'She Is the People's Countess'

Card of horse leaping over prison wall

ment which had sentenced her to death and then condemned her to prison for life. No cup of tea can ever have tasted quite like that one.

On Thursday morning, 21 June, the party undertook the long train journey to Holyhead to catch the evening boat to Dublin. 'It was a strange journey,' Esther wrote. 'We left Euston by the early morning boat-train. Irish men and women sang patriotic songs on the platform, and friendly porters looked on smiling.'[265]

The London Irish crowd sang 'The Soldier's Song' as Constance stood to attention on the platform.

> As the train was leaving, someone called for 'Three cheers for the Countess,' and with a happy gesture, she kissed the bunch of roses she held in her arms and scattered them among her admirers.'[266]

She might well have been on stage, the leading lady in one of Casimir's plays, accepting the plaudits of the audience. She knew well how people appreciated a dramatic gesture.

> When we arrived at Holyhead the platform was packed with people waving flags and singing and cheering wildly. I remember standing by Constance's side trying to get on the gangway of the boat. Her clear voice called out,

> 'Which is the right side for us to get on?'
>
> A coal-black face was thrust out of an engine-room, and with a broad grin replied: 'It's always the right side if you're on it,' and disappeared again amid the laughing cheers of the crowd.
>
> Once in the boat there was nothing but kindness. In the cabin the stewardess provided for Constance and her friends a breakfast including lovely grapes and peaches. They pressed round her full of delight and smiling welcome. Alas! these friendly people were all drowned later on when the boat was torpedoed.
>
> We zigzagged across the water, and at last arrived at Kingstown Harbour, where the people were delirious with excitement and pleasure. It was difficult to catch the train for Dublin.[267]

Constance was the last prisoner to return and the fervour of her welcome surpassed all the others.

> The journey home ... culminated in scenes of enthusiasm as great or surpassing those which had greeted the men. Constance, in her womanhood and particular presence, in her character of rebel leader, befriender of Dublin's poor, and, above all in her imprisonment, had been transformed and, with the released men, became a powerful force in the currents then shaping Irish political life.[268]

Her friend, Ella Young, wrote of the disappointment of the crowd on Monday when she did not return with de Valera and the others: 'Where is the Countess Markievicz?' was the cry. 'We want the Countess.'

> She is not coming into Dublin till tomorrow. There will be a real reception for the Countess. It takes a day to prepare it. She is the people's Countess, and we will give a proper welcome to her.[269]

The boat landed at Kingstown in the late afternoon where welcoming crowds lined the pier. *The Irish Times* reported that young men tried to get into her carriage and fought with railway officials. Constance and her friends intervened and persuaded them to follow in the next carriage. Meanwhile preparations were underway at Westland Row station.

> A short time before the train was due a body of men in civilian attire marched up the platform in military order and halted at a word of command.

The boat train from Kingstown arrived at Westland Row shortly after six o'clock.

> When Madame Markievicz appeared at the carriage door those nearest shook her hand and those behind waved hats and handkerchiefs, cheering all the while. A passage was cleared to the motor car in which Madame Markievicz, her sister, and Dr Kathleen Lynn, took their seats. A command was given to the bodyguards and the motor car, the wagonettes and the crowd moved slowly towards the station exit.[270]

Constance was carried in the same car in which she set out from Liberty Hall to Dublin Castle fourteen months previously. Esther kept a record of the scene:

> Stepping down from the train was like plunging into the waves of the Atlantic – we were swallowed up. The deputations of welcome did their work somehow, and in time 'the Countess' and her friends were placed in cars which were to drive them to Liberty Hall for the official welcome.[271]

Kathleen Tynan witnessed the scene at Westland Row:

> All the Dublin women and babies were out, and small boys were balancing themselves dangerously on the spiked area railings... A little later she (Constance) passed, standing up, holding out her hands to the crowd who were clasping them and kissing them.... A few seconds later she was gone – the crowd swept after her, and the street was empty with the sadness settling down on it of a summer evening in the city.[272]

The streets were lined with people flouting tricolour flags in defiance of the official ban while the parade had contingents from Cumann na mBan, the Irish Citizen Army and the Volunteers. The demonstrations were illegal and participants would usually be punished but the authorities held back. A pipe band waited on the south bank near Liberty Hall. The cavalcade moved down Great Brunswick (now Pearse) Street, into Tara Street and across the Liffey by Butt Bridge to Liberty Hall.

Ella Young provides one of the most exuberant reports of the homecoming. In prose that mimics the language of the Celtic sagas Constance appears a figure from mythology:

> ... the Countess entered Dublin in the midst of a long procession, with banner after banner and brass band; with riders on horseback; with running boys waving branches; with lumbering floats drawn by big slow-footed good-natured Clydesdale horses; with trade-guilds carrying emblems; with public notabilities in uniform; with ragged urchins from the slums – a glad and multitudinous company laughing, shouting and singing.... Upon a float piled high with flowers and greenery the Countess stood, very fair to look on, radiant and slender.[273]

Dublin welcome

'She Is the People's Countess'

For over a year Eva and Esther had worked as visitors, messengers, agitators, counsellors and unpaid secretaries for Constance and now she was moving away from them. From this day on she would belong to the people who greeted her with such fervour. She was their high representative, the repository of their dreams, beloved by the people to an extent that very few figures in history ever achieve. All the barriers of accent, creed and class that separated her from the people were blown away in that emotional, passionate welcome as the open motor car moved through a mass that had begun to think of themselves as a nation.

Esther viewed proceedings from a distance behind the leading car:

> We simply could not move at first. Constance had to stand nearly all the time so that she could be seen by the vast crowds. It seemed as if all of Dublin must be there. It felt hours long before my car arrived at Liberty Hall and I was admitted. Traffic all along the line was controlled by the 'rebel' band, the police most sensibly remaining in the background.[274]

Kathleen Lynn said it was as though they were greeting royalty, but this was no servile crowd gazing at a foreign monarch. The Unionists of Dublin, and there were many of them, pulled down the window shades and blocked their ears. The documentary film, *Mise Eire*, used the scenes of Constance's return to portray a sense of national awakening. The camera sweeps over the sea of faces that merge like grains of sands into a force vaster than themselves. This had become much more than the return of an individual.

The cavalcade stopped at Liberty Hall, partially rebuilt, but still showing the scars of the previous year's bombardment. It was a sombre setting for a homecoming, but symbolic rather than practical. A banner with the words 'Cead Mile Failte' was draped across the entrance; women held flags at the windows. Again it is the outsider, the idealistic Englishwoman, Esther Roper, who provides the most dramatic image of the interior of the building from which Constance started out on the day of her appointment with history:

> When I did get into that shattered building, roofless and windowless, which in the old days had been so full of life, I could feel as real only those sombre figures in mourning – the widows of the men executed in Easter Week – who had come to welcome back their friend.

RETURN OF I.R.A. PRISONERS, JUNE, 1917.
COUNTESS MARKIEVICZ ARRIVES AT LIBERTY HALL, DUBLIN.

Céad Míle Fáilte

It was a highly charged reunion resembling a scene from a Greek drama. Liberty Hall with its charred beams and broken floors formed the background for the widows dressed in black as they waited for the one who had gone to the land of the dead and came back again. Among the widows were Agnes Mallin, Mrs Pearse, Kathleen Clarke, Lillie Connolly, and Maud Gonne. They did not grieve for the deaths of their loved ones or blame Constance for having survived. Her return with her arms full of flowers was a vindication of their sacrifice. The widows were dedicated to the Republic and welcomed her as a companion in struggle.

Constance wrote about the return in a fragment among the Hannah Sheehy-Skeffington papers:

> And so home – to Dublin, to Liberty Hall, blackened and roofless, 'old scenes, old songs, old friends again such as were left … Dublin turned out en masse, itself again. The nightmare over, the dawn breaking... One felon home again.[275]

After some time Constance appeared at a window and tried to speak to the cheering crowd: 'I am going home now to rest in order that I may start work at once.'

Ireland was her home, but she no longer had a dwelling. Josslyn had disposed of Surrey House and St. Mary's was leased. For the immediate future she would stay with Kathleen Lynn at 9 Belgrave Road, Rathmines. On the way they stopped at the College of Surgeons where Maeve Cavanagh ('the poet of the Revolution') presented her with a nosegay of flowers. Detectives and army intelligence officers followed at a discreet distance. There was one more part to the homecoming:

> Her last welcome came from Poppet, for whom over a year's absence had not been enough to obliterate the memory of the sound of a familiar step and voice.[276]

She made a brief appearance to a crowd outside Kathleen Lynn's house. An officer of the British General Staff (presumably in plain clothes) made a note of her short speech:

> I thank you more than I can say for the welcome back to Dublin you have given me – I find Ireland rebel at last (loud cheers)
>
> We shall all go on working until Ireland is Free once more (loud and prolonged cheers and shouts).
>
> I will now only say goodnight to you, but we will meet again tomorrow – the next day - and every day – and we will all go on working until Ireland is a Republic.[277]

On the following morning Kathleen Tynan was amazed to encounter Constance in a fashionable drapery shop:

> We were at another counter a little later when Madame came in with her dog and, standing quite near us, proceeded to buy herself a length of tulle to wear around her neck according to the fashion of the moment.[278]

Constance and Poppet, 1917

Constance made contact with Canon MacMahon of Holy Cross, College, Clonliffe and asked to be received into the Catholic Church. On Sunday, 24 June, she was baptised in Clonliffe College. Eva and Esther, Agnes Mallin and some Dublin friends attended. She adopted the name Anastasia, after a Fourth Century Christian martyr. The name in Greek means Resurrection, one who is reborn, appropriate for a woman who was condemned to death and reprieved. In a telescoped version of the usual progress through the sacraments she received her First Communion with the Sisters of Charity, Upper Gardiner Street shortly afterwards and was confirmed at St. Mary's, Haddington Road.

Some saw her reception into the Catholic Church as a manoeuvre to bring her closer to the majority religion. 'Her acceptance of Ireland was as complete as she could make it,'[279] O'Faolain commented. But we can see from her prison writings and drawings that the conversion was no cynical gesture, but an integral part of her spiritual development. She genuinely accepted the Catholic religion, even if she resisted attempts by individual clerics to dictate in political matters.

'The clergy generally never quite approved of so independent a rebel as Madam,' according to Hannah.

> As to her religion generally I would say she belonged to the Church of St. Francis rather than that of Paul. The ritual, the ceremonies, the music & beauty of the Catholic Church, its art and cultural background attracted the mystic in her. She defended the Socialist Connolly against an attack by a Jesuit, Father McKenna. She held Socialism possible with the Church: individual clerics she often sharply disagreed with. Over her bed was a picture of DaVinci's Christ.[280]

Constance with a nun, 1917

Diana Norman thought she was ahead of her time and in tune with the 'Liberation Theology' of the late twentieth century.[281] Esther considered she was attracted by the mystical richness of the Catholic Church.

Constance was a political celebrity and in constant demand for nationalist ceremonies and public events. She had no income as her property was still legally under her brother's control. Michael Collins, on behalf of the Irish National Aid Association, sent money. She wrote with the acknowledgement: 'I was left with no clothes and could not get at my own money.'[282] In a sense all of nationalist Ireland was her home and she was often on the move. The author has met people whose grandparents told of visits from Constance where she sat in the kitchen with her feet on the stove and smoked cigars like a man.

The Irish Citizen Army welcomed her back into the ranks. On 12 July the new Commandant, James O'Neill wrote from Liberty Hall:

> At the army council meeting of the above held on Monday, 9th July it was decided to ask you to accept the office of Chief of Staff to the army. Which will carry with it the rank of Major and which means that you will be second in command. I may mention that in selecting you for this office the council has not done so as a mark of respect for you nor out of sympathy with you for what you have suffered but simply because they realise your worth as a military officer and they hope you will soon be free to take up your duties as above if you will accept same.[283]

Publicity photo of Constance, 1917

She was happy to accept the promotion although this did not mean a return to a military role as the Irish Citizen Army did not regain the position it held in 1916. Constance identified with the reorganized Irish Volunteers which was transforming itself into the Irish Republican Army. In the months after her release she sometimes signed herself as 'Prisoner 12, Aylesbury, IRA.' Her role would be primarily political apart from training with the Fianna.

Father Albert wrote to Eva on 29 June to say he was sorry to miss her in Dublin:

> I called to see her [Constance] on Wednesday night. She looked splendid ... the awful treatment she received in jail has told on her very much. I hope she will take a rest and care of her health until she is strong again.[284]

Eva replied on 5 July:

> I was very sorry not to have the pleasure of meeting you in Dublin after our long correspondence, especially as I wanted to thank you

for the splendid way you kept me posted in news of great interest to my sister. It was a wonderful welcome she got. I shall never forget the drive through Dublin.

The letter has an intriguing postscript: 'I enclose a little photo I took in Aylesbury. I thought it might amuse you.' Alas, the letter and photograph have long parted company.[285]

People who had been dismissive of Constance in the past came forward to revise their opinions. Lennox Robinson, manager of the Abbey Theatre, who created a parody of her in his 1915 novel, *Young Man from the South*, wrote in early July:

> I don't, you know, see eye to eye with you, there's much I could blame you for but – like Willie Redmond – you never asked anyone to do what you weren't ready to do yourself and I do admire your sincerity and courage.[286]

She was a national celebrity and much sought after for photo opportunities.

REPUBLICAN TRIPLETS.
Constance, Kathleen, and Grace. Born July 1917.

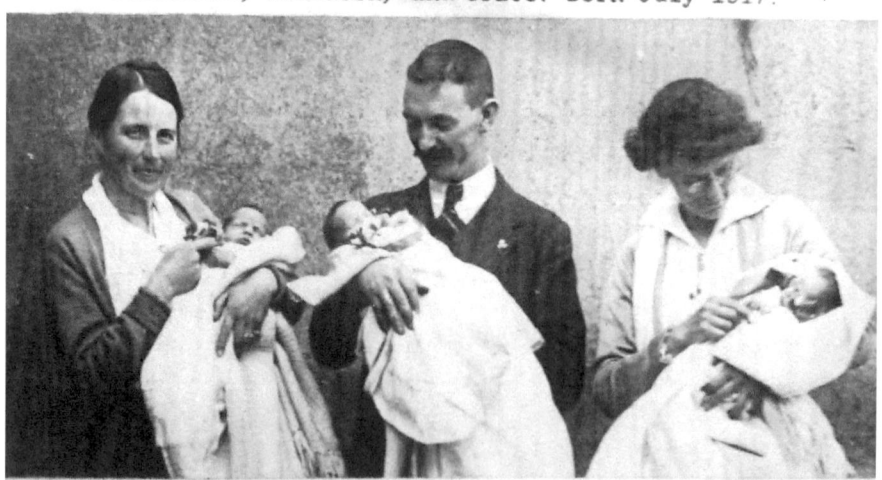

Daughters of Mr. and Mrs. Fullerton - Irish Citizen Army - with Countess Constance de Markievicz, Dr. Kathleen Lynn, and their father, representing Mrs. Grace Plunkett.

Republican triplets – Constance & Kathleen Lynn with babies

It was the 19 July before she got around to writing to Josslyn about the state of her finances:

> Thanks for the accounts. I have been too busy & occupied to think about them 'til today. What has happened to the 300 & something I was to have received when I was in jail?[287]

Apparently he sent an account showing she owed him £145-9-8. She was dumbfounded: 'What's it all for?' The wrangle over money with Josslyn would continue over the summer. She complained of lack of funds on 10 September. Only four days previously Strahan's informed Josslyn that they had moved all her belongings into Laurence Ginnell's house at 143 Leinster Road.

> The National Aid gave me a cheque to 'take a holiday' & I get expenses when I go to speak at meetings & I can get a dinner for 3d at Liberty Hall – pea soup, bread and tea; a much better dinner than you get in jail so I have moved along somehow 'til now, but now I am starting a house again. I want a little cash. Yours, Con.[288]

Josslyn still had loose ends to complete, but at the end of the summer was able to return Constance's chequebook.

Constance's chequebook

In late July she had the sad task of writing to the newly-widowed wife of William Partridge:

> Dear Mrs. Partridge, I was greatly grieved to hear the sad news. Mr. Partridge as you know is the man I have to thank that I am a Catholic and it was never my fate to know a nobler or braver man. I know he

is happier now than he was sick and suffering here. God will bless him. I am writing to ask you if it will be possible to postpone the funeral to Sunday as I don't think I could get down 'til the last train on Sat. night. He would have liked it and I greatly desire to show my respect & affection for him this last chance I shall have in this world. I should esteem it a great favour if you could grant my request.[289]

She never forgot William Partridge and wore around her neck the rosary beads he gave her in the College of Surgeons. After the Rising he was imprisoned in Dartmoor where the prison work and harsh conditions led to a rapid deterioration in health. He was moved to Lewes Prison where he had better treatment and was released on health grounds in April 1917. He went to stay with his family in Ballaghadreen, County Roscommon where he died on 26 July.

Constance delivered the funeral oration in which she described Partridge as 'the purest-souled and noblest patriot Ireland ever had.' She wore her Citizen Army uniform from St. Stephen's Green along with the tunic which belonged to Michael Mallin. Some of the accounts have her firing three shots over the grave.

22

Aftermath

Constance was back in business as never before in the hurry and scurry of politics. She plunged into revolutionary activity with relish and, for the rest of her life, would have no settled home. She invariably carried a sketchbook and continued to paint and draw, but much of the work was political propaganda in response to the War of Independence and Civil War. She painted some fascinating watercolours in Holloway Prison in 1918-19 and during a period in Scotland in the early 1920s, but never again the quantity and quality of work from the long months in Aylesbury.

Eva continued to campaign for her pacifist ideals; shortly after Constance's release her pamphlet, *Rhythms of Art,* was published in London by the League of Peace and Freedom. In the middle of a violent age she stressed the importance of beauty and art with reference to her experience in Ireland:

> Thus the 'Dark Rosaleen' is a far more powerful poem than 'Rule Britannica' because the rhythm that finds vent in rebellion, imperfect as it must be, or else it could not find vent in violence, is still a more subtle and beautiful rhythm than the vibration that expresses itself in the ponderous pomposity and violence of Empire.[290]

Despite increasing pain from cancer she continued to edit *Urania* and write poetic dialogues, pamphlets, poems and prose. She worked hard to complete the meditative work she regarded her greatest achievement: *A Philosophical and Poetical Approach to the Study of Christ in the Fourth Gospel,* published in 1924. At the same time she developed her poetic talent and achieved a classical simplicity in the collections: *The Shepherd of Eternity* in 1924 and *The House with the Three Windows*, with an introduction by Evelyn Underhill, published after her death in 1926. The masthead of *Urania* was adapted to include a quote from her work which remained in place until the final issue in 1940.

Constance maintained the connection with Eva during her years of political agitation and imprisonment, but her energies were devoted to the realization of the Irish Republic in which she believed with a mystical intensity. She continued to write songs, articles and plays as part of the effort to create the republic. With the exception of the watercolours painted in Holloway Prison and the occasional portrait or landscape, most of her artwork was in response to the moment, lacking the depth of the work in Aylesbury. Her attacks on the British Army and the Irish Free State were pasted on lamp-posts and city walls. She reverted to the warrior archetype of Maeve, but retained the sense of the sorrow and pity she learned from her period in Aylesbury.

Some people believe that Constance broke off relations with her family and abandoned her daughter. During the years of prison and life on the

Constance, Maeve and Eva

run it was impossible to maintain any semblance of family life, but the occasional meeting with Maeve, sometimes facilitated by Eva, took place.

She did not visit Lissadell between her visit with Stasko in 1915 and her mother's funeral in 1927. Underneath the brave exterior she feared rejection at a face-to-face meeting. She had abandoned the ancestral and colonial mentality, but through all the upheavals tried to maintain good relations with the family. There was frequent correspondence with Josslyn about family matters, but they found it hard to reconcile their differences. She saw much more of her mother and daughter in the years before her death.

'There was no one ever like her,' she wrote to Esther after Eva's death in 1926.

> She was something wonderful and beautiful, and so simple and thought so little of herself. I don't think she ever knew how much she was to me.
>
> I am so vague and stupid and can't express myself.
>
> But her gentleness prevented me getting very brutal and one does get very callous in a War. I once held out and stopped a man being shot because of her. And she was always there when I was down and out, she and you...
>
> I had always had a funny habit, since Aylesbury, of referring anything I was doing to her. Every sketch I made I wondered how she would like it, and I looked forward to showing it to her. If I saw anything beautiful, I thought of her and wished she was there to enjoy it.

From 1916 onwards writers on the period focused on Constance; R.M. Fox attempted to redress the balance with a chapter on Eva in *Rebel Irishwomen*:

> In life she never desired to dominate; in death she dominates no less by the strength of her belief and the loveliness of her poems.

The sisters were vital and unique figures to people who knew them. George Russell wrote in the mid-1930s:

> When I look back along the aisle of memory I can conjure up the image of Eva Gore-Booth as I saw her a quarter of a century ago, like a star half-hidden in mist ... a little breathless, always in pursuit of the

spirit, just as her sister Constance, was a little breathless in pursuit of her national ideals.

During these years Yeats had little contact with the sisters. The death of Eva in 1926, followed by Constance in July 1927, gave him the impetus to include them in his ruminations on futility and mortality. Soon after the latter's death he began work on a new poem, 'In Memory of Eva Gore-Booth and Con Markiewicz'. He adopted the Polish spelling of her name and called her 'Con' which was only ever used by family and close friends. 'In Memory' has become one of his most popular poems largely because of the fluency of the evocative lines and the image of 'two girls in silk kimonos, both beautiful, one a gazelle.'

Eva and Esther's grave in Hampstead

The opening lines ensured that Yeats' view of the sisters has remained the prism through which many view them. Unfortunately he was not content to use them as symbols of a vanished order, but he went on to excoriate their political beliefs. The phrases 'conspiring among the ignorant' and 'skeleton gaunt/an image of such politics' have become attached to them in the memory of most educated people. D.J. Smith wrote in 1983: '... one may be unable to think of Con otherwise than in the way Yeats left her.' Her first biographer, Sean O'Faolain, thought likewise and followed the template even in the title of his biography *Constance Markievicz: The Average Revolutionary* in 1934.

In the centenary of the Easter Rising we cannot see the sisters in the same way their contemporaries viewed them. To them they were flesh and blood, but to us they are figures of the mind, coming alive in their words and images. They were united by that bond formed in childhood and by their hatred of injustice and oppression. We can never be certain what drove them to struggle for a fairer social system. Part of it was the idealism of the age, part a result of being born into a colonial aristocratic elite and partly an innate sense of fairness. Their aristocratic background gave them the confidence to challenge the power of empire – they knew the hidden places were decisions were made.

Their hatred of empire did not make them enemies of the English people or of England. While feeling deeply Irish they were representative of a strand among the elite who turned against monolithic institutions in search of more human ways to organize society. The reported quip from Casimir that Constance's execution would plunge half of Debrett's into mourning had some validity. They were also part of a remarkable and idealistic generation of social, political and artistic radicals that included William Morris, George Bernard Shaw, Emmeline Pankhurst, Keir Hardie, James Connolly, H.G. Wells, Beatrice Webb and many others.

Constance and Eva worked without stint in different ways to create a society based on free and equal relationships. We live in a different age where some of their aims have been achieved, but which is dysfunctional in many ways. Their belief in their ideals should encourage us to dream beyond what appears possible. We can learn from their creative energy and their idealistic view that people can change the world. Their paths led them far from conventional relationships, but they recognized the importance of family ties which remained strong despite the strains of clashing beliefs. The history and heritage of the Gore-Booth and Markievicz families were of enormous importance in their lives.

Constance was accurate in her prediction that her enemies would make a monster of her while her friends would create a heroine. The desire to give women their rightful place in history has temporarily rebounded against Constance's reputation in that some historians disregard her to make room for others who have been ignored. Much of the criticism directed against her has been based on superficial knowledge and the trend to view things in the simplistic terms of an impatient media culture. She has become an archetypal figure on which people can project their need to denigrate or worship.

But she was much more than a blank canvas and those who take the trouble can discover the passionate idealist who tried to change the world, aware of the high cost in happiness, lost relationships and damaged reputation.

Eva's approach was always more gentle; she absorbed the arguments of her opponents and attempted to change them by persistent persuasion. She could produce art with social concerns, but turn inward to write poems of exquisite beauty and intensity. Her life in London meant she was absorbed in completing her theological book and battling with cancer, remote from the bitter quarrels that damaged idealism for decades in Ireland. Her contributions to culture and politics were forgotten; her books went out of print. Except for a few, Gifford Lewis and Emma Donoghue especially, she was ignored until the valiant efforts of Sonja Tiernan reclaimed her for new generations who can appreciate her ability to see beyond the limitations of class and gender. Her emphasis on the spiritual life as an essential component of human liberation made her a marginal figure, ahead of our times as much as her own.

Constance and Eva were complex individuals, but a century later we can rediscover them as creative spirits, burning with vitality, two valiant idealists as true as steel in their beliefs who well deserve their place in the pantheon of the world's wild rebels.

Lissadell 2010: The light of evening fades as the sky darkens and the stage lights come on. Cohen's crooning voice flows from the speakers into the summer night. He sings songs of hope emerging from defeat and despair. It is easy to imagine the spirits of Constance and Eva haunting these dark trees and woodland paths. The darkness deepens around the trees, blotting out the hills as gigantic clouds sail in from the Atlantic and it does not seem fanciful to imagine the ghostly sisters smiling down from whatever afterlife they inhabit. Eva's elegy to Constance in her Christmas card of 1916 attests to her living presence a century later:

> Nay on that undreamed judgement day
> When on the old world's scrap-heap flung,
> Powers and empires pass away,
> Radiant and unconquerable
> Thou shalt be young.

Endnotes

Prologue
1 Constance letter to Josslyn Gore-Booth, 17/10/1916, Lissadell Papers (LP), PRONI.
2 Constance letter to Esther Roper, *Prison Letters*, p. 311

1 – 'The Hour So Anxiously Awaited...'
3 Nora Connolly O'Brien, *Memories of a Rebel Father*, p. 266
4 Sidney Gifford in Joy (ed.) *The Irish Rebellion*, p. 358
5 William O'Brien, *Forth the Banners Go*, p. 253
6 Thomas O'Donoghue, BMH,WS
7 Frank Robbins, *Beneath the Starry Plough*, p. 110
8 O'Brien, op. cit., p. 285
9 Constance de Markievicz, *Eire*, 26/05/1923
10 Max Caulfield, *The Easter Rebellion*, p. 92
11 J.H. Cox, 1916 Files, BMH
12 C. Day Lewis, 'Remembering Con Markievicz', *Complete Poems*, p. 663
13 Margaret Skinnider, *Doing My Bit for Ireland*, p. 111
14 James Connolly quoted in Greaves, p. 403
15 Constance de Markievicz, *Women in Easter Week* in *Prison Letters*
16 Constance de Markievicz, 'A memory', *Eire*, 26/05/1923

2 – Eva and Constance – 'The World's Great Song'
17 Eva Gore-Booth, 'Inner Life of a Child' in *Poems of Eva Gore-Booth*
18 Esther Roper, *Poems of Eva Gore-Booth*, p. 7

19 Constance Gore-Booth, Diary, National Museum
20 W.B. Yeats, *Letters Vol. 1*, 21/06/1893
21 W.B. Yeats to Susan May Yeats, 23/11/1894, *Letters Vol. 1*, p. 413
22 W.B. Yeats, *Memoirs*, pp. 78-9
23 W.B. Yeats to Eva, quoted in *Poems of Eva Gore-Booth*, Complete Edition, p. 5
24 Esther Roper, ibid, p. 112
25 Stanislaw Markiewicz, *Biography of Countess Markievicz*, p. 134
26 AE, *The Living Torch*, p. 166
27 R.M. Fox, *Rebel Irishwomen*, p. 44
28 Hannah Sheehy-Skeffington Papers, NLI
29 R.M. Fox, *Rebel Irishwomen*, op. cit., p. 42
30 Eva Gore-Booth, *Political Writings*, p. 146
31 Esther Roper, *Prison Letters*, p. 14

3 – The Rebellion Begins

32 Constance de Markievicz, *Women of Easter Week*
33 Kathleen Lynn, BMH WS
34 Dr DeBurgh Daly, letter to Josslyn Gore-Booth, LP
35 Walter McKay, Trial of Countess Markievicz, Markievicz file, PRO, Kew
36 Anne Marreco, *The Rebel Countess*, p. 203
37 Letter to Josslyn Gore-Booth, June 1916, LP
38 Markievicz Police File, PRO, Kew
39 Caulfield, op. cit., p. 44
40 Elizabeth Bowen, *The Shelbourne*, p. 156
41 Ulick O'Connor, *A Terrible Beauty is Born*, p. 86
42 Kathleen Behan, *In Their Own Voice*, p. 66
43 F.A. McKenzie, *The Irish Rebellion*, p. 52
44 Frank Robbins, *Under the Starry Plough*, p. 96
45 James Duncan petition, RCSI Archives
46 Margaret Skinnider, op. cit., p. 120
47 R.M. Fox, *History of the Irish Citizen Army*, p. 163

4 – 'The Red Angel of the Revolution'

48 Margaret Skinnider, *Doing My Bit for Ireland*, p. 119

49 Thomas O'Donoghue, BMH WS 1666, p. 21

50 Sean O'Faolain, *Countess Markievicz*, p. 219

51 Thomas O'Donoghue, op. cit.

52 Sean O'Faolain, op. cit., p. 221

53 James Duncan op. cit.

54 Alfred Bucknill, BMH, WS

55 Max Caulfield, *The Easter Rebellion*, p. 276

56 Esther Roper, *Prison Letters of Countess Markievicz*, p. 21

57 Leonard Cohen, 'Anthem', *The Future*, 1992

5 – In Kilmainham

58 Anne Marreco, *The Rebel Countess*, p. 207

59 Seamus Kavanagh, BMH WS

60 Captain Wheeler, Constance Markievicz Prison File, PRO

61 William Oman, BMH, WS

62 F.A. McKenzie, *The Irish Rebellion*, p. 94

63 Anne Haverty, *Constance Markievicz*, p. 158

64 St. John Irvine, quoted in Bateson, *Rising Dead*, p. 33

65 F.A. McKenzie, op. cit., p. 93

66 Kathleen Lynn Diary, RCPI

67 Elsie Mahaffy Diary, Trinity College

68 Alfred Bucknill, BMH WS

69 John Cowell, *A Noontide Raging*, p. 94

70 Constance de Markievicz statement on trial, LP

71 Anne Haverty, op. cit., p.161

72 Dr C.D. McAdam, *New York Times* 15/05/1916 quoted in McConville, p. 579, n. 89

73 Sir Horace Plunkett quoted in Marreco, *The Rebel Countess*, p. 210

74 Sidney Czira, BMH WS p. 5

75 Constance letter to Gertrude Bannister, Roger Casement Papers, Ms 13,075 (1), NLI

76 Brigid Lyons Thornton in *A Curious Journey*, a documentary film by Kenneth Griffiths

77 Circular letter in Colonel Moore Papers, NLI

78 Hannah Sheehy-Skeffington Papers, NLI

6 – Two Trials

79 Sean Enright, *Easter Rising 1916, The Trials*, p. 1

80 Note on William E. Wylie, BMH WS

81 Constance wrote two accounts of her court-martial, LP

82 Alfred Bucknill, BMH WS

83 William E.Wylie, Memoir, PRO, Kew

84 Esther Roper, *Prison Letters*, p. 28

85 Brian Barton, *From behind a Closed Door*, p. 80

86 Wylie op. cit., p. 30

87 Charles Lysaght, review of O'Broin: *W.E. Wylie* in *Studies*, vol. 79, no. 315 (Autumn 1990), p. 325

88 Elsie Mahaffy Diary, TCD Rare Books & Manuscripts

89 Enright, op. cit., p. 192

90 Sir John Maxwell, quoted in Enright, op. cit., p. 34

7 – 'My Sister's Dead Body …'

91 Esther Roper, *Prison Letters*, p. 15. See also Leon O'Broin, W.E. Wylie, p. 14. The journalist Henry Nevinson also believed Asquith and Lord Oxford secured the reprieve for Constance: *Irish Times*, 16/06/1934

92 Esther Roper, op. cit., p.14

93 Eva Gore-Booth Papers UCD Archives

94 Eva Gore-Booth in Hannah Sheehy-Skeffington Papers, NLI

95 Esther Roper, op. cit., p. 27

96 Quoted in Haverty, op. cit., p. 162

97 A.A. Dickson Papers, IWM

98 Eva Gore-Booth, *Political Writings*, p. 192

99 Eva Gore-Booth, *Prison Letters*, p. 46

100 Esther Roper, op. cit., p. 54

8 – *Eva and Esther in Dublin*

101 Sidney Gifford in Joy, *Irish Rebellion*, p. 346

102 Esther Roper, op. cit., p. 55

103 Hannah Sheehy-Skeffington Papers, NLI

104 Susan Mitchell to Josslyn Gore-Booth, LP

105 Eva Gore-Booth, *Prison Letters*, p. 51

106 Eva Gore-Booth, ibid, p. 51

107 Constance deMarkievicz, *San Francisco Examiner*

108 Eva Gore-Booth to Hannah Sheehy-Skeffington, NLI

109 Constance deMarkievicz letter to Stasko, NLI

110 Crozier to Josslyn Gore-Booth, LP

111 Eva Gore-Booth to Josslyn, LP

112 Eva Gore-Booth Papers, UCD Archives

113 R.M. Fox, *Rebel Irishwomen*, p. 45

114 Eva Gore-Booth, *Prison Letters*, p. 53

115 Eva Gore-Booth Papers, UCD Archives

116 Hilary Pyle, *Cesca's Diary*, p. 226

9 – Sorting Out

117 Constance to Eva, 16/05/1916, NLI

118 Eva to Josslyn, LP

119 Eva Gore-Booth to Fr O'Ryan, Hannah Sheehy-Skeffington Papers, NLI

120 Constance to Josslyn, LP

121 Crozier to Sir Herbert Samuel, 03/07/1915, LP

122 Hannah Sheehy-Skeffington Papers, NLI

123 Royal Commission of Enquiry, Westminster, May, 1916, p.7

124 Charles DeBurgh Daly to Josslyn, LP

125 Arthur Sandbach to Josslyn, LP

126 G. Ball to Josslyn, 01/08/1916, LP

10 – 'Paying the Price...'

127 Constance deMarkievicz to Eva, 08/08/1916, NLI

128 Eva Gore-Booth, *Death of Fionavar*, p. 11

129 Constance to Eva, 08/08/1916, *Prison Letters*, p. 150

130 J.F. Cunningham letter in Constance Prison file, PRO, Kew

131 Casimir Markiewicz to Josslyn, 16/08/1916, LP

132 Stanislaw Markiewicz to Josslyn, 16/08/1916, LP

133 G.B. Shaw, in MacArdle, *The Irish Republic*, p. 174

134 W.B. Yeats to Ezra Pound, *The Poems*, p. 613, n.1. He made a similar remark to his wife George when writing *On a Political Prisoner* in 1918: 'I'm writing one on Con to avoid writing one on Maud.' ibid

135 Kathleen Tynan, *The Years of the Shadow*, p. 204

136 General Maxwell, 16/07/1916, Markievicz Prison File, PRO, Kew

137 Constance to Eva, n/d, Ms 5763, NLI

138 Constance to Eva, n/d, *Prison Letters*, p. 144

139 Sir John Leslie to Eva, n/d, *Prison Letters*, p. 42

140 Hannah Sheehy-Skeffington Papers, NLI

11 – Roger Casement

141 Esther Roper, *Prison Letters*, p. 77

142 Eva Gore-Booth to Lord Sumner, Eva Gore-Booth File, PRO, Kew

143 W.B. Yeats to Eva Gore-Booth, 23/07/1916, *Review of English Lit.*, July 1963

144 Eva Gore-Booth, For God and Kathleen Ni Houlihan, *Prison Letters*, p. 82

145 Sir E. Troup to Dryhurst, 20/07/1916, Constance Markievicz Prison File, PRO, Kew

146 Constance to Eva, n/d, *Prison Letters*, p. 143

147 Irish Times, 03/08/1916, p. 3

148 E.O'Farrell, 26/07/1916, Constance Markievicz Prison File, PRO, Kew

149 Constance to Eva, n/d, quoted in Van Voris, *Constance Markievicz*, p. 217

150 Supt. Lewes report, Constance Police File, PRO, Kew

151 Constance to Eva, 08/08/1916, *Prison Letters*, p. 150

152 Esther Roper, *Prison Letters*, pp. 65-6

12 – Aylesbury: 'It's Queer and Lonely Here...'

153 May Sharpe, *Story of Chicago May*, p. 196

154 S.F. Fox

155 Constance, *San Francisco Examiner*

156 Sean McConville, *Irish Political Prisoners 1868-1922*, p. 8

157 Hannah Sheehy-Skeffington Papers, NLI

158 Constance, New Ireland, 15/04/1922

159 May Sharpe, op. cit., p. 200

160 Constance to Eva, 08/08/1916, *Prison Letters*, p. 149-151

161 Josslyn to Eva, n/d, LP

162 Constance note, n/d, *Prison Letters*, p. 145

163 Constance, *San Francisco Examiner*, op. cit.

164 Constance to Eva, *Prison Letters*, NL

165 Esther Roper, *Prison Letters*, p. 69

166 Constance, New Ireland, 15/04/1922

13 – September 1916

167 Eva Gore-Booth, *Death of Fionavar*, p. 15

168 New York Times, 10/09/1916

169 Constance to Eva, n/d, *Prison Letters*, p. 144

170 E.W. Sharp, report to Prison Governor, Constance Markievicz Prison File, PRO, Kew

171 E. O'Farrell to Troup, 16/09/1916, Constance Markievicz Prison File, PRO, Kew

172 Esther Roper, *Prison Letters*, p. v

173 Ibid, p. 71

174 Constance, *San Francisco Examiner*

175 Constance in New Ireland, 15/04/1922

176 S.F. Fox, Constance Markievicz Prison File, PRO, Kew

177 Constance to Eva, 21/09/2016, *Prison Letters*, pp. 151-6

14 – 'Life's Secret Forces...'

178 Esther Roper, *Poems of Eva Gore-Booth*, p. 25

179 Eva Gore-Booth, 'The Tribunal', *Political Writings*, p. 155

180 Helena Molony, BMH, WS

181 Esther Roper, *Prison Letters*, p.69

182 Constance in New Ireland, 08/04/1922

183 Eva to Helena Molony, n/d, BMH Archives

184 May Sharpe, op. cit., p. 199

185 Nuala O'Faolain, *Chicago May*, p. 211

186 Sean O'Faolain, *Constance Markievicz*, pp. 239-40

187 Esther Roper, *Prison Letters*, p. 68

188 Sidney Gifford, *The Irish Rebellion of 1916*, p. 342

189 Colonel Moore Papers, NLI

190 Constance in New Ireland, 08/04/1922

191 Esther Roper, *Prison Letters*, p. 70

192 S.F. Fox, Constance Markievicz Prison File, PRO, Kew

15 – Settling Accounts

193 Constance to Josslyn, 17/10/1916, LP

194 J.A. Cooper to Cochrane & Co., 21/10/1916, LP

195 Lady Gore-Booth to Josslyn, n/d, LP

196 Eva to Kathleen Lynn, November 1916, Allen Library, Dublin

197 Eva to Josslyn, recd. 07/11/1916, LP

198 Eva to Josslyn, recd. 11/11/1916, LP

199 Eva to Josslyn, recd. 18/11/1916

200 Casimir Markiewicz to Josslyn, 09/11/1916, LP

201 Eva to Josslyn, recd. 23/11/1916

202 Eva to Kathleen Tynan, Nov. 1916, quoted in Tiernan: *Eva Gore-Booth*, p. 205

203 Susan Mitchell to Josslyn, 25/11/1916, LP

204 Maria Perolz to Josslyn, 30/11/1916, LP

205 Eva to Josslyn, n/d, LP

206 Winifred Carney to Home Sec., 1/12/1916, Constance Prison File, PRO, Kew

207 Eva to Helena Molony, n/d, BMH

208 William Patrick Partridge, p. 285

209 Esther Roper, intro. to *Buried Life of Deirdre*

16 – Christmas 1916 – 'What I Was Born to Do'

210 J.R. White to Henry Duke, Dec. 1916, Constance Prison File, PRO, Kew

211 Fr. Albert Bibby to Eva, 23/12/1916, NLI

212 Constance to Eva, 29/11/1916, NLI

213 Eva Gore-Booth, *Inner Life of a Child*

214 John O'Dowd to Home Sec., Prison File, PRO

215 Van Voris, *Constance Markievicz*, p. 228

17 – 1917 – 'Dim Sunshine and Pearly Waves...'

216 Stasko to Eva, 04/03/1917, LP

217 CP Scott to Eva, 02/01/1917, LP

218 Eva to Josslyn, 24/12/1916, LP

219 Eva to Josslyn, 17/01/1917, LP

220 H.O. to John O'Dowd, 11/01/1917, Constance Markievicz Prison File, PRO, Kew

Endnotes

221 Susan Mitchell to Josslyn, 05/01/1917, LP

222 Josslyn to Morduant, 05/02/1917, LP

223 Morduant to Josslyn, 07/02/1917, LP

224 Mrs. DeBurgh Daly to Josslyn, 20/02/1917, LP

225 Father James Sherwin to Josslyn, 21/02/1917, LP

226 Josslyn to Father Sherwin, 23/02/1917, LP

227 Josslyn to Morduant, 27/02/1917, LP

228 Morduant to Josslyn, 01/03/1917, LP

229 Sean McConville, *Irish Political Prisoners*, p. 548

230 Mrs Rudnose-Browne to Kathleen Lynn, Allen Library

231 J.F. Cunningham to Henry Duke, Constance Markievicz Prison File, PRO, Kew

18 – 'In Prison All Her Life…'

232 Arthur Griffith letter, Allen Library

233 Report by Matron Sharp, Constance Markievicz Prison File, PRO, Kew

234 Constance Prison File

235 Eva to Helena Molony, BMH Molony File

236 Constance to Eva, 29/01/1917, NLI

237 Art O'Brian letter, 23/02/2017, Constance Markievicz Prison File, PRO

238 Quoted in McConville, p. 547

239 Dr Fox report in Prison file

240 Alfie Byrne MP, 14/01/1917 in Prison file

241 David Lloyd George, 07/03/1917, quoted in *Irish Republic*, p. 198

242 Constance to Eva, 27/02/1917, NLI

243 McConville, *Irish Political Prisoners*, p. 548

19 – 'Where I Would Like to Be…'

244 Lady Gore-Booth to Josslyn, 12/03/1917, LP

245 Dryhurst to Troup, 27/03/1917, Prison File

246 Stasko to Eva, 04/03/1917, LP

247 Eva to Father Albert, recd. 06/03/1917, Capuchin Archives

248 Father Albert to Eva, NLI

249 Susan Mitchell to Josslyn, 29/03/1917, LP

250 Father Albert to Eva, 30/03/1917, NLI

251 Esther Roper, *Prison Letters*, pp. 67-8

252 Barclay to Troup, 26/03/1917, Prison File

253 Father Albert to Eva, 03/04/1917, NLI

20 – 'The Brave Soul'

254 Eva to Helena Molony, BMH

255 Cumann na MBan letter, c. March 1917, private collection

256 Father Albert to Eva, 25/04/1917, NLI Ms33

257 Constance to Eva, 14/05/1917, NLI

258 Casimir to Josslyn, 02/06/1917, LP

259 Constance to Eva, 09/06/1917, NLI

260 Dorothy MacArdle, review of *Prison Letters*, *Irish Press*, 28/05/1934

21 – 'She Is the People's Countess'

261 Kathleen Lynn, flyer in NLI

262 Esther Roper, *Prison Letters*, p. 72

263 S.F. Fox, p. 14

264 Get source

265 Esther Roper, op. cit., p. 72

266 Van Voris, *Constance Markievicz*, p.231

267 Esther Roper, op cit., p. 72

268 McConville, *Irish Political Prisoners*, p. 553

269 Ella Young, *Flowering Dusk*, p. 132

270 *Irish Times*, 22/06/1917, p. 5

271 Esther Roper, *Prison Letters*, p. 73

272 Kathleen Tynan, op. cit., p. 279

273 Ella Young, op. cit.

274 Esther Roper, op. cit., p. 73

275 Hannah Sheehy-Skeffington Papers, NLI

276 Sean O'Faolain, op. cit., p. 249

277 Constance Markievicz Police File, PRO, Kew

278 Kathleen Tynan, op. cit., p. 279-80

279 Sean O'Faolain, op. cit. p. 249

280 Hannah Sheehy-Skeffington Papers, NLI

Endnotes

281 Diana Norman, *Terrible Beauty*, p. 173

282 Quoted in Anne Haverty, *Constance Markievicz*, p. 179

283 James O'Neill to Constance, 12/07/1917, Allen Library

284 Father Albert to Eva, 29/06/2017, NLI

285 Eva to Father Albert, n/d, Capuchin Archives

286 Lennox Robinson to Constance, NM, EH1994

287 Constance to Josslyn, 19/07/1917, LP

288 Constance to Josslyn, 10/09/1917, LP

289 Constance to Mrs Partridge, July 1917, NM

22 – Aftermath

290 Eva Gore-Booth, 'Rhythms of Art', *Political Writings*, p. 168

List of Illustrations

Frontispiece: Eva's bookplate by Constance, National Museum of Ireland (NMI), 1916 Collection

p. 2 – Con and Eva in 1890s, Lissadell Papers (LP), Public Record Office of Northern Ireland

p. 5 – Constance in Irish Citizen Army uniform, National Library of Ireland (NL)

p. 7 – The Spark, NL

p. 7 – Poppet's dog licence, Bureau of Military History

p. 9 – Constance sketch of Margaret Skinnider, NL

p. 10 – Peter the Painter, NL

p. 13 – Constance and Eva by Sarah Purser, author photo, courtesy of Merrion Hotel

p. 16 – Esther Roper sketched by Eva, LP

p. 17 – Fitzroy Square, author photo

p. 18 – Eva and Esther in Paris, LP

p. 21 – Kathleen Lynn with Constance, NL

p. 23 – University Club, author photo

p. 26 – Constance in action, Kilmainham Gaol

p. 32 – Constance aiming pistol, NL

p. 33 – Damaged portrait of Queen Victoria, Royal College of Surgeons of Ireland (RCSI)

p. 36 – William Partridge, NMI

p. 37 – Examination Hall, College of Surgeons, RCSI

p. 38 – Maedbh by Constance, NMI

p. 39 – Bucknill and Maxwell, LP

p. 44 – Constance's pistol, NL

List of Illustrations

p. 45 – Detail from *The Arrest* by Kathleen Fox, Sligo County Museum

p. 48 – *Evening World* headline, Michael Barry

p. 49 – Constance: mug-shot photographs, LP

p. 51 – Father Albert Bibby, Capuchin Annual, 1966

p. 56 – Constance walking to Red + ambulance, NL

p. 62 – Extract from trial record, LP

p. 65 – Constance after court-martial, Kilmainham Gaol

p. 68 – Constance and Eva: newspaper photograph, Kilmainham Gaol

p. 71 – Eva, LP

p. 74 – Painting of Susan Mitchell by Constance, LP

p. 77 – Surrey House, author photo

p. 79 – Constance prison file photographs, LP, original in Clare County Library

p. 80 – Eva note to Hannah, NL

p. 81 – Josslyn and Molly Gore-Booth with baby, LP

p. 88 – Hall at 34 Camden Street, author photo

p. 92 – Maeve de Markievicz in war work fete in 1916, LP

p. 93 – Strahan bill for removals, LP

p. 96 – Scout, NMI

p. 99 – Winged horses from Fionavar, author photo

p. 100 – Page from Fionavar, author photo

p. 101 – Casimir photograph by Constance, courtesy of Tadeusz Malkiewicz, Krakow

p. 103 – 1916 Memorial cards, LP

p. 104 – General Maxwell's note, National Archives, Kew

p. 104 – Note smuggled from Mountjoy Jail, NL

p. 109 – Casement memorial card 1916, LP

p. 110 – Crowd outside courthouse, Capuchin Annual, 1966

p. 115 – Stasko and Poppet 1915, LP

p. 116 – Esther Roper, LP

p. 118 – Aylesbury Women's Prison, LP

p. 120 – Dr Fox at work in her study, Life of SF Fox

p. 125 – Pin-cushion made in prison, NMI

p. 125 – Apron from Aylesbury Prison, Sligo County Museum

p. 128 – Agnes Mallin and children in 1916, LP

p. 130 – Water decoration from Fionavar, author photo

p. 131 – Trees decoration from Fionavar, author photo

p. 131 – The rose, author photo

p. 136 – Picture by Eva, LP

p. 142 – Upon our cheeks verse from Prison Journal, NMI

p. 143 – Maeve and Gaga, LP

p. 144 – Lissadell in the early 1900s, LP

p. 146 – *Urania*, London School of Economics, Fawcett Library

p. 148 – The Prisoner by Constance, Allen Library

p. 152 – Handkerchief made in prison, Allen Library

p. 156 – Dr S.F. Fox in 1938, Life of SF Fox

p. 160 – Christmas card by Constance, Allen Library

p. 162 – Buried Life of Deirdre, NL

p. 163 – Deirdre by Constance, LP

p. 164 – Captain Jack White in 1930, author photo

p. 165 – Prison Journal rules, NMI

p. 166 – Constance behind bars (when my fancies), NMI

p. 168 – Eva's Christmas card, LP

p. 170 – Live Dangerously, NMI

p. 171 – Eva verse from card, LP

p. 172 – Constance drawing of rose verse, NMI

p. 173 – Magi, NMI

p. 177 – Woman on shore, NMI

p. 180 – In the sheen, NMI

p. 183 – Woman with crystal, NMI

p. 183 – Bright horseman, NMI

p. 188 – Maedhbh and Maca, NMI

p. 189 – Clare Annesley, NMI

p. 190 – Scene from Eva's card, LP

p. 194 – The Watcher, NMI

p. 195 – Letter with birds at cell window, NL

p. 197 – Thrush sketch, NMI

p. 198 – Sketch of winged horse, NMI

p. 200 – 'Where I would like to be…' NMI

List of Illustrations

p. 201 – Hope, NMI

p. 202 – Blue bird poems and picture, NMI

p. 202 – Dr S.F. Fox's initials

p. 204 – Prison breakout, NMI

p. 205 – The Owl, NMI

p. 206 – St Patrick's Day card, Allen Library

p. 209 – The Satyr, NMI

p. 212 – Eva drawing of angel, LP

p. 213 – Mutilated prison letter, NL

p. 214 – Aylesbury prison pass, NL

p. 216 – St Francis, NMI

p. 220 – Poster, LP

p. 222 – Freedom woman, NMI

p. 223 – Horse over prison wall card, NL

p. 226 – Dublin welcome, LP

p. 228 – Cead Mile Failte, Kilmainham Gaol

p. 229 – Constance and Poppet in 1917, LP

p. 230 – Constance in Sligo 1917, Kilmainham Gaol

p. 231 – Countess Markievicz 1917, Kilmainham Gaol

p. 232 – Constance, Kathleen Lynn and babies, Allen Library

p. 233 – Constance's chequebook

p. 236 – Constance, Eva, Maeve and Poppet, LP

p. 238 – Eva and Esther's grave, author photo

Bibliography

Archives:

Allen Library, Dublin, Frederick J. Allen Papers, Ms 26,765

Art O'Brien Papers, NLI, Ms 8435/28,

Bureau of Military History, Witness Statements and Helena Molony Papers

Capuchin Archives, Church St., Dublin

Roger Casement Papers, NLI, Ms 13,075

Eva Gore-Booth Papers, UCD Special Collections

Eva Gore-Booth File, NLI, Ms 13,177/ Ms 21,815

Kilmainham Gaol Archives

Lissadell Papers, PRONI, Belfast

Patricia Lynch and RM Fox Papers, NLI

Constance Markievicz file, 1916 Collection, National Museum, Collins Barracks, Dublin

Constance Markievicz files, National Archives, Kew, PRO HO 144/158/31618

Royal College of Physicians of Ireland Archives

Royal College of Surgeons in IrelandArchives

Military Archives, Cathal Brugha Barracks, Rathmines, Dublin

Hannah Sheehy-Skeffington Papers, NLI, Ms 41,189/Ms 24,189/Ms33,605-6

Newspapers:

An Phoblacht, 05/04/1933

Daily Mirror

Eire

Irish Independent

Bibliography

The Irish Times

Le Miroir

New Ireland

San Francisco Examiner, 07/12/1919, p.16

Books:

AE: *The Living Torch*, Macmillan Co., New York, 1937

Anon: *Selina Fitzherbert Fox 1871-1958*, London, n/d

Arrington, Lauren: *Revolutionary Lives: Constance and Casimir Markievicz*, Princeton University Press, 2016

Barone, Rosemary: *The Oak Tree and the Olive Tree*, Irish Academic Press, Dublin, 1994

Barton, Brian: *From Behind a Closed Door: Secret Court Martial Records of the 1916 Easter Rising*, Blackstaff Press, Belfast, 2002

Bateson, Ray: *The Rising Dead: RIC and DMP*, Irish Graves Publications, Dublin, 2012

Bateson, Ray, *They Died by Pearse's Side*, Irish Graves Publications, Dublin, 2010

Bowen, Elizabeth: *The Shelbourne*, George G. Harrap and Co., London, 1951

Cartwright, Colin: *Burning to Get the Vote: The Women's Suffrage Movement in Central Buckinghamshire, 1904-1914*, University of Buckingham, 2013

C. Day Lewis: *Complete Poems*, Stanford University Press, 1996

Caulfield, Max: *The Easter Rebellion*, Gill and Macmillan, Dublin 1995

Joe Connell: *Rebels' Priests*, Kilmainham Tale 10, Dublin 2014

Joe Connell: *Unequal Patriots*, Kilmainham Tale 11, Dublin 2015

Joseph E.A. Connell Jnr: *Dublin in Rebellion, A Directory 1913-1923*, Lilliput Press, Dublin 2009

Nora Connolly O'Brien: *Portrait of a Rebel Father*, Four Masters, Dublin, 1975

Cowell, John: *A Noontide Raging: Brigid Lyons Thornton*, Currach Press, Dublin, 2005

Coxhead, Elizabeth: *Daughters of Erin*, Secker and Warburg, London, 1965

Devine, Francis and Manus O'Riordan: *James Connolly, Liberty Hall and the 1916 Rising*, Irish Labour History Society, Dublin, 2006

Enright, Sean: *Easter Rising 1916: The Trials*, Merrion Press, Kildare, 2013

Findlater, Alex: *1916 Surrenders: Captain H.E. De Courcy-Wheeler's Eyewitness Account*, Dun-Laoghaire County Council, Dublin, 2016

Foster, Roy: *W.B. Yeats: A Life Vol. II, The Arch-Poet 1919-1939*, Oxford UP, 2003

Fox, R.M.: *History of the Irish Citizen Army*, James Duffy, Dublin, 1943

Fox, R.M.: *Rebel Irishwomen*, Talbot Press, Dublin 1935

Foy, Michael and Brian Barton: *The Easter Rising*, Gloucestershire, Sutton, 2004

Geraghty, Hugh: *William Patrick Partridge and His Times (1874-1917)*, Curlew Press, Dublin 2003

Gore-Booth, Eva: *Broken Glory*, Maunsel, Dublin, 1918

Gore-Booth, Eva: *Buried Life of Deirdre*, Longmans, London, 1930

Gore-Booth, Eva: *Death of Fionavar*, Erskine Macdonald, London, 1916

Gore-Booth, Eva: *Three Resurrections and the Triumph of Maeve*, Longmans, London, 1905

Greaves, G. Desmond: *Life and Times of James Connolly*, Lawrence and Wishart, London, 1986

Haverty, Anne: *Constance Markievicz: Irish Revolutionary*, Pandora, London, 1988 (revised edition, Lilliput Press, Dublin, 2016)

Hughes, Brian: *Michael Mallin*, O'Brien Press, Dublin, 2012

James, Dermot: *The Gore-Booths of Lissadell*, Woodfield Press, Dublin, 2004

Joy, Maurice: *The Irish Rebellion and Its Martyrs*, Devin Adair, New York, 1916

Kiberd, Declan: *1916 Rebellion Handbook*, Mourne River Press, Dublin, 1998

Lewis, Gifford: *Eva Gore-Booth and Esther Roper: A Biography*, Pandora, London, 1988

Macardle, Dorothy: *The Irish Republic*, Corgi, London, 1968

McCarthy, Cal: *Cumann na mBan and the Irish Revolution*, Collins Press, Cork, 2007

McConville, Sean: *Irish Political Prisoners, 1868-1922*, Routledge, London, 2003

McCoole, Sinead: *Guns and Chiffon*, Stationery Office, Dublin, 1997

McCoole, Sinead: *No Ordinary Women: Irish Female Activists in the Revolutionary Years 1900-1923*, O'Brien Press, 2004

McGowan, Joe: *Constance Markievicz: The People's Countess*, Sligo, 2000

McIntosh and Urquhart, *Irish Women at War 20th Century*, Irish Academic Press, Kildare, 2010

McKenzie, F.A.: *The Irish Rebellion: What Happened and Why*, London, 1916

McNally, Michael: *Easter Rising 1916: Birth of the Irish Republic*, Osprey, Oxford, 2007

Marreco, Anne: *The Rebel Countess: Life and Times of Constance Markievicz*, Weidenfeld andNicolson, London, 1967

Bibliography

Norman, Diana: *Terrible Beauty: A Life of Constance Markievicz*, Hodder and Stoughton, London, 1987

O'Broin, Leon: *Dublin Castle and the 1916 Rising*, Helicon, Dublin, 1966

O'Broin, Leon: *W.E. Wylie and the Irish Revolution 1916-21*, Gill and Macmillan, Dublin, 1989

O'Connor, Ulick: *A Terrible Beauty is Born*, Hamish Hamilton, London, 1985

O'Faolain, Nuala: *The Story of Chicago May*, Michael Joseph, London, 2005

O'Faolain, Sean: *Constance Markievicz: The Average Revolutionary*, Jonathan Cape, London, 1934

Oikarinen, Sari: *A Dream of Liberty: Constance Markievicz's Vision of Ireland, 1908-1927*, Suomen Historiallinen Seura, Helsinki, 1998

Paseta, Senia: *Irish Nationalist Women, 1900-1918*, Cambridge University Press, 2013

Pyle, Hilary: *Cesca's Diary 1913-1916: Where Art and Nationalism Meet*, Woodfield Press, Dublin, 2005

Pyle, Hilary: *The Red-headed Rebel: Susan L. Mitchell*, Woodfield Press, Dublin, 1998

Quigley, Patrick: *The Polish Irishman: Life and Times of Count Casimir Markievicz*, The Liffey Press, Dublin 2012

Robbins, Frank: *Under the Starry Plough: Recollections of the Irish Citizen Army*, Academy Press, Dublin, 1987

Roper, Esther (ed.): *Poems of Eva Gore-Booth, Complete Edition*, Longmans, London, 1929

Roper, Esther (ed.): *Prison Letters of Countess Markievicz*, Virago Press, London, 1987

Scott, Ciara: *Madame Countess de Markievicz*, Kilmainham Tale 6, Dublin, 2013

Scoular, Clive: *Maeve de Markievicz: Daughter of Constance*, Scoular, 2003

Sharpe, May: *Chicago May: Her Story*, Sampson Low and Co., London, 1929

Skinnider, Margaret: *Doing My Bit for Ireland*, Republican Publications, Dublin, 2014

Stallworthy, Jon: *Between the Lines: Yeats' Poetry in the Making*, Oxford University Press, 1963

Steele, Karen: *Women, Dress and Politics during the Irish Revival*, Syracuse University Press, 2007

Stephens, James: *The Insurrection in Dublin*, Colin Smythe Ltd., Buckinghamshire, 1972

Taillon, Ruth: *When History Was Made*, Beyond the Pale, Belfast, 1996

Tiernan, Sonja: *After Such Knowledge: A Life of Eva Gore-Booth*, Manchester University Press, 2012

Tiernan, Sonja (ed.): *Political Writings of Eva Gore-Booth*, Manchester University Press, 2015

Townshend, Charles: *Easter 1916: The Irish Rebellion*, Penguin Books, London, 2006

Tynan-Hickson, Katherine: *The Years of the Shadow*, Constable and Co., London, 1919

Van Voris, Jacqueline: *Constance de Markievicz in the Cause of Ireland*, University of Massachusetts Press, Amherst, 1967

Walsh, Edward and Constance Cassidy: *Countess Markievicz, 1868-1927*, Lissadell Press, Sligo, 2007

Ward, Margaret: *Hannah Sheehy-Skeffington: A Life*, Attic Press, Cork, 1997

Ward, Margaret: *In Their Own Voice: Women and Irish Nationalism*, Attic Press, Cork, 1995

Ward, Margaret: *Unmanageable Revolutionaries*, Pluto Press, London, 1989

White, Capt. James: *Misfit, a Revolutionary Life*, Livewire Publications, Dublin, 2005

Yeates, Padraig: *A City in Wartime: Dublin, 1914–1918*, Gill and Macmillan, Dublin 2012

Yeats, W.B.: *Collected Letters Vol. 1, 1865-1895*, Oxford UP, 1986

Yeats, W.B.: *Collected Letters Vol. 3, 1901-1904*, Clarendon Press, Oxford, 1994

Yeats, W.B.: *Memoirs*, Macmillan, London, 1973

Yeats, W.B.: *The Poems* (ed. Daniel Albright), Everyman Library, London, 1992

Young, Ella: *Flowering Dusk*, Longmans Green and Co., New York, 1945

Misc:

Condren, Mary, 'Eva Gore-Booth' in *Field Day Anthology Vol. IV*, Cork University Press, 2002

Donoghue, Emma: 'How could I fear and hold thee by the hand? The Poetry of Eva Gore-Booth,' in Eibhear Walsh (ed.) *Sex, Nation and Dissent in Irish Writing*, Cork University Press, 1997

Farrell, Brian: 'Markievicz and the Women of the Irish Revolution' in *Leaders and Men of the 1916 Rising* (ed. Martin), Methuen and Co., London, 1967

de Markievicz, Constance: 'Conditions of Women in English Jails' in *New Ireland*, 15/04/1922

Bibliography

de Markievicz, Constance: 'Countess Markievicz on English Jails,' *New Ireland*, 08/04/1922

de Markievicz, Constance: 'Hymn on the Battlefield,' *Workers' Republic*, 13/11/1915

de Markievicz, Constance: 'In Kilmainham' *New Ireland*, 9/02/1918

de Markievicz, Constance: 'In Mountjoy,' *New Ireland*, 16/02/1918

de Markievicz, Constance: 'My 1916 Lover' in 1916 Collection, National Museum

de Markievicz, Constance: '1916' in *The Nation*, 23/04/1927

de Markievicz, Constance: 'Some Women of Easter Week' in *Prison Letters*

Markiewicz, Stanislaw: Memories of Madame Markievicz, Ms 44,619 in National Library of Ireland

Ni Chumhaill, Eithne: History of Cumann na mBan, *An Phoblacht*, 05/04/1933

Smith, D.J.: The Countess and the Poets, *Journal of Irish Literature* vol. xii, no.1, Proscenium Press, Delaware, 1983

Tiernan, Sonja: 'Countess Markievicz and Eva Gore-Booth,' Biagini and Mulhall (ed.): *The Shaping of Modern Ireland*, Irish Academic Press, Kildare, 2016

Tiernan, Sonja: 'No Measures of Emancipation or Equality will Suffice,' O'Connor and Shepard (ed.): *Women, Social and Cultural Change in 20th Century Ireland*, Cambridge Scholar's Publishing, Newcastle, 2008

Tiernan, Sonja: 'Engagements Dissolved: Eva Gore-Booth, Urania and the Radical Challenge to Marriage in McAuliffe and Tiernan (eds.) *Tribades, Tommies and Transgressives: Histories of Sexualities* Vol. 1, Cambridge Scholars Publishing, Newcastle, 2008

Yeats, W.B.: Letter to Eva Gore-Booth, *A Review of English Literature* IV, 3/07/1963

Film:

Constance Markievicz: A Documentary (Video Productions, Dublin, 2016)

Curious Journey – The 1916 Rising (Kenneth Griffith, 1974)

Mise Eire (George Morrison, 1959)

1916: Seachtar na Casca (TG4, Dublin, 2014)

Websites:

www.bureauofmilitaryhistory.ie

www.kilmainhamtales.ie

www.lissadellhouse.com

www.richmondbarracks.ie

Index

Abbey Theatre, 50, 232
Adeline, Lady, 148–9
Aethnic Union, 146
Annesley, Lady Clare, 143, 185, 187, 205
Asquith, Herbert, 66, 72, 161
Aylesbury Women's Prison, 3, 96, 117–28

Ball, G., 95
'Ballad of Reading Gaol, The', 141
Bannister, Gertrude, 51, 108–9
Barton, Brian, 62
Bateson, Ray, 25
Battersea, Lady, 148–9
Behan, Kathleen, 27
Bennett, Louise, 192
Bibby, Father Albert, 50–1, 104, 165, 199, 205–7, 210–12, 231
Blackader, C.J., 58–63
Blake, William, 14, 172, 197, 213, 218
'Blue Bird, The', 201
Bowen, Elizabeth, 27
Bread, 76, 93
Brockway, Fenner, 145
Broken Glory, 110, 123, 162
Bucknill, Alfred, 39, 46, 56–8, 64
Buried Life of Deirdre, The, 13, 162
Byrne, Alfred (Alfie), 112, 151, 161, 192, 222

Carney, Winifred, 10, 116, 120, 146, 161

Casement, Roger, 6, 8, 51, 107–16
Cathleen Ni Houlihan, 102, 142
Caulfield, Max, 8, 25
Cavanagh, James, 28
Cavanagh, Maeve, 228
Cave, George, 191–2, 203
Ceannt, Eamonn, 71
Celtic Renaissance, 2, 16, 168, 204
Chambers, Robert, 134
Chicago May, *see* May Sharpe
Churchill, Winston, 16
Clarke, Kathleen, 88, 91, 228
Clarke, Tom, 7, 11, 50, 55, 88, 91, 97
Cohen, Leonard, 1, 41, 240
Colbert, Con, 5, 71
College of Surgeons, 30–41
'College of Surgeons', 41
Collins, Michael, 5, 230
Colum, Mary, 150
Colum, Padraig, 150
Connolly, James, 4–5, 7–9, 11, 20, 73–5, 101–2, 239
Connolly, Joseph, 37, 42
Connolly, Lillie, 38, 89, 104, 128, 218, 228
Connolly, Nora 'Nono', 4, 38, 140
Connolly, Sean, 21, 37
'Conscientious Objectors', 145
Constance Markievicz: The Average Revolutionary, 238
Cooper, J.A., 153–4, 158

Index

Cox, J.H., 8
Cumann na mBan, 19–21, 28, 46, 91, 162, 211, 225
Cunningham, J.F., 100, 183–4

Daly, De Burgh, 22–4, 56–7, 60–1, 94–5, 181
Daly, Edward, 51
Death of Fionavar, The, 82, 98, 123, 129, 143, 150, 202, 204
Defence of the Realm Act, 5, 54
Devil's Disciple, The, 85
Dickson, A.A., 70
Doing My Bit for Ireland, 30
Donoghue, Emma, 240
Dryhurst, Frederick, 111, 203
Duffy, George Gavan, 60, 107–8, 157, 166
Duke, Henry, 134, 164, 183, 220
Duncan, James, 28–9, 36
Dunn, Andy, 139

'Easter 1916', 102
Emmet, Robert, 46
Enright, Sean, 54
Ervine, St. John, 44

Fianna Éireann, 4, 71
FitzGerald, Mabel, 49
Fitzgerald, Miss, 24–5
Foley, Breda, 120
Fox, Kathleen, 43–4
Fox, R.M., 35, 50, 82, 98, 237
Fox, Selina F., 118–20, 124, 137, 148, 152, 156, 183, 202, 220–2
ffrench-Mullen, Madeline, 37, 41, 46
French, Lord, 66
'From the West Coast', 200
Fry, Roger, 17

'Garden of Love', 172
George, David Lloyd, 161, 174, 193, 220
Gifford, Sidney, 76, 140, 150
Ginnell, Laurence, 220, 233
Goff, Bridie, 80, 88, 90

Gonne, Maud, 14, 103, 168, 228
Gore-Booth, Eva
  as pacifist, 3, 35, 69, 78, 235
  campaign for Casement reprieve, 107–10
  conscientious objector campaign, 145–6
  death of, 238
  early years of, 12–15
  nature of relationship with Esther Roper, 16
  poetry of, 156, 18, 129, 191
  reincarnation and, 13, 163
  relationship with Constance, 14, 170
  spirituality of, 12, 18, 99, 235
  telepathy and, 114–16, 140
  women's suffrange and, 16–7, 217
Gore-Booth, Josslyn, 24, 77, 81, 90–5, 123, 153–60, 174–82, 233
Gore-Booth, Lady Georgina (Gaga), 1, 86, 94, 143, 155, 170, 213
Gore-Booth, Mabel, 12, 16, 123, 170
Gore-Booth, Molly, 123
Gore-Booth, Mordaunt, 12, 123, 179, 181–2
Gore-Booth, Sir Henry, 1
Gore-Booth, Sir Robert, 13
Gregory, Lady, 102, 190
Grennan, Julia, 46
Griffith, Arthur, 185

Healy, Tim, 60, 151, 203
Hearst, William Randolph, 185
Heuston, Sean, 5, 71
Hill, Lady Frances Charlotte Arabella, 12
Holohan, Gary, 89
House with the Three Windows, The, 235

'In Kilmainham', 51–2
'In Memory of Eva Gore-Booth and Con Markievicz', 1, 238
'In Mountjoy', 97

'In the West the Waves are Green', 182
Independent Theatre Company, 85
Inner Life of a Child, The, 12
Irish Citizen, 87
Irish Citizen Army, 4, 6, 8–11, 20, 26–8, 31–2, 54, 91, 146, 210, 225, 231
Irish National Aid and Volunteers Dependents Fund (INAVDF), 91, 230
Irish National Relief Fund, 191
Irish Rebellion, The, 28
Irish Rebellion of 1916 and Its Martyrs, 150
Irish Volunteers, 6, 10, 225
Irish Women Workers Union, 182

Joy, Maurice, 150

Kavanagh, Seamus, 42
Kelly, Tom, 210
Kempson, Lily, 26, 133, 135, 140
King George V, 109

Lahiff, Michael, 24–5
Lavery, Sir John, 107
Law, Bonar, 220
Le Fanu, F.S., 181
Leslie, Sir John, 105, 165
Lewes Prison, 151, 161, 164–5, 183, 215, 233–4
Lewis, C. Day, 9
Lewis, Gifford, 83, 240
Lissadell House, 1, 12, 14
Lowe, W.H.M., 34, 39, 43
Lynch, Bessie, 80, 84–5, 87–9, 140, 159–60, 179, 198, 206
Lynn, Kathleen, 4, 20–1, 31, 46, 50, 116, 157, 183, 220, 222, 227–9
Lysaght, Charles, 63

Macardle, Dorothy, 218
MacBride, John, 51, 103
MacDermott, Sean, 7, 73
MacDonagh, Thomas, 11, 50, 55
MacNeice, Louis, 24
MacNeill, Eoin, 8

'Magi', 173
Mahaffy, Elsie, 46, 48, 63–4
Mallin, Agnes, 74, 78, 128, 196, 228–9
Mallin, Michael, 8, 22, 25, 29, 31, 37–8, 42–3, 65–6, 71, 234
Markievicz, Casimir Dunin, 6,–7, 11, 66, 76, 85–6, 89, 91, 94, 96, 100, 140, 157–8, 174, 216
Markievicz, Countess Constance
    and Mauser pistol, 'Peter the Painter', 10–11, 43
    as first woman elected to Westminster, 2
    as modern Joan of Arc, 130–1
    death of, 238
    election as president of Cumann na mBan, 162
    in Aylesbury Prison, 112–28
    in Kilmainham Gaol, 47–53
    in Mountjoy Jail, 70, 73, 96–106
    Catholicism and, 40–1, 43, 105–6, 147, 189, 229–30
    Last Will of, 41
    marriage to Casimir Dunin-Markievicz, 7, 16, 40, 94
    presented to Queen Victoria, 14
    prison journals of, vii, 3, 96, 141–2, 163, 165
    release from prison and homecoming, 221–230
    role in 1916 Rising, 20–41
    surrender of, 42–7
    trials of, 54–66
Markievicz, Maeve Alys, 41, 91, 143, 199, 236–7
Markievicz, Stasko, 16, 23, 35, 91, 101, 174, 199
Marreco, Anne, 11, 37
Maxwell, John, 38, 54, 66, 79, 103–4, 110, 182
McAdam, Cecil D., 48
McDonnell, Lord Anthony, 195
McGuiness, Joseph, 215
McKay, Walter, 23, 56–8, 60–2, 83

Index

McKenzie, F.A., 28, 44–5
McMahon, Father, 105–6, 229
Memory of the Dead, The, 10
'Men of Easter Week, The', 53
Mise Eire, 227
Mitchell, Susan, 73–4, 77, 80–1, 92–3, 139, 160, 177–8, 180
Molony, Helena, 116, 120, 146–7, 161, 178, 187, 210, 222
Morrell, Lady Ottoline, 138

No Conscription Fellowship, 145
Norman, Diana, 230

O'Brien, Art, 91, 191, 195
O'Brien, Constable, 21, 24
O'Brien, William, 7, 10, 102
O'Connor, Ulick, 27
O'Donoghue, Thomas, 6, 32, 34
O'Dowd, John, 171, 176
O'Farrell, Edward, 112, 134
O'Faolain, Nuala, 148
O'Faolain, Sean, 24, 28, 30, 34–5, 63, 148, 208, 238
O'Hanrahan, Michael, 51
Oman, William, 43
O'Neill, James, 231
'On a Political Prisoner', 131
On Bloodstained Wings, 213
One and the Many, The, 98
O'Ryan, Father, 78, 80, 90

Pankhurst, Cristabel, 16
Pankhurst, Emmeline, 16, 100, 195, 239
Partridge, William, 29, 35–7, 41–2, 66, 121, 128, 161, 233
Pearse, Padraic, 11, 38–40, 50, 55
Perilous Light, The, 129
Perolz, Marie, 6, 38, 69, 84, 116, 133, 139, 156, 159, 182, 222
Philosophical and Poetical Approach to the Study of Christ in the Fourth Gospel, A, 235
'Pinehurst', 172

Plunkett, Countess, 70
Plunkett, Horace, 48
Plunkett, Joseph, 11, 51, 70, 193
Poole, Christopher, 25, 27
Poppet, 7, 87, 104, 113–6, 169, 229
Power, Jenny Wyse, 7
Prison Letters of Countess Markievicz, 125, 135, 219
Purser, Sarah, 13, 16

Queen Victoria, 33

Rebel Irishwomen, 237
Rhythms of Art, 235
Rising Dead RIC & DMP, The, 25
Robbins, Frank, 6, 28, 37, 46
Robinson, Lennox, 232
'Roger Casement', 110
Roper, Esther, 3, 13, 15–16, 19, 40, 60, 72–3, 76–83, 107–9, 116, 123, 125, 135, 185, 221, 227
'Rosary, The', 41
'Rose Tree, The', 172
Rossa, Jeremiah O'Donovan, 19
Rudnose-Browne, (Mrs (Brownie), 167, 178–9, 183
Ruskin, John, 166
Russell, George (AE), 16–17, 66, 93, 204, 237
Russell, Mrs Violet, 81, 139
Ryan, Ellen, 120
Ryan, Nell, 146

'Sad Years, The', 216
Samuel, Herbert, 92, 110, 112, 151
Sandbach, Arthur, 94–5
Scanlan, Thomas, 174
Scott, C.P., 174, 193
Scott, Father, 147
Separation Women, 43–4
Sharp, E.W., 132–4, 185
Sharpe, May, 117–18, 121, 128, 147
Shaw, George Bernard, 102, 108, 239
Sheehy-Skeffington, Frank, 27, 35, 69, 78, 87, 110, 129

Sheehy-Skeffington, Hannah, 17–19, 27, 35, 53, 69, 76, 82, 90, 93, 96, 120, 228, 230
Shepherd of Eternity, The, 235
Sherwin, Father James, 181
Shiubhlaigh, Maire Nic, 21
Shorter, Dora Sigerson, 216
Skinnider, Margaret, 9, 20, 29–31, 36–8, 41–2, 139–40
Smith, D.J., 238
Spark, The, 7
Stephens, James, 28
'Statues, The', 38
Surrey House, 5, 17–18, 35, 76–7, 81, 92–3
'Survival', 171
Sword of Justice, The, 123

Theosophy, 100, 168, 218
Thornton, Brigid Lyons, 46, 51
Three Resurrrections and the Triumph of Maeve, The, 98, 171
'Thrush, The', 193, 196–7
Tiernan, Sonja, 129, 240
Transport Union, 7
Trench, Frances, 83
Tribunal, The, 145

Troup, E., 110–11, 134, 203, 208
Tynan, Kathleen, 103, 159, 225, 229

Underhill, Evelyn, 235
University Club, 23
Unseen Kings, 162
Urania, 146, 235–6

Voris, Jacqueline Van, 165, 172

Walsh, William, 49
Webb, Beatrice, 239
Wells, H.G., 239
Wheeldon, Alice, 207
Wilde, Oscar, 141
Wheeler, de Courcy, 42–3, 56, 61
White, Jack R., 164, 186, 222
Winder, G.W., 118, 132, 134
Women's Peace Crusade, 145
Wylie, William Evelyn, 55, 58–9, 61–4

Yeats, Lily, 48
Yeats, William Butler, 1, 14, 38, 100, 102, 108, 117, 132, 142, 172, 190, 201, 218, 238
Young, Ella, 168, 224, 226
Young Man from the South, 232

About the Author

Patrick Quigley is a retired public servant. His novel, *Borderland* (Brandon, 1994), was translated into German and broadcast on RTÉ radio. He was awarded a Pro-Memoria medal by the Polish Government in 2014 for *The Polish Irishman: the Life and Times of Count Casimir Markievicz* (The Liffey Press, 2012).